POWER, CULTURE, AND PLACE

ESSAYS ON NEW YORK CITY

POWER, CULTURE, AND PLACE

ESSAYS ON NEW YORK CITY

John Hull Mollenkopf
EDITOR

RUSSELL SAGE FOUNDATION

NEW YORK

The Russell Sage Foundation

The Russell Sage Foundation, one of the oldest of America's general purpose foundations, was established in 1907 by Mrs. Margaret Olivia Sage for "the improvement of social and living conditions in the United States." The Foundation seeks to fulfill this mandate by fostering the development and dissemination of knowledge about the political, social, and economic problems of America. It conducts research in the social sciences and public policy, and publishes books and pamphlets that derive from this research.

The Board of Trustees is responsible for oversight and the general policies of the Foundation, while administrative direction of the program and staff is vested in the President, assisted by the officers and staff. The President bears final responsibility for the decision to publish a manuscript as a Russell Sage Foundation book. In reaching a judgment on the competence, accuracy, and objectivity of each study, the President is advised by the staff and selected expert readers. The conclusions and interpretations in Russell Sage Foundation publications are those of the authors and not of the Foundation, its Trustees, or its staff. Publication by the Foundation, therefore, does not imply endorsement of the contents of the study.

Library of Congress Cataloging-in-Publication Data

Power, culture, and place : essays on New York City / John Hull Mollenkopf, editor.
   p. cm.
  Bibliography: p.
  Includes index.
  ISBN 0-87154-603-5
  1. New York (N.Y.)—Politics and government. 2. New York (N.Y.)—Economic conditions. 3. New York (N.Y.)—Civilization.
  I. Mollenkopf, John H., 1946–
F128.47.P88 1988
974.7'1—dc19
                        88-39077
                        CIP

The paper used in this publication meets the minimum requirements of American National Standard for Information Sciences—Permanence of Paper for Printed Library Materials, ANSI Z39.48-1984. ∞

10 9 8 7 6 5 4 3 2 1

The preparation of this volume was sponsored by the Committee on New York City of the Social Science Research Council.

Ira Katznelson, Chair
New School for Social Research

M. Christine Boyer
Cooper Union

Manuel Castells
University of California, Berkeley

Michael P. Conzen
University of Chicago

Kenneth T. Jackson
Columbia University

Diane Lindstrom
University of Wisconsin

John Hull Mollenkopf
The Graduate Center, City University of New York

Elizabeth Roistacher
Queens College, City University of New York

Mary P. Ryan
University of California, Berkeley

Martin Shefter
Cornell University

Olivier Zunz
University of Virginia

David L. Szanton, Staff
Social Science Research Council

Contributors

Thomas Bender, New York University

James Beshers, Queens College and The Graduate Center,
City University of New York

Amy Bridges, University of California, San Diego

Peter G. Buckley, Cooper Union

Norman I. Fainstein, Baruch College, City University of New York

Susan S. Fainstein, Rutgers University

Ira Katznelson, New School for Social Research

William Kornblum, The Graduate Center, City University of New York

Diane Lindstrom, University of Wisconsin–Madison

John Hull Mollenkopf, The Graduate Center,
City University of New York

Martin Shefter, Cornell University

William R. Taylor, State University of New York, Stony Brook

Emanuel Tobier, New York University

Acknowledgments

The impetus for establishing the Committee on New York City at the Social Science Research Council came from Kenneth Prewitt, then president of the Council and now with the Rockefeller Foundation; David L. Szanton of the Council staff; and Ira Katznelson, dean of the New School Graduate Faculty. They formed an organizing group that included Herbert Gutman of the CUNY Graduate Center History Program, Thomas Bender of the New York University Department of History, and myself. At that point, the Russell Sage Foundation, particularly Peter de Janosi, expressed confidence in the project by providing an initial planning grant. Beginning in 1983, more than 75 scholars representing different disciplines, generations, and ideological commitments participated in planning sessions to formulate a research agenda. These discussions led, in early 1984, to three small conferences on how economic, cultural, and political perspectives might illuminate the mercantile, industrial, and postindustrial phases of New York's development. The papers were extensively revised and augmented with postconference reflections to form the present volume. Reviewers Nathan Glazer and Louis Winnick provided helpful criticisms, as did Priscilla Lewis, director of publications at the Russell Sage Foundation.

This preparatory work convinced the Council to establish the Committee on New York City in May 1985. The Russell Sage Foundation graciously provided major funding for the committee, while the Spencer Foundation and the Robert F. Wagner Sr. Institute of Urban Public Policy at the City University Graduate Center have provided additional support. Three working groups are bringing economic, political, and cultural perspectives to bear on analyzing how the city's built environment, patterns of inequality, and competitive position in the system of cities have evolved over time. These efforts are chaired respectively by M. Christine Boyer, Manuel Castells and myself, and Martin Shefter. In December 1987 the Council launched an additional effort to create a historical and analytical atlas of New York City, led by Michael Conzen and Ira Katznelson.

Support from spouses is much evident in this book, ranging from toleration of our frequent weekend meetings to intellectual criticism and coauthorship. In my own case, Kathleen Gerson has provided constant stimulation, insight, and understanding. Sadly, one who inspired our efforts is no longer with us. Herbert Gutman's brilliance at bringing cultural and political perspectives to bear on the formation of the working class in American cities and his passion for the historian's craft inspired the committee's efforts. We dedicate this volume to his memory.

J. H. M.

Contents

Introduction

This volume uses the special vantage point of New York City to explore the economic, political, and cultural facets of urban development in the United States. While focusing on these themes within the city, it also asks how developments in the nation's largest and most important city have helped shape broader patterns throughout this country and the world. The contributors do not attempt to resolve long-standing debates about the relative importance of economic, political, and cultural factors in explaining social development, but they do try to frame the crucial issues concerning the interaction of these factors during the mercantile, industrial, and postindustrial transformations of New York City and the larger society.

A number of methodological and substantive assumptions underlie this effort. First, we believe that the emergence of modern, urban, post-industrial society can be successfully understood only through a conscious analysis of the interplay among power, culture, and economic structure; each dimension must be given its analytic due; and their intersections must be explored. By contrast, the social science disciplines have at best tended to abstract the realms of polity, economy, and culture from one another, and, at worst, have dismissed or assumed away important interactions among them.

Admittedly, it is easier to assert the need for truly interdisciplinary research than to bring to life a genuine dialogue among the disciplines. The essays in this volume do not always transcend their disciplinary origins. Nevertheless, this volume and the Social Science Research Council's Committee on New York City are committed to bringing economic, political, and cultural perspectives into fuller engagement with each other.

Our second point of departure is the belief that understanding society requires a sense of place. The pursuit of generalizable results has sometimes led scholars to downplay the variations arising from the particularities of place. Indeed, disciplinary specialization practically requires the homogenization of space and place. But economics, politics, and culture exist not in abstraction but in places, and socially constructed places affect the interaction of social forces over time. To borrow a metaphor from Herman Melville, places constitute the "loom of time" upon which choice, constraint, and chance weave history.[1] Places certainly result from past choices and conflicts, but they also constrain and encourage future choices and conflicts, thus imparting a distinct pattern to historical development.

A third, closely related assumption is that large cities have driven nineteenth and twentieth century development and will probably continue to do so in the twenty-first century. The close link between urbanization and industrial capitalism makes the first part of this claim almost self-evident. For the current period, this claim is more controversial. In recent decades, the outward migration of jobs and population and the rise of new urban centers have created the multinucleated metropolitan realm to replace earlier, more self-contained central cities. We believe, however, that large cities, understood in this new metropolitan context, will continue to dominate human settlement patterns and that large central cities will continue to produce system-changing trends.

Finally, we believe that New York is an ideal laboratory in which to substantiate the validity and usefulness of our methodological assumptions. Its population and its annual budget exceed those of many nations. Three-fourths of those who work in its economy live within its political boundaries. For a century and a half, it has been North America's largest city, home to the largest concentration of corporate headquarters, a global financial center, and the focus of an international nexus of culture and communication. As the continent's largest port, New York was a leading point of connection with the outside world, particularly Europe. Today, four-fifths of all transborder data-flows and half of all international air cargo shipments pass through New York City.

This nodal position in the national and global network of cities has opened New York to a worldwide range of influences, whether Asian and Caribbean emigration, foreign direct investment in the United States, or avant-garde ideas in the arts. It is thus a study in cultural, economic, and political contrasts. New York's connections to the world have facilitated its role as a source of innovations—from mortgage-backed securities to break dancing—that, in turn, strongly influence the rest of the world. Perhaps more than other world cities, New York intensifies and combines social forces, ranging in scale from local to global, that elsewhere may be hidden, latent, or segregated from one another.

In short, this volume argues that urban studies should be revived as a fruitful and suggestive basis for the social sciences. The city gave birth to the social sciences and motivated many classic studies, ranging from Friedrich Engels on Manchester and Charles Booth on London to Robert A. Dahl on New Haven. We believe a renewed urban focus can enlighten and enliven many of the most important issues currently engaging social scientists.

Among these are such methodological and epistemological issues as whether to rely upon individualist explanations, as opposed to more holistic or systemic explanations, or whether to stress meaning and interpretation, as in the work of Clifford Geertz, or whether to emphasize causal explanation. By concentrating large numbers of different kinds of people and social strata in close physical proximity, urban areas provide fertile soil for contrasting and comparing these approaches. Large cities also highlight a number of issues central to the theoretical growth of the social sciences, including class formation, the development of state capacities, and the mediation of economic trends by politics and culture.

How, for example, do rapid changes in economic structure influence broad patterns of social and political stratification? The essays in this volume delineate the enormous social, political, and cultural divisions and revisions arising in what might be called the first, second, and third industrial revolutions, or the mercantile, industrial, and postindustrial eras. In each era, the creation of new social forms and the simultaneous decay of old forms created an uneven and complicated impact across the class structure.

How, given these complicated effects, have groups entering or being created in the rapidly changing urban setting become incorporated into the economy, polity, and culture? How can a common polity, a shared civic culture, be created from so many distinct and conflicting streams? Is the process characterized by upward mobility, a closed opportunity structure, or both? What explains the fate of various groups? Is an underclass a permanent feature of rapid periods of structural change? New York City has constantly generated new inequalities, with new groups clustered seemingly permanently at the bottom. Yet many of these groups have improved their economic position over time through a complex political struggle. Intense political struggles have also taken place between decaying economic forms, whether artisan production in 1810 or garment loft factories in the 1980s, and rising forms, such as the nineteenth century factory system or the present-day growth of advanced corporate services.

The current theoretical interest in analyzing the evolution of state capacity and autonomy can also be advanced through studies of New York City. State intervention has fostered and shaped the city's physical and economic growth. This has been most obvious in large public capital investments like the Erie Canal, the subway system, and Kennedy Airport, but it has also been true in more subtle ways. New York's defeat of Philadelphia's Second Bank of the United States in 1836 provides an example of how political advantage helped shaped financial markets not only in New York but throughout the nation. Reciprocally, the concentration of wealth and poverty in New York inevitably turns economic trends into political issues. Class differences in New York have been enormous for a century and a half, yet outbreaks of class violence or class politics have been episodic at most. The essays in each section of this volume show how political order and civic culture have mediated economic tensions.

This mediation certainly took place outside the strictly political realm as well. A common culture was forged out of disparate and competing voices, in part because this culture expressed some cleavages among groups while dampening others. Certain city spaces were delineated as the turf of class and ethnic subcultures, while others developed a much more public, heterogeneous character. This volume speculates on the implicit rules governing the evolution of such spatial differentiation, and on how these rules related to the political and economic dimensions of power. From the debate over the creation of Central Park to conflict over access to park space on the city's rim 140 years later, New York City offers much material for reflection on these issues.

A final, crucial theoretical question concerns the degree of and limits to local autonomy. Anthony Giddens has written that the city was central to social theory until the advent of the nation-state, which usurped the city's rights and powers. Much neoclassical and neo-Marxist thinking has reinforced this position. Leading economists, sociologists, and political scientists have concluded that competition for investment prevents cities from exercising political power over economic arrangements, at least in terms of redistribution. Some neo-Marxists have portrayed cities as the product of the mode of production and its discontents, with local politics following the functional imperative of promoting the former and suppressing the latter.

Other scholars, drawing on what is an older tradition in the United States, resist writing off local autonomy. The community-studies literature took for granted the importance of the urban realm. The Chicago School of sociology saw the city as society writ small. While recognizing that things change as the scale of analysis shifts from the nation to the city, Robert Dahl's classic study of New Haven and Browning, Marshall, and Tabb's recent prize-winning study of California cities recognize that cities are places where larger forces can be affected as well as observed and understood.[2] According to this view, despite the loss of authority to higher jurisdictions and the vulnerability to global market and demographic trends, actions in urban polities can have real, systemic consequences because they exercise real, if constrained, authority over core economic and cultural activities.

New York City offers a test case for the relative theoretical sturdiness of these two views. What city has been more subject to global forces of economic and demographic change? Yet what city has attempted more government intervention, whether through an elaborate local welfare state, the regulation of housing markets, or the promotion of its own economic expansion? The evidence in these essays can help us determine the extent to which cities use larger forces to chart their own course or are merely subject to them.

Skeptics may challenge both the assumption that place-centered, interdisciplinary, historical research is badly needed and the belief that New York offers an excellent starting point for such work. New York City's distinctiveness may cause particular doubt about the latter point. After all, New York City is an outlying case on many of the dimensions often used to compare cities. It is older, larger, denser, and more heterogeneous than other American cities. It is more Roman Catholic than most and more Jewish than any. It houses disproportionate numbers of rich and poor alike. It has a larger public labor force, more kinds of public services, and greater governmental regulation of housing markets than other cities. And while New York City might be the nation's most cosmopolitan city, it also has parochial worlds like the Satmar Chassidim in Williamsburg or the Italian-Americans of Bensonhurst. How, then, can New York City be taken as representative of anything?

We believe that New York City is more archetypical than atypical. By concentrating extremes, it reveals forces, trends, and conflicts that are latent elsewhere. As a world city, it is among the first to feel trends arising elsewhere. As a center of influential economic, political, and cultural institutions, it creates and propagates widely felt innovations. Despite decentralization and new sources of competition, it has been economically dominant for more than a century. New York's disproportionate influence on national political development continues today, despite the city's dwindling fraction of the national vote. From the political machine (and its Progressive opponents) to the New Deal, the liberal reforms of the 1960s, and the fiscal crisis of the 1970s, New York has provided a template for national patterns. A third of all foundation dollars, three national news operations, most of the leading magazine and book publishers, two newspapers with a claim to national standing, the main fine arts market, and many nationally significant cultural institutions are all located in New York City.

It is surprising, then, that New York has received so little comprehensive scholarly attention. Numerous monographs have appeared on particular aspects of the city's history, but they are fragmented and lack a common theoretical focus. Scholars have produced more synthetic work on Boston or Chicago, or even on New Haven, than on New York. A quarter century has passed since the last comprehensive research program on New York City's political system or its economy. Even if the skeptic rejects the claim that New York provides a basis for theoretical development in the social sciences, the need for greater comprehensive scholarly attention can hardly be denied.

E. B. White once wrote that "by rights New York should have destroyed itself long ago, from panic or fire or rioting or failure of some vital supply line in its circulatory system or from some deep labyrinthine short circuit."[3] The essays in this volume do not achieve an analytic synthesis of economics, politics, and culture in New York, but they do suggest reasons why, for now, such a fate has been avoided.

In the essays opening the discussion of each period, Diane Lindstrom, Emanuel Tobier, and Norman and Susan Fainstein provide ample evidence that mercantile, industrial, and postindustrial economic transformations posed major social challenges. Lindstrom shows that overall economic growth was accompanied by increasing class inequality in the antebellum period. Tobier shows how the tremendous economic drive at the turn of the century produced new tensions over land use in the central business district and the expanding outer borough housing markets. The Fainsteins in turn examine how state intervention to reshape the city to promote corporate functions and metropolitan decentralization generated new kinds of conflict. These essays give ample evidence that economic development consistently produced sharp conflict but never a fatal crisis.

One source of order may emerge from learning to live with disorder. For the mercantile and industrial eras, cultural historians Peter G. Buckley and William R. Taylor examine the cross-class use of public spaces, the forging of street life, and how the popular culture industry selected aspects of that street culture and introduced them into national discourse. Sociologists William Kornblum and James Beshers follow this theme into the contemporary period by examining the reconstituted white ethnic enclaves along Jamaica Bay and their conflicts with emerging black and Hispanic communities over access to public spaces like the Gateway National Recreation Area.

These essays suggest that the social construction of public space has important consequences for economic, social, and political order. Groups expend great energy to carve out and protect niches in a shared spatial context. No group can completely dominate or control that shared space, yet the rules of the game favor and protect some competing elements while dampening the expression of others. Order and disorder are not polar conditions; order is built instead upon the particular way disorder takes place.

In the third essays for each period, political scientists Amy Bridges, Martin Shefter, and I argue that the framework of political participation also helps to harness conflict. For Bridges, the political interests of the urban immigrant working class were defined by America's (and New York's) great political invention—the professional political party or machine—because universal white male suffrage preceded the formation of that class. Shefter traces how the nineteenth century machine-reform dialectic was transposed into the relatively stable, and for a time uncontested, pluralism of the 1950s and early 1960s. My essay analyzes how the enormous economic, fiscal, and racial traumas of the late 1960s and 1970s affected the position of different groups in the political arena and speculates on why it remained stable nonetheless.

The three last, reflective essays take up and reformulate issues embedded in earlier sections. Thomas Bender argues for a renewed analytic focus on public, civic culture and the social and physical spaces in which it is generated as a way of overcoming weaknesses in the "new social history." I reflect on the paradox that political parties have decayed as a means of representation at the same time that state efforts to shape the physical environment have become more pervasive. Finally, Ira Katznelson takes a step back from empirical analysis to consider how major social theorists have understood what the city meant and how its growth in turn affected their thinking. In different ways, each essay provides a comment on the relationships among power, culture, and place.

These essays only begin to substantiate the assumptions that provide the starting point for this volume. While reading the essays, the reader will want to think of them as open questions. Do culture, politics, and economics really have an equally significant influence on New York's development? How do they intersect? Do the essays bear out the contention that the particular shared spatial context helps shape how these domains are woven together? What distinct pattern, if any, has New York stamped on larger social trends? Has New York driven larger development patterns or has it progressively lost ground to external forces?

In the coming years, the Committee on New York City will pursue the general issues raised here by focusing on the built environment, metropolitan dominance, and the dual city. These topics have been chosen because they allow economic, political, and cultural perspectives to be brought to bear on central theoretical issues.

The working group on the built environment will examine how economic and political developments, market forces, individual designers and builders, city planners, and the diverse cultures of the city interacted to give the city its physical shape. This group will examine not only the making of the physical city but also its use and meaning. It will explore the physical dimensions of topics that the two other groups are analyzing, mindful of how such dimensions as class, gender, race, ethnicity, technology, and economic function are variously intermingled and geographically segregated.

The effort to understand metropolitan dominance will study New York's "foreign policy"—how New York has influenced the wider economy, political system, and culture despite frequent adverse changes in its competitive environment. If New York institutions have fostered important national economic, political, and cultural changes, then investigations of the activities of these institutions should reveal largely unexplored relations between economic, political, and cultural development. This working group will examine the impact of the current reorganization of the global economic system on the relative standing of New York and its elites.

The third research effort will analyze the economic, social, and political ramifications of the current "postindustrial revolution." Manufacturing decline, the rise of services, and internationalization of the city's businesses and population have been particularly rapid since the 1960s. Racial and ethnic succession, the rise of new social strata and the decline of old ones, and economic restructuring have posed severe challenges to the city's economy, polity, and civic culture. Trends toward polarization and a new middle class are both evident, undermining old patterns of inequality even as new ones are created. Though the main framework for this research will be contemporary, an effort will be made to contrast findings with studies of earlier moments of economic transformation, particularly the industrial revolution of the late nineteenth and early twentieth centuries.

We anticipate that subsequent volumes will flow from each of these efforts and trust that they will build on this volume's strengths while avoiding its shortcomings.

John Hull Mollenkopf

1. Herman Melville, *Moby Dick* (New York: Random House, [1851] 1950), 213.
2. Robert Dahl, *Who Governs* (New Haven: Yale University Press, 1961); Rufus Browning, Dale Marshall, and David Tabb, *Protest Is Not Enough* (Berkeley: University of California Press, 1984).
3. E. B. White, *Here Is New York* (New York: Harper, 1949), 24–25.

POWER, CULTURE, AND PLACE

ESSAYS ON NEW YORK CITY

PART I

The Mercantile Era

1

Economic Structure, Demographic Change, and Income Inequality in Antebellum New York

Diane Lindstrom

The years from 1815 to 1860 brought unprecedented and sweeping economic change to the United States. Surging nonagricultural output accelerated the nation's underlying growth rate. Vigorous capital investment in new technologies fueled the rise of manufacturing and mining. It also precipitated a sharp shift toward greater income and wealth inequality. By the eve of the Civil War, the distinctly modern patterns of industrialization, rapid economic growth, and substantial income inequality were fully shaped.

This transformation vitally affected American cities. Urban areas increasingly attracted nonagricultural employment; cities had traditionally housed services, but now they began to accommodate growing shares of manufacturing. They could not provide the requisite labor force out of their own natural increase in population. Given relatively low fertility and high infant and child mortality rates, urban growth depended on immigration. The waves of foreign and domestic migrants in turn greatly altered urban demography and economy. In the 1840s and 1850s, they fueled the highest decennial rate of urbanization ever experienced in the United States. The mix of age, sex, and skills among migrants also exacerbated inequality.

This essay traces the relationships among economic structure, demographic change, and inequality within the nation's largest city, New York. After reviewing New York's population history, it turns to the issues of sectoral growth and employment, particularly the relative contributions of commerce and industry. An examination of New York's occupational mix in 1855 highlights the demand for skills. A series of net migration estimates outlines the labor market response. Finally, relying on recent research on income equality, the essay speculates on the impact of structural change on individual well-being.

The Rise of New York

Around the year 1803, the population of New York City surpassed that of Philadelphia, and New York City has never relinquished its claim to the title of the nation's largest city. Table 1.1 presents New York's success against other seaboard centers, against all U.S. urban areas, and against the nation as a whole. Compared with its seaport rivals, New York's growth spurted in the 1790s. The events of the first two decades of the nineteenth century evidently affected the great Eastern seaports more or less equally, since they all grew at roughly the same rate. But beginning in the 1820s, New York pulled away from its rivals, topping one million people on the eve of the Civil War.

By most measures, New York enjoyed spectacular growth. Except for the 1810s, a poor decade for all cities, New York roughly doubled the national rate of population increase. Excluding new entrants to the urban system in the last two antebellum decades, New York accounted for a whopping 22 percent of the national urban population growth in the 1840s and 1850s.[1] Other large cities shared some of this success. John Sharpless and Allan Pred cogently argue that if we view cities as competitors for migrants, "the very largest cities were—on the average— capturing 2½ times their just share of the total increase in the nation's urban population in the decades immediately prior to the Civil War."[2] In sum, while several cities grew to extraordinary size, articulating the urban system, New York outdistanced the others to attain a secure place at the top of the urban hierarchy.

Economic Structure

Historians have traditionally linked urban economic with urban demographic growth. In New York's case, they have emphasized how the city became the nation's "commercial emporium." By 1800, New York was the nation's leading port. Over the next sixty years, it tightened its grip on America's interregional and international trade. Nonetheless, New York's growth required more than commercial supremacy. Despite Al-

Table 1.1 Population, Increment in U.S. Population Share, and Decennial Rates of Increase for New York, Philadelphia, and Boston, and Their Suburbs, 1790–1860

City	1790	1800	1810[a]	1820[a]	1830[a]	1840[a]	1850[a]	1860[a]
New York	33,131	60,515	119,734	152,056	242,278	391,114	696,115	1,174,779
Increment change[b]		0.30	0.51	– .02	0.30	0.41	0.71	0.74
Philadelphia	44,096	61,559	112,210	137,097	188,797	258,037	408,762	565,529
Increment change[b]		0.04	0.39	– .13	0.05	0.4	0.25	0.04
Boston	18,320	24,937	49,654	63,247	88,354	124,037	208,972	288,735
Increment change[b]		0.00	0.22	– .03	0.03	0.04	0.17	0.02
Percent change								
New York		82.7%	97.9%	27.0%	59.3%	61.4%	78.0%	68.8%
Philadelphia		39.6	82.3	22.2	37.7	36.7	58.4	38.4
Boston		36.1	99.1	27.4	39.7	40.4	68.5	38.2
U.S. Population		34.8	36.4	33.1	34.1	32.7	35.9	35.5

Source: George Rogers Taylor, "American Urban Growth Preceding the Railway Age," *Journal of Economic History* (September 1967): 311; and idem, "The Beginnings of Mass Transportation in Urban America," *The Smithsonian Journal of History* 1 (Summer 1966): 36.

[a] These data include the following suburbs: for New York, the four boroughs incorporated in 1898; for Philadelphia, the county; and for Boston, the contiguous towns with their boundaries as of 1840. For 1790 and 1800, the boundaries were slightly smaller. See Taylor, "The Beginnings of Mass Transportation," 36.

$$b = \frac{\text{Pop. City}_t}{\text{Pop. U.S.}_t} - \frac{\text{Pop. City } t - 10}{\text{Pop. U.S.}_{-1} t - 10}$$

lan Pred's label of the "mercantile city era," New York also created a strong and viable manufacturing sector during this era.

Customs data attest to New York's commercial success. Table 1.2 shows imports and exports at the state level for the antebellum era. New York led by the 1790s, and the gap between New York and its rivals widened right up to the eve of the Civil War. New York's share of domestic exports never approached that of its imports, largely because of Southern shipments of cotton directly to Europe. The import data merit close attention. New York's share of all U.S. imports rose from less than one-quarter in the 1790s to better than two-thirds by the 1850s. In contrast, Pennsylvania's trade dwindled steadily. The completion of the Delaware and Raritan Canal in the 1830s enabled many Philadelphia merchants to import their foreign goods via New York. Similarly, in 1848, the Cunard Line shifted its western terminus from Boston to New York. These events signaled New York's hegemony over its immediate rivals. Boston might sustain an East Indian trade and Baltimore a Latin American commerce, but New York dominated. By the 1850s, its share of foreign imports to the United States exceeded that of the four great Eastern seaports combined in 1800. New York had become the distribution center for the East, South, and West.

Superior access to foreign and particularly English goods, credit, and information underwrote New York's commercial supremacy. "All [foreign goods] dwarfed into insignificance in comparison with textiles, which, as Britain's chief article of export and the United States' chief article of importation, towered above all else in the world of commerce."[3] New York enjoyed a virtual monopoly; in 1860, when the United States imported $120 million of textiles, some $101 million entered New York.[4] Thus, even in the antebellum period, merchants throughout the country flocked to New York to purchase their stock of textiles and most other foreign wares.

New York's control over the expansion of commerce depended on major improvements in transportation and communication. Foreign trade, however important, became less of a factor over time. Robert Lipsey estimates that the share of U.S. exports in the national income fell from 10 to 15 percent in the 1790s to 6 percent in the 1850s.[5] When canals, steamboats, and railroads slashed overland transport costs and times, a revolution occurred in domestic commerce. With greatly reduced shipping charges, farmers produced more crops for markets and used the resulting higher cash income to purchase goods they formerly made themselves. This multiplied the quantity of goods in trade. Transport advances also facilitated information flows. The sheer volume of

Table 1.2 Import Duties, Imports, and Domestic Exports for New York, Massachusetts, and Pennsylvania, 1790–1860 (in percentage of U.S.)

	Import Duties[a]					Imports			
	1790–1800	1801–1810	1815–1816	1821–1830	1831–1840	1841–1850	1851–1860
New York	23.2	28.0	35.7	46.3	57.8	60.0	64.4
Pennsylvania	22.2	19.1	18.7	14.5	8.6	6.8	5.5
Massachusetts	18.0	23.7	16.9	18.9	13.8	18.6	14.2

Domestic Exports

	1790–1800	1801–1810	1811–1820	1821–1830	1831–1840	1841–1850	1851–1860
New York	19.2	19.0	19.1	23.9	20.2	26.7	34.8
Pennsylvania	18.8	13.2	8.2	5.9	3.4	3.8	2.3
Massachusetts	14.0	15.4	9.0	7.3	5.8	6.7	6.7

Source: Robert Greenhalgh Albion, *The Rise of the New York Port (1815–1860)* (New York: Scribner's, 1939), 391; Adam Seybert, *Statistical Annals* (Philadelphia: Dobson, 1818), 425–37; and Charles H. Evans, *Exports, Domestic and Foreign*, 48th Cong., 1st sess., H.R., Misc. Doc. 49, Pt. 2 (Serial 2236), 1884, 98–101, 234–36.

[a]Specifically, gross amount of duties on merchandise, tonnage, fines, penalties, and forfeitures.

business travel ensured the dissemination of economic information. News circulated much more quickly with innovations in postal, newspaper, and telegraph services.

Allen Pred argues that this revolution in transportation and communications reinforced the advantage of those in the existing urban system and of New York in particular.[6] Declining freight costs extended large city market areas, often undermining urban growth along the improved transport lines and encouraging it at the termini. Goods moving longer distances were likely to be routed through major centers. New York not only garnered more trade, it enjoyed earlier and greater access to information. New York had the most vessels in trade with European and Southern ports. In the North, canal boats, railroads, and packets constantly plied the trade routes so that New York merchants quickly learned of new business opportunities. Pred calculates that by the early 1850s, the city was the destination of several million business trips.[7] It accounted for 18 percent of national newspaper circulation and 22 percent of letters mailed, but for only 2 percent of the population.[8] New York had become the national center, relegating other cities to regional and subregional status.

Commercial supremacy fostered financial leadership. Philadelphia's loss of federal deposits in the Second Bank of the United States signaled a shift in banking preeminence from Chestnut Street to Wall Street. By 1861, New York's banking capital of $72 million far exceeded Philadelphia's $12 million and Boston's $34 million.[9] Similar if not equivalent success came in fire and marine insurance.[10] By the 1850s, the New York Stock Exchange was attracting those who wished to trade in securities, particularly those of the railroads.

These well-known elements are only part of the story, however. Traditionally, historians have tended to assume that industrialization drove urbanization only after the Civil War. Census data indicate, however, that manufacturing had long been a major contributor to urban income and the prime source of urban employment. When asked to report sectoral employment, 73 percent of New Yorkers in 1820 listed manufacturing.[11] The proportion fell over time to 68 percent in 1840, and 33 percent in 1860. But this precipitous decline must be viewed with caution since the early enumerations allowed only three sectors of employment (agriculture, commerce, and manufactures). New York, like most cities, "was no less committed to manufacturing enterprise in the early decades of the century than after the Civil War."[12]

Even if manufacturing had occupied a preponderant share of the labor force before 1840, Allan Pred suggests that its growth depended upon the commercial sector.

Urban industries, almost without exception, either processed import or export commodities . . . [entrepôt manufactures] or provided printed materials, ships and other capital goods vital to the perpetuation of trade . . . [commerce-serving manufactures] or catered to the household and construction demands of the local mercantile population and the classes serving that population [local market manufactures].[13]

Table 1.3 shows that this assertion does not hold in New York for 1840, the end point of Pred's mercantile city era, when relatively robust data are available.[14] Roughly one-third of manufacturing was commercially stimulated, while the remainder consisted of local market output. This table and the employment data permit the inference that New York did not make a later shift from commerce to manufacturing but relied heavily upon manufacturing and handicrafts in its early, pre-1840 development. Indeed, commercially stimulated manufacturing became *more*, not less, important in the period from 1840 to 1860.

Table 1.3 reveals extraordinarily rapid growth. Per capita value-added in manufacturing probably doubled between 1840 and 1860. The selection of 1840 implies a bias since it was a depression year. Still, these figures attest to vigorous growth, particularly in textiles and apparel, which became the city's largest industry. The ready-made clothing industry boomed in the late antebellum period, and printing and publishing also rose rapidly, challenging foods for second place. The decline in leather's share defies ready explanation.

By the standards of the day, New York housed large and efficient manufacturing firms. On the whole, its individual businesses had larger capitalization, more output, and more employees than the national average.[15] If efficiency is defined simply as more value-added per unit of labor or capital, New York bested the national average in both categories. Such size and efficiency follow from the city's huge market area: it paid to invest in the most technologically advanced machinery and to run it more often.

According to Dorothy Brady, large urban industries made major contributions to American industrialization.[16] They introduced and diffused new lines of manufactures. By the 1820s, the seaports had become centers of capital goods production. Finally, they initiated mass production of consumer goods. Seaport cities offered their manufacturers the latest information, superior access to capital, and the most highly skilled craftsmen.

The defects of census enumeration prevent an exact tracing of sectoral growth in New York's income and employment, but crude income statistics can be constructed for 1840.[17] They indicate that some $19 million

Table 1.3   Value-Added in New York County Manufacturing, 1840 and 1860s (expressed as a percentage of total value added)

	1840	1860
Entrepôt		
Foods	8.2[a]	11.9%
Tobacco	1.0	1.6
Wood products	1.8	4.0
Leather products	11.2	5.1
Total	22.2	22.6
Commerce-serving		
Printing and publishing	7.4	11.3
Paper	0.2	1.7
Transportation equipment	3.1	2.9
Total	10.7	15.9
Local market		
Textiles and apparel	13.8	19.5
Furniture	5.3	4.0
Chemicals	6.5	3.5
Stone, clay, and glass	4.4	3.1
Metals	7.0	7.4
Machinery	7.4	7.7
Miscellaneous	22.7	16.3
Total	67.1	61.5
Total Value-Added	$12,054,000–$20,374,000	$65,417,338
Per Capita	$38.55–$65.15	$80.40

Source: Secretary of State, Compendium, 1840 (Washington, D.C., 1841), 131–37; and Secretary of the Interior, Manufactures of the United States, 1860 (Washington, D.C., 1865), 379–84.

[a] Includes lumber.

to $21 million originated in commerce, another $2 million in navigation, and $11 million to $12 million in manufacturing. Commerce brought in more income, but these data do not indicate that it necessarily employed more New Yorkers. Commerce required massive stocks of capital tied up in goods in transit and inventory, while manufacturing depended upon labor. So in these value-added statistics, which measure the joint contributions of capital and labor, commerce absorbed more of the former and manufacturing more of the latter. Neither sector explained the growth of the other, but when combined they generated tremendous increases in New York's income and employment.[18]

The Labor Force

In pursuing the relationship between urban economic growth and demographic change, we would like to know not only the intensity of sectoral demands for labor, but also their preference in terms of ethnicity, gender, and skills. Labor markets were segmented even in the formative period as identifiable groups filled defined occupational niches. To capture this process over time would require census-type data spanning the period and listing basic demographic detail, occupational title, and wage (as a proxy for skill) for each worker. Unfortunately such data do not exist; the best that can be retrieved readily are the occupational statistics for New York County in 1855. Table 1.4 summarizes the job titles by sector and reports every title with at least 1,000 workers.

The table sheds considerable light upon the issue of employment multipliers. Though economists, geographers, and historians debate the relative importance of commerce and manufacturing, these two sectors combined did not employ half of New York's labor force in 1855. With a labor force share of 37 percent, manufacturing was the largest of the categories in the table. Trade occupied about 10 percent, roughly the same amount as three other categories—transportation, construction, and other services except household. The single largest occupational title was servant; it constituted some 16 percent of the entire county labor force. The primary sector, farming and forestry, had all but disappeared. So, with some 60 percent of its workers in the services, New York was, in 1855, as it had been in the late colonial period, preeminently a service economy.[19]

These sectoral data permit some tentative observations about the demand for skills. Agriculture, transportation, and private households employed the unskilled. Excluding clerks, 30 percent of these categories were unskilled. Trade and other professional services attracted the skilled, but these sectors still had less than 20 percent skilled workers. In between lay construction and manufacturing. Their high wages suggest that most construction workers ought to be considered skilled. Manufacturing defies simple generalization, since it contains more than 150 occupational titles. A perusal of the titles in Table 1.4 shows a preponderance of unskilled jobs. Summing these crude estimates, roughly two-thirds of New York's labor force in 1855 seems to have worked at essentially unskilled jobs.

Table 1.4 Distribution of Employment in New York County, 1855

Sector	Number	Total	(Percent)
Primary			
Fisheries, forests, farms	674		.3
Construction			
Carpenters	6,901		
Masons	3,634		
Painters	3,400		
TOTAL (including unenumerated)		16,963	8.7
Manufacturing			
Bakers	2,856		
Blacksmiths	2,611		
Bookbinders	1,365		
Boot and shoe makers	6,745		
Butchers	2,643		
Cabinet makers	2,606		
Coopers	1,018		
Dressmakers	7,436		
Hat and cap makers	1,422		
Machinists	1,714		
Milliners	1,585		
Printers	1,901		
Ship carpenters, etc.	1,146		
Stone and marble cutters	1,755		
Tailors	12,609		
Tobacco manufacturers	1,996		
TOTAL (including unenumerated)		71,900	36.9
Transportation, Communication, and Other Public Utilities			
Boatmen	1,004		
Carters and draymen	5,338		
Drivers	1,741		
Porters	3,052		
Sailors	4,717		
TOTAL (including unenumerated)		18,266	9.4
Wholesale and Retail Trade, Finance, Insurance and Real Estate			
Dealers (unspecified)	1,025		
Grocers	4,079		
Merchants	6,001		
Peddlers	1,889		
TOTAL (including unenumerated)		19,675	10.1

Table 1.4 (*continued*)

Sector	Number	Total	(Percent)
Other Services (except household)			
Boardinghouse keepers	1,014		
Lawyers	1,112		
Physicians	1,252		
Police	1,164		
Teachers	1,268		
TOTAL (including unenumerated)		16,239	8.3
Private Household and Miscellaneous			
Clerks	13,897		
Laborers	2,592		
Laundresses	2,563		
Servants	31,749		
TOTAL (including unenumerated)		50,936	26.2

Source: New York State Census, 1855, 178–95.

Large cities provided unusual opportunities for female employment, even if women encountered a segregated labor market. Unfortunately, the published censuses list occupation by gender only in the manufacturing sector. According to the 1860 count, 27 percent of New York County's manufacturing workers were women.[20] Almost three-quarters of them worked in just one of the twenty standard industrial classifications (SICs), apparel, mostly in the burgeoning men's clothing industry.[21] The other major SICs employing women were printing and publishing (accounting for 6 percent of women in manufacturing) and miscellaneous (7 percent). More than 85 percent of all women, but only 38 percent of all men, worked in these three sectors.

Women were even more crowded in the service sector. Some were boardinghouse keepers and teachers, but Table 1.4 suggests that their numbers must have been modest. The main source of income for the majority of women workers was domestic service, employing 32,000, or 8,000 more than the total female labor force in manufacturing. Laundresses ranked third behind service and the sweated trades. Probably nine out of ten female workers fell into the unskilled category. But they did find jobs. In the nation, only one of ten women worked for pay, but in New York the proportion was almost one out of three.[22]

Similar, if less rigorous, segregation may be inferred for the ethnic population. Studies of antebellum Boston and Philadelphia show strong variations in sectoral employment by place of birth.[23] The native-born found work in construction, transportation, trade, government, and professional service. The non-Irish foreign-born tended to concentrate in the first two areas and manufacturing. Together, the Germans and the American-born "dominated the most desirable skilled occupations."[24] The Irish were mired in personal service, day labor, carting, and lesser manufactures such as handloom weaving. New York probably replicated these patterns, especially since 84 percent of the foreign-born were either Irish (53 percent) or German (31 percent) on the eve of the Civil War.[25] Sex ratio statistics support such an inference. While German men exceeded their female counterparts (64,000 to 56,000), Irish women, the backbone of domestic service, outnumbered Irish men (117,000 to 87,000).

Migration

A natural population increase alone could not satisfy the enormous demand for labor produced by urban economic growth. To achieve the population growth described earlier, New York relied heavily upon *immigration*. This section uses forward census survival techniques to offer age- and sex-specific net migration estimates for New York County between 1810 and 1860.[26] It then speculates as to how this migrant influx altered the age, gender, and ethnic distribution of the population.

Table 1.5 shows extraordinary rates of immigration. Except for the 1810s, when cities in the aggregate did not increase their share of national population, migration accounted for two-thirds to four-fifths of New York's population growth. As we would expect, it peaked in the 1840s, as famine and revolution rocked Europe. Two contradictory biases in these data should be noted. Because these data encompass a decade, and because conservative mortality estimates were selected, these statistics underestimate actual migration.[27] However, they measure only the potential labor force, those aged ten to sixty in the first observation period. Since children under ten are highly likely to be native-born, generalization from the labor force to the entire population would overestimate the migrant share. Even allowing for these biases, Table 1.5 shows high rates of net immigration. By contrast, Kelley and Williamson report that the net immigrant share amounted to only 39.3 percent of total urban population increase in less developed countries during the dynamic 1960s.[28]

Table 1.6 describes net migration by age and sex. Between 1810 and 1860, an overwhelming proportion of the immigrants were young

Table 1.5   Share of Population Increase in New York County
Attributable to Net Migration*

	1810–1820	1820–1830	1830–1840	1840–1850	1850–1860
Male	28.9%	72.0%	72.5%	84.9%	78.7%
Female	22.3	62.9	66.4	75.9	73.4
AVERAGE	25.2	67.2	69.3	80.6	75.8
Increase in Population					
Male	6,328	18,939	32,883	64,801	69,999
Female	7,791	20,711	34,859	59,339	85,674

Source: Lindstrom, "Northeastern Migration, 1810–1860."
*10>20–20>30 to 50>60–60>70 only.

adults. According to the last column, almost three-quarters of the male and four-fifths of the female migrants arrived in New York County during their teens and twenties. The impact of this youthful influx appears clearly in the census: from 1830 on, New York County had more people in their twenties than in their teens. Moreover, the number of net migrants in this age category exceeded their cohort who had been New York residents for a decade.

If New York drew the young, the middle-aged looked elsewhere. The final column in Table 1.6 shows that the proportion of migrants fell off quickly with age, rising only slightly for the last category, those in their fifties or sixties. Negative signs appear sporadically for the thirty-to-forty-year-olds, which means that these ages saw more outmigrants than immigrants. Perhaps these prime age adults had accumulated their grubstake and moved West, or they may have taken their skills to another urban site. In any event, relatively few people between twenty-five and fifty-five sought residence in New York. This would appear to confirm a conclusion drawn from the occupational profile: most urban jobs were for the unskilled with modest chances for advancement.

Finally, Table 1.6 shows a rise in the migration rates of the older population. While their absolute numbers appear small in comparison to the migrant stream, they came to constitute a sizable share of their age cohort. One wonders why the aged would migrate to New York, where mortality rates for their age group were so high, unless the city offered employment or housing with their mature children. The elderly complete a U-shaped pattern, which emphasizes immigration of both the youthful and the aged.

Table 1.6 Age-Specific Migration Rates and Sex Ratios
for New York County, 1810–1860

	1810–1820	1820–1830	1830–1840	1840–1850	1850–1860	Percentage Total Migrants 1810–1860[a]
Male						
5>10–15>20		30.7%[a]	21.8%	45.1%	30.2%	
10>20–20>30	34.6%	98.5	109.5	169.9	94.5	73.3
20>30–30>40	−9.6	36.2	32.7	37.3	27.7	24.2
30>40–40>50	−6.0	1.7	−7.6	7.0	6.0	1.8
40>50–50>60	−17.6	−14.3	−8.3	14.1	−5.2	− .8
50>60–60>70	46.6	−10.2	0.9	33.5	10.9	1.5
Average[a]	7.3	42.2	43.4	62.1	34.8	
Female						
5>9–15>19		51.1%	44.0%	57.9%	41.2%	
10>20–20>30	19.1%	77.5	105.6	141.7	109.9	84.6
20>30–30>40	−2.7	28.4	10.8	6.8	13.3	10.5
30>40–40>50	4.4	7.3	−3.4	3.1	5.2	1.8
40>50–50>60	−15.2	−4.8	3.6	13.8	3.8	1.0
50>60–60>70	29.2	2.0	9.4	24.0	18.4	2.1
Average[a]	6.9	37.6	38.9	46.5	38.2	

	Sex Ratios (number of females for every 100 males)					
	1810	1820	1830	1840	1850	1860
Age						
10>20	113.3	118.4	115.9	121.2	116.5	107.2
20>30	91.6	100.1	105.7	112.8	108.4	125.6
30>40	90.7	99.2	95.0	88.8	88.2	96.6
40>50	93.0	101.7	105.5	100.2	86.3	88.3
50>60	101.4	98.3	116.1	122.4	102.6	97.0
60>70	102.2	99.1	123.8	139.6	126.1	121.5
Average	99.1	105.5	107.3	108.7	102.9	106.7

Source: Diane Lindstrom, "Northeastern Net Migration, 1810–1860" (Paper presented at the Columbia University Seminar in Economic History, 1983), Table 22.

[a]10>20–20>30 to 50>60–60>70 only. For a description of the derivation and interpretation of the statistics, see notes 27 and 28.

New York's migration patterns show greater gender balance than would be anticipated, since two-thirds of New England's outmigrants and American immigrants were male.[29] According to Table 1.5, male immigrants only slightly exceeded female between 1810 and 1840. The 1840s brought a surplus of 8,500 males, the 1850s a surplus of 7,800 females. Clearly, cities kept more than their "just" share of migrating females, tipping the urban gender balance. For every 100 males, the nation as a whole had 95 to 97 females; New York had 99 to 109. Table 1.6 again shows a U-shaped pattern, this time for sex ratios, as women substantially outnumbered men in the age ranges of ten to twenty and sixty to seventy. The first peak primarily reflects higher rates of female immigration, the second represents both higher migration and male mortality. These data, then, highlight the propensity for women, who initially were less inclined to migrate, to move to and remain in New York. They probably left home seeking marriage or employment, neither of which appeared likely in their rural area or town. In spite of a highly segregated market that allocated few well-paying jobs to their sex, New York did provide employment. This, in turn, explains the high female labor force participation rate observed in New York County.

By the end of the period, New York was populated largely by the foreign-born. Given the port's role in international trade, New York naturally became the center of immigration. Albion reported that 69 percent of all immigrants between 1821 and 1860 arrived at the city's docks, a statistic higher than New York's share of national imports or tonnage.[30] By the 1855 State Census, 51 percent of the New York County population had been born abroad.[31] Nearly 37 percent were born in New York County, but many were the children of immigrants. That left less than 12 percent of the population who came from areas in the United States outside New York County. This domestic migration was drawn largely from nearby states; of the 12 percent, 5 percent were born in New York, 2 percent in New Jersey, and 1 percent each in Connecticut, Massachusetts, and Pennsylvania.

The foreign-born probably crowded out potential domestic migrants. This appears to be particularly true for unskilled labor, which would be provided by either American farm children or the foreign-born. The Irish, who tended to remain in New York, filled both male and female unskilled slots. Germans met success in more skilled markets, but so too did the native-born. While their numbers were modest, Albion stressed their importance: "All of [the merchant princes], however, whether born in England, France, Holland, Long Island, or New York City itself, were swamped by the mighty invasion of business and maritime talent from New England in general and Connecticut in particular."[32] "New

Englanders not only beat the old New Yorkers at the commercial game, but had the effrontery to boast about it."[33]

Inequality

Sectoral, migration, and occupational statistics all point to substantial urban wealth and income inequality. Economists have put cities at the heart of American inequality. For example, Robert Gallman notes that in 1860, while the top 1 percent of families held 24 percent of U.S. wealth, the top 1 percent in the cotton South held 30 percent, and the top 1 percent in three large sample cities controlled 45 percent.[34] This should occasion little surprise; most of the youthful influx to New York must have been, in economists' terms, near-zero wealth holders. Changes within manufacturing towards more capital and higher technology widened the skilled-unskilled wage gap. And the sector characterized by the highest level of income inequality, the services, grew rapidly throughout the period. Increasing concentration of income and wealth did not mean that the poor became poorer, rather that their position, when judged in comparison to those above them, had worsened.

Jeffrey Williamson has analyzed antebellum urban inequality.[35] He finds that real unskilled wages rose a healthy 61.6 percent (or 1.21 percent annually) between 1820 and 1860.[36] This testifies to the beneficial effects of long-term growth upon material well-being. But the urban inequality index showed a dramatic shift from an index of 110 (Jeffersonian democracy equals 100) in 1816 to more than 180 in 1856.[37] "In four short decades, the American Northeast was transformed from the 'Jeffersonian ideal' to a society more typical of developing economies with wide pay differentials and, presumably, marked inequality in the distribution of wage income."[38] Williamson decomposed his inequality index into income and expenditure effects. The income side traced nominal pay ratios—that is, the skilled wage divided by the unskilled wage. For the expenditure series, Williamson constructed cost-of-living indices for the urban unskilled, skilled, and rich. Each consumed a different market basket composed of food, clothing, and servants. Most of the antebellum surge in inequality came from the income side as the skilled-unskilled wage gap widened. Some could be attributed to expenditures, as the cost of necessities rose slightly more rapidly than that of luxuries.

The inequality index climbed unevenly. Williamson summarized:

Nominal pay differentials rose by 23.7 percent from 1820 to 1836. An application of the "rich" and unskilled cost of living indices to the nominal pay structure suggests that *real* pay differentials rose by 37.3 percent over the same sixteen years. . . . In contrast, nominal pay differential stabilized in the early forties, but cost-of-living movements reinforced this tendency too. While nominal pay differentials rose by only 1 percent between 1836 and 1844, in real terms they declined by 12 percent. The story is repeated during the second epic surge in nominal inequality following 1844. While nominal pay differentials increased by 21.5 percent during this second wave of industrialization, they rose in real terms by an incredible 34.5 percent, roughly matching the pre-1836 period.[39]

The unskilled not only found themselves poorer in a comparative sense, but in some years became absolutely poorer. In 1856, the real wage of the urban unskilled had declined to four-fifths of its 1844 level.[40] Moreover, "*all* of the excessive rise in the poor's cost of living (over and above that of the rich) between 1844 and 1856 can be attributed to the relative rise in food prices."[41]

These striking statistics may well minimize inequality, since housing costs are not included in the market basket. Rents must have soared with massive migration. As only 2 percent of New Yorkers held land, most had to rent.[42] Even here, the differential between the rich (and/or skilled) and unskilled cost of living widened. Looking at forty developing countries, Kelley and Williamson found that although both urban luxury and squatter rents rose, the latter climbed more rapidly.[43] Poor New Yorkers may have evaded the effect of rising rents by doubling-up; which nevertheless constituted a decline in their living standard.

Wealth differences could have been even larger. The migration statistics identified an influx of propertyless young and the exit of much smaller numbers of people with some property in their thirties and forties. Edward Pessen confirmed this; he calculated that the share of nonbusiness wealth held by the city's top 4 percent climbed from 49 percent in 1828 to 66 percent in 1845.[44]

Conclusion

The threads of economic structure, demographic change, and economic inequality can be tied together neatly. Commercial supremacy and quickening industrialization created jobs and pulled up wages, which in turn explain the enormous migration into New York County. Seeking the unskilled, urban employers attracted foreigners, women, and the young. This altered the original urban demographic profile and contributed to the unprecedented surge in income inequality. The waves of newcomers, especially in the 1840s and 1850s, must have depressed unskilled wages. But economic development appeared to be far more significant in accounting for inequality, as it handsomely rewarded those with skills and capital. Finally, income inequality surged forward in two episodes. The first occurred in 1820 to 1836, the second from 1844 to 1856.

Why this trend toward increasing inequality prompted only modest discontent is a matter for speculation. On the one hand, one might offer a "rising tide lifts all boats" explanation. Real incomes rose for skilled and unskilled alike. The middle and upper classes, who enjoyed tremendous improvements in their well-being, could now purchase an abundance of goods and services. They began an exodus from the crowded city center, isolating themselves from the increasingly foreign poor. If these favored groups did not achieve all of their economic aspirations, they could migrate elsewhere or anticipate their children's successes. Furthermore, New York's abundant jobs provided unusual opportunities for the unskilled. The foreign-born experienced sharp onetime gains over their home-country conditions. One need only reflect upon the options available in Ireland or the German states during the 1840s.

But this explanation is too facile. If average incomes rose at unprecedented rates, they exhibited sharp variations. Surely the unskilled recognized the decline in their living standard during the late 1840s and the early 1850s. Yet the most riotous period occurs in the Civil War era. Why so late? At least part of the answer lies in the demographic and occupational profiles presented here. The unskilled usually entered jobs without traditions of organized protest. Even when they joined the crafts, they encountered hostility from those already there who saw them as competitors pulling down wages. Unions performed poorly in the antebellum years anyway, forming in tight labor markets and disappearing during depressions. More important, the bulk of the unskilled fell into three overlapping categories: the young, the foreign-born, and females. Their basic characteristics mitigated against class consciousness in republican America. So protest tended to take individualized forms: rowdiness, delinquency, or emigration.

New York City differed from other large Northern cities only by the scale of change. All witnessed historically rapid demographic growth fed by immigration. Their economies prospered with growing and increasingly specialized hinterlands. Large-scale manufacturing firms tended to locate outside the center city to secure water power or to enjoy lower land rents. This hastened the process of suburbanization as well as increasing the commitment of cities to services and light industry.

Lastly, the premium upon capital and skills more than the influx of immigrants made extraordinary inequality a hallmark of urban America.

Notes

1. Allan R. Pred, *Urban Growth and City Systems in the United States, 1840–1860* (Cambridge: Harvard University Press, 1980), 32.
2. Pred, *Urban Growth*, 32.
3. Robert Greenhalgh Albion, *The Rise of the New York Port [1815–1860]* (New York: Scribner, 1939), 57.
4. Albion, *The Rise of the New York Port*, 59.
5. Robert Lipsey "Foreign Trade," in *American Economic Growth*, ed. Lance E. Davis, Richard A. Easterlin, and William N. Parker (New York: Harper & Row, 1972), 554.
6. Pred, *Urban Growth*, 142–65.
7. Pred, *Urban Growth*, 223–24.
8. Pred, *Urban Growth*, 223–24.
9. Pred, *Urban Growth*, 220.
10. For a discussion of the business system, see Thomas Cochran, *Frontiers of Change: Early Industrialism in America* (New York: Oxford University Press, 1981), 11–37, 116–27.
11. These data are drawn from Diane Lindstrom and John Sharpless, "Urban Growth and Economic Structure in Antebellum America," in *Research in Economic History*, ed. Paul Uselding, vol.3 (New York: JAI Press, 1978), 166.
12. Lindstrom and Sharpless, "Urban Growth," 168.
13. Allan R. Pred, *The Spatial Dynamics of United States Urban Industrial Growth 1800–1914: Interpretative and Theoretical Essays* (Cambridge: M.I.T. Press, 1966), 214.
14. Since Standard Industrial Classifications are used, aggregations beyond Pred's manufacturing categories occurred. We biased the data in favor of Pred's argument by putting the aggregated data in question under commerce-serving or entrepôt categories.
15. Lindstrom and Sharpless, "Urban Growth," 174–75.
16. Dorothy Brady, "Comment," in *The Growth of Seaport Cities, 1790–1825*, ed. David Gilchrist (Charlottesville: Eleutherian Mills-Hagley Foundation, 1967), 92–97.
17. From Lindstrom and Sharpless, "Urban Growth," 178.
18. Lindstrom and Sharpless, "Urban Growth," 182–85.
19. Jacob Price, "Economic Function and Growth of Port Towns in the Eighteenth Century," in *Perspectives in American History*, ed. Donald Fleming and Bernard Bailyn, vol. 8 (Cambridge: Harvard University Press, 1974), 184–85.

20. Secretary of the Interior, *Manufactures of the United States, 1860* (Washington, D.C., 1865), 379–84.

21. New York and Philadelphia accounted for about two-thirds of ready-made clothing. See Diane Lindstrom, "The Industrial Revolution in America," in *Region und Industrialisierung*, ed. Sidney Pollard (Göttingen: Vandenhoeck and Reprecht, 1980), 83.

22. W. Elliot Brownlee and Mary M. Brownlee, *Women in the American Economy* (New Haven: Yale University Press, 1976), 3.

23. See John Sharpless, *City Growth in the United States, England and Wales, 1820–1861* (New York: Arno Press, 1977), 248; and Theodore Hershberg, Bruce Laurie, and George Alter, "Immigrants and Industry: The Philadelphia Experience, 1850–1880," in *Philadelphia: Work, Space, Family, and Group Experience in the Nineteenth Century*, ed. Theodore Hershberg (New York: Oxford University Press, 1981), 106–13.

24. Hershberg, Laurie, and Alter, "Immigrants and Industry," 109.

25. U.S. Census Office, *Eighth Census, 1860, Population* (Washington, D.C., 1865), 609.

26. To get county-level net migration estimates, I applied an age-sex and county-specific death rate to the population in one decade and compared the result with the same population in the next decade. For example, if an urban county has 10,000 10>20-year-old males in 1810, I multiplied the 10,000 by the inverse of the death rate (1.0–.06075) to get a survival estimate, 9,303. In the absence of migration, I predicted that there should be 9,303 20>30-year-old males in 1820. If the actual number was higher, immigration occurred; if it was lower, outmigration took place. To get migration rates, I divided the number of migrants by the predicted population. To continue the example, if the census reported 10,000 20>30-year-old males in 1830, net immigration equaled 697 and the rate (697 divided by 9,303) was 7.49 percent.

27. These data cannot measure those who within a census decade migrate and die, migrate and return, or migrate more than once. The death rates were drawn from Maris Vinovskis's analysis of bills of mortality for Massachusetts towns over 10,000. I would assume that these rates are lower than what actually occurred in New York, but the alternative set available, Jaffe and Lourie's, yield implausible estimates. See Maris Vinovskis, "Mortality Rates and Trends in Massachusetts Before 1860," *Journal of Economic History* (March 1972): 24.

28. Allen C. Kelley and Jeffrey G. Williamson, "What Drives Third World City Growth?" (Paper presented to the Conference on Urban Processes and Policies in Developing Countries, Chicago, May 10–13, 1982), 24.

29. Diane Lindstrom, "Northeastern Net Migration, 1810–1860" (Paper presented at the Columbia University Seminar in Economic History, 1983).

30. Albion, *The Rise of the New York Port*, 389.

31. Superintendent of the Census, *Census of the State of New York for 1855* (Albany, 1857), 112–18.

32. Albion, *The Rise of the New York Port*, 241.

33. Albion, *The Rise of the New York Port*, 250.

34. Robert E. Gallman, "The Pace and Pattern of American Economic Growth," in *American Economic Growth*, ed. Davis, Easterlin, and Parker, 30. Gallman does find higher concentrations in sugar-producing rural Louisiana.

35. Jeffrey Williamson, "American Prices and Urban Inequality Since 1820," *Journal of Economic History* (June 1976): 303–13. These generalized urban data ought to mirror the experiences of New York. First, the author based his expenditure series on New York wholesale price indices. The nominal pay statistics came from a variety of reports on wages by occupation and not locale. Most were derived from manufacturing and building trades, which constituted shrinking shares of New York's employment. Had Williamson measured the skilled-unskilled wages in the service sector, he might have found even greater inequality.

36. Williamson, "American Prices," 313.

37. Williamson, "American Prices," 305.

38. Jeffrey Williamson and Peter Lindert, *American Inequality: A Macroeconomic History* (New York: Academic Press, 1980), 68.

39. Williamson, "American Prices," 316.

40. Williamson, "American Prices," 317.

41. Williamson, "American Prices," 319.

42. Calculated from the *New York Census, 1855*, 8.

43. The index (urban squatter divided by urban luxury) rose from a base of 100 in 1960 to 131 in 1973. Kelley and Williamson, "Third World City Growth," 28.

44. Edward Pessen, *Riches, Class, and Power Before the Civil War* (Lexington, Mass.: Heath, 1973), 33–37.

2

Culture, Class, and Place
in Antebellum New York

Peter G. Buckley

New York City witnessed changes of unprecedented scale between 1820 and 1860. The dimensions of this demographic, economic, and spatial transformation have been finely sketched by Diane Lindstrom, among others. This period encompassed the highest decennial rate of urbanization ever experienced by an American city: an almost ninefold increase in population, from a town containing 120,000 people to a metropolitan area of over one million. New York established and maintained both mercantile and manufacturing supremacy over its rivals, Baltimore, Philadelphia, and Boston. The early introduction of regular packet lines secured a near monopoly of information encounters with Europe. The line of residential settlement moved from Canal Street to Thirty-third Street, and the city annexed, economically if not legally, the sleepy village of Brooklyn.[1]

Such changes in scale tend to disguise equally significant changes in social structure through the years of what used to be called the Jacksonian Revolution. By 1860 nearly half the city's population was foreign-born—200,000 from Ireland alone. Inequalities of wealth, income, and perhaps opportunity were widening. Changes in the labor market, especially in the consumer goods trade, fractured the artisanal system of production, for the first time aligning the interests of masters against those of journeymen.[2]

Population and riches were spread unevenly over the procrustean grid of new streets laid out in the Commissioners Plan of 1811. As New

York marched "uptown," it crystallized into its differing social constituents and functions. Notable pockets of destitution appeared at the Five Points, just north of City Hall, and at the waterfronts. The Fifteenth Ward, surrounding Washington Square, contained the most visible and extensive area of luxury housing for the elite. The recent historiography of local politics, grounded in Edward Pessen's careful analysis of the links between wealth and office holding, suggests that the elite's control of political power was not entirely overturned, despite the extension and widespread exercise of the suffrage. By 1860, New York's society thus seems to have had little left of the "Era of the Common Man."[3]

This portrait of a divided city contrasts sharply with the established accounts of urban cultural development over the same period. If the figure of the common man received less than his fair share of wealth and political power, he apparently experienced absolute gains in his acquaintance with, and access to, newspapers, books, music, art, and staged performance.[4] A whole range of technological improvements in paper production, press machinery, and engraving, together with the spread of literacy, made print a majority culture—extending to all social classes—for the first time. In 1820, New York City had only one stage that offered extended dramatic entertainment and no public library or gallery open to "non-subscribers." By 1860, it boasted twelve theaters, six lecture rooms, five photographic and two art galleries, and numerous smaller sites for commercial entertainment. The families of skilled or craft workers could afford entrance to all of these places.[5]

In scale terms, this expansion in cultural offerings could be seen as the unfolding of the promissory note of democracy, perhaps serving an integrative function—assimilating immigrants or pacifying the mob—where so many other rungs in the social ladder had failed. However, cultural forms and options do not appear to have proliferated any more evenly over the face of the city than did people or wealth. The common man or woman was not given an admission ticket to forms already existing in 1820. New genres of performance, particularly melodrama, burlesque, and minstrelsy, developed along Chatham Street and the Bowery, catering to (and frequently staffed by) the vigorous popular audiences of the Lower East Side. The arrival of the Penny Press, after 1834, totally altered the content, circulation, and financing of newspapers. The "news" now included extended narratives of urban crime, amusement, and the antics of elite society, in contrast to the dry coverage of shipping and politics undertaken by the subscription-based mercantile sheets. At the same time, new kinds of genteel aesthetic discrimination arose within elite circles to accommodate the introduction of

Italian opera, symphonic music, and "serious" narratives of discovery and history.

An absolute link between cultural forms and class would caricature the actual intermingling of audiences and tastes that undoubtedly took place. A plebeian loafer, like Walt Whitman, learned to love Italian opera by 1849, despite his early reservations about its social exclusiveness. And members of New York's upper classes, such as the famous diarist George Templeton Strong, were not above a visit to P. T. Barnum's gaudy museum on lower Broadway. Antebellum urban culture was Jacksonian to the extent that older lines between the vernacular and the polite broke apart. Yet the very pervasiveness of popular commercial culture produced a heightened concern among the elite or the "respectable" to establish new boundaries between the rough and the genteel. After about 1840, guidebooks, moral tracts, and personal accounts present a simple historical map to the changing amusements of New York. From the single Park Theatre of 1820, urban culture had grown and divided along two routes: the popular and plebeian course followed Chatham Street and the Bowery, with their menageries, oyster cellars, melodrama houses, and concert saloons; the other followed Broadway, with its dry-goods houses and lecture rooms, to the Fifteenth Ward and the Astor Place Opera House.

All maps are partial and incomplete. However, this geographical metaphor proves useful in bringing to earth cultural processes that are often left hovering above the "real" social changes in urban society. Cultural forms not only contain a description of such changes but are also a vital part of them. The divisions of class and ethnicity in the "mercantile period" extended beyond the workplace or formal politics, to the street, to cultural spaces and options, and to representations of the city itself. Indeed, the greatest episode of collective violence between 1820 and 1860, the Astor Place riot of May 1849, arose from the seemingly insignificant matter of an English actor's right to play Macbeth.

This essay visits briefly five locations that attracted much cultural attention in the period: the Five Points, the Fifteenth Ward, the Bowery, Barnum's Museum, and the Central Park. The sites, in both their fictional and their real dimensions, show that antebellum urban culture was not, to paraphrase Clifford Geertz, a single system of signification, but rather an articulation of difference, deeply rooted in class and politics. But despite sharp and growing inequalities, perhaps because of them, all parts of the social spectrum engaged in constructing, and in some cases sharing, this culture of differences.

The Five Points

In January 1843, Richard Henry Dana, Jr., the very model of Bostonian conservatism, traveled to New York City on important legal business.[6] Dana's journal entries from the visit provide an interesting account of the "Broadway" axis of polite culture. Using Theodore Sedgwick's house on Ninth Street as a base, he journeyed downtown to the fraternity of Wall Street lawyers, and, after breakfasting with the U.S. District Attorney, worked his way back to the Sedgwicks', calling on William Cullen Bryant, Julia Ward Howe, John O'Sullivan, and John Jay's daughters. After dinner, Dana thought he might round off a constructive day by having a nightcap at Daniel Lord's in St. John Square. On leaving this house, however, an altogether different aspect of the city imposed itself:

> Passing down Broadway, the name of Anthony st., struck me, & I had a sudden desire to see that sink of iniquity & filth, The "Five Points". Following Anthony st. down, I came upon the neighbourhood. It was about half past ten, & the night was cloudy. . . . Several of [the] houses had wooden shutters well closed & in almost [each] such case I found by stopping & listening, that there were many voices in the rooms & sometimes the sound of music & dancing. On the opposite side of [the] way I saw a door opened suddenly & a woman thrust into the street with great resistance & most foul language on her part.[7]

Dana continued his encounter with the "Points," examining all the "obscure and suspicious looking places" and receiving from prostitutes "many invitations to walk in & see them, just to sit down a minute, &c., followed usually by laughter & jeers when they saw me pass on without noticing them." On impulse, he entered an "establishment," telling the girl that he "had no object but curiosity in coming into the house." She did not seem to be surprised at the request. Fearing that he might be robbed or be caught in a police "descent" without sufficient excuse for being there, he quickly retraced his steps and emerged back into the map of the city he understood:

> From these dark filthy, violent & degraded regions, I passed into Broadway, where lighted carriages with footmen, numerous well dressed passers by, cheerful light coming from behind curtained parlor windows, where were happy, affectionate & virtuous people connected by the ties of blood & friendship & enjoying the charities & honors of life. What mighty differences, what awful separations, wide as that of the great gulf & lasting for eternity, do what seem to be the merest chances place between human beings, of the same flesh and blood.[8]

For the contemporary reader there is, perhaps, something inevitably comic about a man in top hat and formal dress wandering through an urban rookery, anxiously inquiring about the conditions of prostitution and vice. The scene has been reproduced too many times on stage and in novels for us to view such an encounter as an authentic experience. Yet at least the anxiety Dana felt appears to have been authentic. For men of his class, the Five Points presented an unreadable, unordered space in which dilapidated buildings hid scenes of human degradation. Even when vice became visible in street altercations it remained "indescribable." Dana seeks (in the longest prose description in his Journal before 1846) to designate the Points as an area of "darkness" in order to heighten the moral "light" coming from "behind curtained parlor windows" on Broadway. This was indeed an effort; Dana remained sufficiently Calvinist to recognize that only "merest chances" had placed him beyond the world of the Points. Had he not "known desires more terrible than those I witnessed" in his own heart? He was disturbed, not comforted, when he returned to the Sedgwick household to see "seated round a pleasant fire . . . a family solely of women, one the beautiful mother of five daughters, all of whom were yet to try the world & be tried by it, another a distinguished writer of moral stories."[9] He did not, of course, tell them where he had been.

Dana's brief voyage ended with personal reflections on "the relations of man to man and man to God" similar to those in *Two Years Before the Mast*. However, the literary setting for these reflections was of relatively recent invention and, for an American city, politically problematic. Charles Dickens had given fictional shape to the Five Points only the year before, in *American Notes*. The "awful separations" of the kind reproduced in Dana's short walk, and in Dickens's description of tenement conditions, were not supposed to exist in a republic that required "independence" and "equality."[10]

Dickens was accused, by New York's radical and popular press, of simply importing London's most notorious purlieu—the Seven Dials—and setting it down close to City Hall and the "sunshine" of Broadway. Dickens does in fact appear to have developed his "Points" to mock the heightened American cultural nationalism of the 1840s. The scavenging pig of New York's poorer streets became more active and "self-reliant" than any of the other urban inhabitants; "in every respect a republican pig, going wherever he pleases, and mingling with the best society, on an equal, if not superior footing."[11] To Mike Walsh, editor of the radical newspaper *Subterranean*, this parody of democratic mixing proved that "Boz" had thrown his lot in with the "accursed aristocrats." Nevertheless, even Walsh acknowledged, when he wished to illustrate the dangers facing the producing class, that New York was now a city, like London, of Sunshine and Shadow, divided by day and night, by rich and poor.

After Dickens, however real the depth of poverty, the Five Points became a fictional localization of republican failure: a place where virtue and independence ceased to exist and where all social distinctions fell apart. Here, blacks slept with whites; the buildings and animals displayed more character than the humans; the women acted more coarse than did the men.

These inversions and mixings, the central element in depicting the Five Points, were only one extreme that threatened the operations of republican virtue in the metropolis. In the same year as Dana's ramble, an ex-mayor of the city, Philip Hone, judged that

> our good city of New York has already arrived at the state of society to be found in the large cities of Europe; overwhelmed with population, and where the two extremes of costly luxury in living, expensive establishments and improvident wastes are presented in daily and hourly contrast with squalid mixing and hapless destruction."[12]

As a good republican, Hone recognized that luxury posed a danger to the polity equal to the "hapless destruction" of permanent poverty. Both resulted in self-interest and idleness, turning a citizen away from the public duty he owed to the commonweal. But if the squalid mixing could be located with certainty within the Five Points, where might evidence of luxury be found? Dana shows little embarrassment in placing "lighted carriages with footmen" in the same sentence as his "happy, affectionate & virtuous people," though most New Yorkers, including the wealthy Philip Hone, would have thought such a display an aping of European aristocratic luxury. Walt Whitman, visiting Grace Church in 1849, saw liveried servants waiting on the street while their "would-be masters" worshiped in a "temple given over to money." In the same decade as the literary localization of the Points, the popular press typed the Fifteenth, or Empire, Ward, which then included Washington and Union squares, as a home for luxury and the *parvenu* elite of "nabobs" and "codfish aristocrats." As with Five Points depictions, tropes of concealment and inversion abounded. The fine fronts of residences and fashionable Parisian dress disguised the origin and moral character of the nabob. Whitman suspected that

> nine-tenths of the families residing in these noble dwellings, have "sprung from nothing," as the phrase is—by which is intended that their parents

were hucksters, laborers, waiters, and so on; which made the said parents not a whit the worse, but, on the contrary, they were perhaps more sensible and respectable than the children.[13]

The new narratives of urban degradation and luxury that emerged in the 1840s provoked one other localization, that of "knickerbocker New York." Appearing in a variety of forms—historical sketches, memorials, addresses, and visual reproductions (or, more usually, imaginings) of past scenes—these works testified to an earlier age marked by a simplicity of manner and a shared knowledge of place and position. In 1845, a retired merchant named Grant Thorburn, one of the initiators of the genre, complained of "the splendid misery" now before him:

> Young Folks smile when their grandmothers tell of the happy days of auld lang syne. But certain it is that fifty years ago the people in New York lived happier than they do now. They had no artificial wants—only two banks—rarely gave a note—but one small playhouse—no opera, no ottomans, few sofas or sideboards, and perhaps not six pianos in the city.[14]

Though Thorburn was addressing his class, especially clerks who were beginning their careers, he carefully extended the old, close relationships of training, family, and credit that supposedly had existed within the mercantile community to cover the rest of society. The hallmark of the knickerbocker New York reminiscence was a belief that the city's street life and public spaces had once been legible. All social classes had encountered each other at street level, so to speak, in face-to-face acts of commerce, charity, amusement, and voluntary association.

Providing a date for the dissolution of this republican town proved difficult, depending upon the generation and concerns of the writer. Even Henry James remembered the Washington Square society of the 1840s adhering to the rules of "republican simplicity." Yet for merchants and professionals who had established their careers before the Panic of 1837, the fracturing of public culture by "insatiate longings," promiscuous street contact, and political rowdyism seemed real enough.[15]

The literary realizations of knickerbocker New York find no basis in a statistical portrait of a republican town unsegregated by wealth or political power. Recent studies of New York's working populations, political factions, and arrangements of land ownership and use during the Early National period reveal that social distinctions and discriminations operated at every level. By 1820, New York's residential space was already differentiated by class, with 80 percent of the two hundred wealthiest families living in only eight streets near the urban core; journeyman mechanics and artisans not boarding with their masters gravitated to the waterfront districts and the northern boundaries of settlement. The rich assumed that local political office holding, and the leadership of charitable and cultural organizations, remained their exclusive province.[16]

Nevertheless, there were ways in which all groups in the city claimed a role in public life. At least through the 1820s, inter-class contact was extensive, and the political, charitable, and social obligations developed among knickerbocker merchants overflowed into the street. The wealthy continued to shop at the public markets, since there was no other outlet for perishable produce until the late 1830s. The Park Theatre and the summer gardens, such as the original Vauxhall, had socially mixed audiences, including prostitutes, even though patrons were distributed in boxes, pit, and gallery according to social rank and gender. No exclusionary behavioral rules, or actual fencing, existed on public property such as City Hall Park or the Battery. The volunteer fire companies were perhaps the greatest testament to the operations of citizenship in a republic; until 1830, they contained all gradations of rank. The occasional street races, hosings, and brawls that then took place among them testified only to company camaraderie and manly spirit and not, as would be claimed later, to the unrestrained antics of plebeians and loafers.

Mechanics and artisans were as keen as the mercantile and professional elite to engage in the public exercise of citizenship. They paraded in the streets to celebrate the virtue of the crafts over private enterprise on every July 4th and Evacuation Day holiday. Through such festivities, public orations, and craft societies, artisans elaborated what Sean Wilentz describes as "an urban variation of the Jeffersonian theme of the virtuous husbandman," one that saw the producing class as the backbone of a republic and as a defense against despotism. But this "variation" did not extend to a political defense of the rights and value of labor until 1828, with the founding of the Working Men's movement. In the early 1820s, journeymen had not yet developed an ideological position independent of masters and entrepreneurs.[17]

Thus, despite a wide variation of income, ownership, and power in 1820, all classes claimed the same terrain of republican understanding and decried luxury and the affectation of "aristocratic" manners and tastes. The rich held to mild, though ideologically significant, self-restrictions on the visual registration of power and wealth. There were so few private carriages in the city in 1820 that it was common to hear "the owner's name called out as the vehicle drove by." When the actor John Henry kept a carriage because of his gout, "he was forced to explain the reason for such pretension by having an emblem of two crutches painted on the door of his carriage with the motto 'This or These.' "[18]

The great fears about the large population centers in a republic—the poor and the mob—had not yet been identified as permanent political threats or assigned definite spaces in the representations of urban life. The Society for the Prevention of Pauperism had linked poverty to the new waves of immigration as early as 1819. Yet apart from the precocious organizers of this group, who learned the language of poverty science from Patrick Colquhoun, the city authorities viewed the poor as an interstitial presence who arrived with bad weather, financial panics, and other disasters. No area was recognized as specializing in degradation such as the Five Points would in the mid-1830s. By that time, evangelical missionaries and health reformers had come to give poverty either a moral character or an environmental cause. By 1844, the New York Association for Improving the Condition of the Poor, anxious to introduce a "comprehensive, uniform and systematic plan" for the forty organizations then dispensing alms, at last gave the poor "a home" and decisively rejected the indiscriminate practices of "outdoor relief."[19]

Recent studies have shown that mob actions were frequent in the early National and Jacksonian periods. They also reveal how rarely the magistracy viewed mobs as political threats to their authority. The customary reading of the "riot act" quelled most disturbances, and few of the rioters arrested ever reached the point of indictment, because the authorities knew either that trial by jury might lead to acquittal or that leniency best maintained their hegemony over notions of justice. Only in 1836, after three years of violent anti-abolitionist rioting, did the state officially grant the mayor power to call in the militia in advance of a crowd. As late as 1849, in the Astor Place Riot, most of the crowd thought that the militia did not possess the legal authority to fire upon citizens.[20]

No doubt knickerbocker New York had its share of the indigent, the rowdy, and the luxurious. Perhaps they were not sizable enough to characterize the whole of city life or to provoke concerted political actions. But the notion of a unified town that the contemporary guides and later recreations of knickerbocker New York give results from more than the intimate scale suggested by the image of "A Walking City." Rather, the mercantile and rentier elite's confidence in its authority and ability to supervise all areas of urban life—from politics, to charity, to culture— also produced this appearance of unity. The public sphere appears relatively seamless because the elite, figuratively and geographically, was at the center of its construction.

Through the 1830s, the march uptown to the new luxuries "above Bleecker" and the challenge posed by the spread of political and cultural forms of representation to other groups both broke apart this confidence of scale and authority. By 1850, New York was firmly characterized, as it is today, by its extremes of wealth and poverty. Few residents openly celebrated being a Fifth Avenue Nabob or a Five-Pointer. Rather, the fractures in New York's antebellum cultural terrain are revealed in the ways differing social classes claimed to be central to the maintenance of republican virtue. Struggle occurred over establishing the boundaries of a virtuous middle ground: a variable, shifting space between "improvident wastes" and "squalid mixing." How did the Fifteenth Ward Nabob or the Bowery B'hoy seek to claim a central place in the changing political and social order of the city? How did each view the other across the perceptual barricades of refinement and rowdiness?

The Fifteenth Ward

By 1850, the author Nathaniel Parker Willis had developed the reputation as the most consistent, if not the most admired, commentator of the fashionable metropolitan scene. In the *Mirror* and later *The Home Journal*, Willis penned hundreds of sketches of society balls, horse races, Parisian fashions, and opera attendance in New York. It struck him that the contemporary urban scene lacked a fashionable "inner republic" to set taste and standards. In 1844, Willis claimed that New York's "uppertendom" (one of his more durable coinings) had never known "so prolonged a state of anarchy as exists at this moment," its "aristocracies lasting but a year or so."[21]

Most popular journalists agreed that a "town" had dissolved into a series of competing elites eager to outdistance each other in conspicuous consumption and cultural pretension. For Democratic radicals such as Mike Walsh of the Sixth Ward Spartan Association, certain public behaviors—the wearing of white kid gloves or attendance at Grace Church or at the Astor Place Opera House—proved that wider inequalities existed in society. Whatever the knickerbocker elite's former claims to leadership, the new wealthy, in their march uptown to the residential luxury "above Bleecker," had severed any relations with republican pieties. In Walsh's words, "the Nabobs of the Fifteenth Ward . . . live off the labor of their fellow citizens."[22]

Though penny press journalists seldom identified real nabobs by name, we do have a substantial record, in Philip Hone's *Diary*, of a circle of acquaintance and a style of consumption that matches the description of nabob life in many details. Hone paid $900 for a front pew in Grace Church after its construction in 1842. He also became one of the original subscribers to the Astor Place Opera House in 1847, which was, according to the *Herald*, "the first authentic organization of the upper classes, congregated under a splendid dome in a respectable quarter of the city."[23] In 1836, Hone sold his fine Broadway house fronting City Hall Park and moved up to Washington Square in the Fifteenth Ward. He complained of being

> turned out of doors. Almost everybody downtown is in the same predicament. We are tempted with prices so exorbitantly high that none can resist, and the old downtown burgomasters, who have fixed to one spot all their lives, will be seen during the next summer in flocks, marching reluctantly north to pitch their tents in places which in their time, were orchards, cornfields or morasses a pretty smart distance from town, and a journey to which was considered an affair of some moment and required preparation before hand, but which constitute at this time the most fashionable quarter of New York."[24]

Here, as so often in Hone's writing, there is a gentle tone of mockery, of both himself and his class. In one sense the image of a nomadic tribe heading to new grazing is exact, given his memory of the area around the Washington Square he had known as a child. Yet the pastoral also serves to distance Hone's reflections from the economic realities and social meanings of the great uptown march of fashion. Being turned out of doors suggests a forced removal, yet Hone received $60,000 for the sale of his Broadway site. Neither were the new homes exactly "tents." Most of his friends also moved to the fine terraced residences built from costly materials leading from Washington and Gramercy parks and, somewhat later, Union Square. This pastoral rhetorically evades questions that Hone himself may have had about the creation of a large fashionable area. How might he justify his increasing acquaintance with luxury? How might his class establish a new set of recognizable boundaries once separated from the downtown world of commerce, friendship, and propinquity?

Between 1820 and 1837, Philip Hone used mercantile capital gained through his auction house to create a large stock of banking, insurance, manufacturing, and real estate investments.[25] Like Grant Thorburn, Hone openly lamented the rise in "artificial wants" that such wealth produced and the sheer number of *nouveaux arrivés* with whom he was now forced to socialize. For instance, the range of society obligations expanded to costume balls, "at-homes," and summers at Saratoga. In 1840, exhausted after "seeing in" the New Year, he remarked that "the extent of the visiting circle in New York has become too great for the operations of one day." Like Willis, Hone agreed that the city's *beau monde* had fallen into different "parishes."[26] The more certain separation of the world of work from the operations of society produced a further problem. After 1836, Hone stopped bringing friends home unannounced for a game of whist and an informal dinner.

This expansion in the size of the wealthy classes required new means for controlling entrance to a social elite above and beyond matters of cash and capital. Acquaintance of the kind once gained by walks on the Battery, through the Tontine Coffee House, or in the pit and boxes of the Park Theatre, was no longer held sufficient or reliable. The street, the theater, and even the new respectable hotels such as the Astor House presented a faceless democracy: character and credit were difficult to decode. Hone was troubled by many of the alternative routines for social intercourse, including those he engaged in himself. The large, though "select," balls at the Wadells' or the Aspinwalls', and the masked fetes of the Brevoorts were "insufferable" in their forced gentility. Hone was also a founder member of the Union Club (1836), and the New York Yacht (1836) and Racket clubs (1844), though he found most of their functions "dismal." In 1832, Hone paid over $750 for a box at the first Italian Opera House in the city, yet when it failed, he praised New Yorkers' "spirit of independence that refused its countenance to anything so exclusive."[27]

The public life of polite society established a new set of routines after 1830: more formal dress codes, later dinner hours, and the regulated spaces of clubs. Hone also found himself besieged at home. Though married throughout his years in the Fifteenth Ward, he was fond of casting himself as an aging, displaced bachelor somewhat above the general grope for luxury which he took to be a trait of the young and the female. In 1838, he founded an informal dining club where he could be *en garçon* with his friends, away from the trials of domestic formality. All French food was banned; instead, "a sumptuary law was enacted confining dinner to soup, fish, oysters, four dishes of meat, with a dessert of fruit, ice-cream, and jelly." Yet Hone also recognized that the new course of refinement, which he invariably took to be French in origin, was necessary for the elite in general. He "suffered" through balls, and justified his support of Italian Opera in the knowledge that through such functions "our young men may be initiated into the habits and forms of social intercourse." Such intercourse was the only guarantee, in a world of instant wealth, that the elite could reproduce itself.[28]

Hone displaced the personal vice of luxury by passing it on to the younger generation (or to women, who were always seen to be more susceptible to its demands).[29] However, the *Diary's* retiring bachelor, with his crusty attitude to luxury, contrasts with the persona of the public servant who remains in the streets and offices. Not only did Hone increase his commitments to charity organizations and cultural institutions after 1836, he also remained active in local politics, refusing to concede any loss of terrain to the growing ranks of the "canaille." Again, Hone casts himself as an unwilling minion to an agency beyond his control:

> I begin to be tired of serving the public without serving myself. I have been a slave all my life to an ungrateful master, but somehow I cannot break the shackles which pride and a foolish love of distinction caused me to assume, and which are now so deeply worn into the flesh that the effort would be painful to cast them off, and I must "go on my way" not rejoicing, but grumbling.[30]

There seemed plenty to grumble about. Though the notion of a virtuous people remained an understated possibility, the arrival of the penny press editor and the professional Democratic politician were transforming the citizens of the city into a mob. Hone thought both unworthy of attention, and therefore his *Diary* is full of railings against and quotes from them.

The popular press was particularly vexing for Hone because it "depraved and vitiated" the direct connections between natural leaders and the people. The old mercantile press had been sold only by subscription, assuring that its readership was both its audience and its subject. Especially after James Gordon Bennett's *Herald* arrived in 1836, the penny press broadened and redefined the boundaries of the "public" so that wholly new areas of urban life—from night court at the Tombs to the costumes at elite balls—became open to continuous surveillance and narration. Its readership could only be those who had no particular stakes in the politics of virtue. Hone guessed that the *Herald* was only "sought after with avidity by all those whose insignificance preserves them from being made its subjects." Such a reading public, Hone thought, merely deserved the kinds of leaders thrown up by a system of "puffery and licentiousness."[31]

He saw these readers in local Democracy. After the 1834 state election day festivities, Hone returned to his house "much indisposed, and retired to bed at an early hour, where I was kept awake during the greater part of the night by the unmanly insults of the ruffian crew from Tammany Hall, who came over to my door every half hour and saluted me with groans and hisses."[32]

Undoubtedly, the Jacksonian Revolution displaced some of the wealthy from local office holding, yet "status anxiety" does not adequately describe the quality of Hone's lament. He is careful in such *Diary* entries to blame the system of "barter, bargain and sale" in the Democratic party, rather than the "people," for such outrages. He uses republican rhetoric to justify his continued presence in the public sphere, taking the lead in many municipal processions in the streets as a matter of "duty." The fact that after 1833 he aided in forming an alternative party, the Whigs, with its own corpus of expedient routines and professionals, did not strike him as a paradox; nor did he express surprise when the Whigs outpaced the Democrats in their manipulation of symbols and print during Benjamin Harrison's "Log Cabin" campaign of 1840. For Hone, the Whigs were not a party as such, but rather, at the national level, a collection of men eager to preserve "experience, talent and integrity."[33] Against the case of Mike Walsh and other "Jack Cades" who gathered mobs, Hone consistently placed the figure of Daniel Webster, who by voice alone could hold a respectable gathering of Whig mechanics for three hours. Hone continued to imagine that the Whig politics was based on "natural" relations between the people and their leaders, in contrast to a politics grounded in party and newspaper reputation.

In a deep sense, then, Hone did not see beyond the Republican town of 1820 and the paternalist assumptions of the older elite. Unlike the younger Dana, he had no desire to encounter the Five Points, having heard quite enough of how the other half lived from below his window. However, far from being an unself-conscious nabob, he struggled with the demands of his class as it learned to live with luxury. Cultural refinement, from matters of dress to musical and literary taste, determined entrance to a social elite once recognizable in the lineaments of family, credit, and public service. In the Whig party, he found an aesthetic of public life and performance that countered the changes in urban politics.

The Bowery

If the Fifteenth Ward was recognized by its fine Whig residential spaces and its institutions of high culture, the Bowery was typed by its popular commercial entertainment and its blend of rowdiness and radicalism. The centerpiece of this milieu, the Bowery Theatre, had certainly not begun life as a plebeian place. Its cornerstone was laid in 1826 by none other than Philip Hone, who used the occasion to lecture on the moral benefits of the stage, provided it remained under the direction of "those whose standing in Society enables them to control opinions." Only a decade later, Hone thought that the theater had become a "haunt of mere Pittites," and reflected that "no act in my public life cost me so many friends."[34]

During the 1830s, the Bowery Theatre's audience and performance styles escaped the supervision of Hone's circle. In 1831, a new manager, Thomas Hamblin, introduced melodrama as the mainstay of New York's popular stage. Blackface acts, "ethnic" or Yankee humor, and Revolutionary drama rounded out the bill. The raucous plebeian audiences that filled the galleries and pit eventually drove the middle classes from the theater altogether.[35] Walt Whitman remembered that

> after 1840 the character of the Bowery . . . completely changed. . . . Not that there was more or less rankness in the crowd even then. For types of sectional New York . . . —the streets East of the Bowery, that intersect Division, Grand, and up to Third Avenue—types that have never found their Dickens, Hogarth, or Balzac . . . —the young shipbuilders, cartmen, butchers, firemen, they too were always to be seen in these audiences, racy of the East River and the Dry Dock.[36]

Whitman's selection of types here conforms to both the street and the theater's reputation as a militantly public zone for working-class amusement. By 1850, the Bowery offered a continuous strip of entertainment featuring menageries, saloons, billiard halls, and "free and easies."[37] To its east, in the "unknown proletarian regions" of "sectional New York," lay the greatest concentration of single young men and women in the city, living in boarding houses and free from the restrictions of family or apprenticeship.[38] However, the Bowery itself was not an area of "darkness," like the Points, but rather a street where colorful plebeian types, such as Whitman's Mose, the Bowery B'hoy, and his G'hal Lize, displayed and enjoyed themselves.[39] Foreign observers were impressed with the increasing velocity of nightlife: "John Bull," claimed an English mechanic, "sits leisurely down and makes a night of it: Jonathan can't keep still, but rushes first to the bar-room of the hotel where he has dined, has a drink, thence to the confectioner's saloon, then to a cigar ditto, next to an oyster ditto, and most likely 'smiles' at each of them."[40]

This Bowery milieu possessed a distinct class character, though, being commercial to the core, its culture was neither "traditional" nor "autonomous." Entrepreneurs, like P. T. Barnum during his tenure at the Vauxhall Garden, specialized in low-cost appropriations from the street, inviting the audience to perform clog dances, breakdowns, glees, and imitations of urban types, while at the same time charging admission. The Bowery assigned to working class amusement its own space and time, removed from the customs of work or "community." According to Charles Haswell, the chief figure of the street, the infamous "B'hoy" with his stovepipe hat, red fireman's shirt, and check trousers, appeared *in propria persona* only on Sundays; for the remainder of the week he became an industrious butcher, clerk, or mechanic.[41]

Though the Bowery was the commercial product of the marketplace for amusement, no one took it to be politically neutral territory. Professional writers (who had their own audiences to develop) celebrated the unfolding of popular commercial culture as the final overthrow of aristocratic privilege. George Foster thought that the numerous "well conducted resorts" on the Bowery proved "that however poor may be the condition of an American family" it was much superior to and more educated than its European counterpart, which had to be supplied with amusements and knowledge from above.[42] Walt Whitman was perhaps the first journalist to read the "glorious jam" of the New York streets as a direct extension of political democracy. In the *Aurora*, a popular newspaper Whitman edited in 1842, he conducted "walks around town" covering the life of fire companies, markets, newsboys, and theaters. The working man and woman's right to be visible in public life became a central aspect of Whitman's understanding of political power, and he wanted his paper to serve the needs of the "would-be *elegantes*" among the producing classes.[43]

Taking to the street in a travesty of upper class manners was transformed into a political right, especially after the Panic of 1837 ended the General Trades Union insurgency from the shop floor. Popular cultural forms presented the elaborate dress and street manners of the B'hoy and G'hal in opposition to the middle class mania for respectability and "self-culture" during the 1840s. The most popular play of that decade, Benjamin Baker's *A Glance at New York*, featured Mose on a spree at the Vauxhall Garden and at a bowling alley.[44] He affects the manners of a dandy, offering critiques of the latest plays and novels, and he also engages in four "regular knock-downs and drag-outs" in the space of forty minutes. Such "musses" testified to his independent character, and all protected the virginity of young sewing girls and the innocence of the rural greenhorns. Later versions of the play invariably include a spectacular conflagration scene in which Mose, always a volunteer fireman, saves a young child from the flames and returns the infant to a weeping mother. The figure of Mose encapsulated the rough, material pleasures of the Bowery, yet the popular theater showed Mose's and Lize's counterparts in the audience that rowdiness, rather than Fifteenth Ward refinement, could sustain the virtues of a republic.

Evangelical opposition to the Bowery saw the common man's decline into the ultimate degradation of the Five Points rather than his ascendancy through commercial amusement. John Todd's *The Young Man* offered little schemas of debauchery that awaited the greenhorn entering the city. Mose became the enticer, not the savior:

> The enticer will court your acquaintance, will take you, at his own expense, to the confectioners, then to the beer-shop, and the oyster-seller. By degrees he leads you on till you find yourself in the billiard room, then the theatre, and probably next entering the door of her whose house is the gate-way to hell.[45]

Those "above Bleecker" had a somewhat broader perspective on the Bowery than these precise evangelical warnings. The Bowery was not a localized danger that led to the Points; rather, its techniques of display and self-promotion threatened to invade all of the city's streets and public institutions. It was precisely this appropriation of the street, the market, and the fire company, and not the potential for "the roughs" to organize workers, that most worried Hone's circle. N. P. Willis thought that the real aristocrats who were destroying the republican town consisted of

> the newsboy who disturbs the decent citizen with his cries in the early morning, the omnibus driver who steers his foaming steed without regard to life or limb, the market women with their bawdy talk, the arrogance of the fire company runner—these are the aristocrats who think only of themselves.[46]

Moreover, the Bowery milieu acquired a formal political presence that challenged the power of the elite in both parties. Out of the networks of male working class sociability—in markets, fire companies, bars, and theaters—emerged locally effective political traditions that blended the rationalist perspective of the workingmen's movements of the late 1820s with the new world of the streets. The most infamous of these was the Spartan Association, formed in 1840 by Mike Walsh, David Broderick, and other members of the Red Rover fire engine company. Walsh must be given the credit for perfecting, if not inventing, the use of crowd action as a political tool. His group successfully infiltrated the Democratic organization through street harangues and storming the long room of Tammany Hall.[47]

These new kinds of political action curiously parallel new forms of writing about the city in terms of personnel and style. Much of what we know about the popular culture of New York comes from those who moved easily between politics and the new means of communication in print and theater. Whitman offers the clearest case, but Walsh too, when not engaging in direct political action, advised workers on what kinds of new writing were suited to their "intelligence." His *Subterranean* became the first periodical in the city to carry extracts from Eugene Sue's *The Mysteries of Paris* (1843), especially after Dickens's *American Notes* proved to Walsh that he was unsuitable for the "B'hoys."

Popular journalism, like the Bowery, was not considered politically neutral terrain. Since 1834, the penny press had claimed to be on "public" duty, assuming the mantle of "independence" in the years when the Workingman's party failed. With the Democratic and Whig organizations in the hands of "regulars" and "placemen," and the police and judiciary subject to the demands of patronage, the popular journalist and writer took up the task of telling the truth about the city.[48]

This may well account for the durable nature of the image of "sunshine and shadow." The rhetoric of exposure sanctioned a drift in many popular novels (such as Ned Buntline's *Mysteries and Miseries of New York* [1848]) into a kind of republican pornography where vice and prostitution illuminate the intimate connections between the vicious poor and the uncaring rich. Moreover, the popular writer had to be part of the people and yet claim a greater knowledge of the threats facing them. An odd blend of self-promotion and loyalty to the producing classes emerges from the pages of Whitman's *Aurora*, Walsh's *Subterranean*, and Levi Slamm's *Daily Plebeian*. They wrote themselves into the streets only to be elevated into political placemen or poets. The resulting ironies were not lost to Whitman:

> Then finding it impossible to do anything either in the way of "heavy business," or humor, we took our cane . . . and our hat, and sauntered down Broadway to the Battery. Strangely enough, nobody stared at us with admiration—nobody said "there goes the Whitman of the Aurora!"—nobody ran after us to take a better and second better look . . . nobody wheeled out of our way deferentially—but on we went, swinging our stick in our right hand—and with our left hand tastily thrust in its appropriate pocket in our frock coat.[49]

The figure of the Bowery B'hoy who so annoyed Hone's circle emerged from this kind of writing and action. The B'hoy may have been a real figure of the streets but he was certainly a type who, though never finding its Dickens, Hogarth, or Balzac, gained its Whitman, Foster, Baker, and Walsh.

The Museum and the Park

The rhetorical and ideological opposition of the Democratic Bowery to the Whig Fifteenth Ward resulted in open conflict during the Astor Place Riot of May 1849. A growing public feud between the great British actor William Charles Macready and the hero of the Bowery's melodramatic stage, Edwin Forrest, provided the immediate context for the riot. On May 10, a crowd of eight thousand people gathered before the Astor Place Opera House to protest Macready's continued presence on an "aristocratic" stage. Unlike previous theatrical disputes, the house was protected by a large cadre of police, and later the militia, with orders from a Whig mayor to protect Macready in "the lawful exercise of his calling." In the melee that followed, twenty-two people lost their lives and the city was placed under martial law for three days.[50]

Blame for this result was apportioned according to the politics of the observer: radical Democrats castigated the mayor, the police, and, above all, the nabobs who had built the opera house and requested the authorities to defend a British actor. The mercantile press delighted in the firm suppression of "the spirit of the mob" that had been so active in Europe during 1848. However, the riot presented evidence to every journalist that extremes of wealth and poverty now characterized the center of urban life:

> It leaves behind it a feeling to which this community has been a stranger—an opposition of classes—the rich and the poor—white kids [gloves] and no kids at all; in fact, to speak right out, a feeling that there is now in this country, in New York City, what every good patriot has hitherto felt it his duty to deny—a *high* class and a *low* class.[51]

After the riot, with the renewal of organized labor agitation in 1850, the need to reconstruct a middle ground for urban culture was clear and pressing. Two reworkings of the "public," without resorting to the temperance tract or the militia, seemed particularly persuasive. One appeared out of the Bowery axis. It celebrated the democratic rights of the public, as consumers, to enter the marketplace of commercial culture. The other took the higher road of refinement in a revised Whiggism, still suspicious of an unregulated market and the influence of party, yet denying evangelical solutions or legislative efforts to police recreation and amusement. In New York, these two solutions to a culturally divided city found their material and geographical expression in P. T. Barnum's American Museum and Frederick Law Olmsted's Central Park.

The American Museum

Despite the gradual effacement of the social origins of the "world's greatest showman" in his autobiography, P. T. Barnum formally began his meteoric career on the Bowery during the Panic of the late 1830s.[52] Barnum tried his hand at the usual range of petty entrepreneurial pursuits: boardinghouse keeper, bootblack manufacturer, and Bible salesman. He first showed a marked edge over the competition in June 1840 during his tenure as director of amusements at the Vauxhall Garden at the northern end of the Bowery. There he dispensed with the regular stock company of performers and "jobbed-in" artists for the night for an ever-changing mix of music, ventriloquism, and enactments of street types such as the Fulton Market Roarer.

> There is no mistake in the performance at this establishment. They are exceedingly various, and full of life and merriment. This is what we want. The public have enough to groan and sigh about at home these times, they go out to such places as Vauxhall to "laugh and grow fat," and Barnum is determined they shall not go in vain.[53]

In order to "laugh and grow fat" at a more central site, Barnum secured, through dubious means, the lease to Scudder's museum on the corner of Broadway and Ann Street, facing both City Hall Park and the elite Astor House Hotel. To this previously respectable location, he imported the Bowery techniques of showmanship and display. In 1844, he transformed the exterior of the building, applying overnight 104 five-foot-high transparencies of the curiosities contained within: "When the living stream rolled down Broadway the next morning and reached the Astor House corner, it seemed to meet with a sudden check. I never saw so many open mouths and astonished eyes."[54] On the inside, Barnum gave similar Bowery treatment to the musty showcases of Scudder's exhibit, which had contained examples of natural creation arranged in Linnaean order. Freaks, national wonders, and a host of "transient attractions" reproduced the "exceedingly various" offering of the Vauxhall Garden.

Since Barnum was eager to attract and develop the largest public possible, he also carefully removed any taint of immorality from the exhibition or his persona. He undertook a fashionably late conversion to the cause of temperance in 1847 and wisely labeled the theatrical space in his museum "a lecture room." On this stage W. H. Smith's temperance drama, *The Drunkard*, became the first play in the United States ever to achieve an uninterrupted run of one hundred performances.[55] Barnum was also evidently the first amusement entrepreneur to introduce the matinee as a regular feature of theatrical practice, allowing women and children to attend a world of pleasure previously associated with the "shadows" of nightlife. Barnum was no humbug or simple pitchman. He offered all this entertainment as a republican gesture. He invited the inquiring public into his museum not to be fooled, but rather to have its credulity tested and its native intelligence exercised. He advertised one of his greatest hoaxes, the Feegee mermaid, for instance, as an authentic wonder of nature *and* as a cleverly sewn together series of animal parts. It was the "duty" of republican citizens to come and seek the truth for themselves.[56]

Barnum cleverly knit together a celebration of market, crowds, respectability, and republicanism. He reassembled a fragmented cultural terrain by containing on one site as many options as possible. In this sense, the museum, despite its visual impact, was a nonplace—a mere extension of the street, the entrance to which was not restricted by class, ethnicity, or gender. The "living stream" of Broadway was checked only by a brief exchange of twenty-five cents at the door.

The Central Park

Olmsted and Vaux's famous "Greensward" plan for The Central Park, which won first prize in the competition established by the Park Commissioners in 1858, presented a different and opposing conception of urban crowding and culture. The Greensward plan, with its emphasis on an uninterrupted sweep of natural scenery, became an integral part of New York's landscape and of the language of park planning; it is thus hard to recapture the design's original contribution or to see how it offered a programmatic solution to the problems of a culturally divided city. In fact, the conception of a park as a unified work of scenic art was a relatively late entry in the field of park functions and uses. As early as 1844, N. P. Willis had editorialized about the need for a large promenade for walking and driving, a place where the middle classes could learn and enact fashion and etiquette. Even Andrew Jackson Downing, the landscape architect whose articles in the *Horticulturalist* supposedly began the legislative drive to establish a large open space, conceived of an urban park as a "drawing room," in which all classes could exchange pleasantries under the shade of trees.[57]

Even after the Central Park site had been formally appropriated, in 1853, and the commissioners had set the terms for the competition, a wide variety of notions existed. *Frank Leslie's*, the most popular illustrated magazine in the city, urged designers to follow "the French, who have wisely allowed the labouring classes to have cafe concerts, cirques, ambulatory exhibitions, and shooting galleries. . . . We must not make our places of public amusement like our fashionable dwellings—the abodes of isolated grandeur."[58]

Almost all of the thirty-three designs submitted did incorporate some elements of the popular carnivalesque: playgrounds, concert halls, skating ponds, or prospect towers. One plan placed a shooting gallery, a third of a mile in length, next to the receiving reservoir; another envisioned a forty-acre amphitheater surrounding a parade ground. All, except Greensward, contained areas for exhibition halls and other forms of architectural embellishment. There was a great fondness of statuary and republican symbolism: a plan labeled "hope" had the entire history of the Revolution told in frescoes on the walls of the old reservoir.[59]

Olmsted's pitch for Greensward as a "single work of art" should be judged in the context of other proposals that saw the park as a potpourri of landscaping tastes and social functions. Only a unified, natural scene could counter the commercial life of the city rather than serve as an extension of the street. In Greensward, all of the infringements of the city were minimized: crosstown traffic disappeared from view in the sunken transverse roads; sharp curves were introduced in the circular drives in order to prevent "opportunities for trotting matches"; the parade ground reappeared as an informal, spacious "meadow." Even the promenade, a requirement of the commission, was subordinated to the unity of the landscape by aligning it with the enormous vista rock above the Seventy-ninth Street crossing.[60]

Such "art" had an implicit social function. It left little room for the planned gregarious activities of any group in New York society other than children. Olmsted hoped that Central Park might offer a varied, though much more controlled, performance than any existing on the street or in Barnum's museum. On entering the park, through gates that represented the various callings in American life, one would leave the anxieties and emulations of social class behind to be "recreated" by the beauties of the landscape.

Like Barnum's Museum, Olmsted presented Vaux's plan as a model of democracy and republicanism. However, the park would incorporate, or rather diffuse, the crowd on a plane of "aesthetic culture" rather than crass commercialism. Moreover, the park promised to be only the first of many locations—galleries, museums, educational institutions—that the state would sponsor in order to "elevate" the mass. Even before joining the park staff as superintendent in 1857, Olmsted had urged his young liberal friends to "get up parks, gardens, music, dancing schools, reunions which will be so attractive as to force into contact the good and the bad, the gentleman and the rowdy."[61] Those who thought such integration impossible were guilty of the "fallacy of cowardly conservatism." He treasured, as an example of this fallacy, an editorial from the *Herald* that predicted that any attempt to impose European notions of civility was doomed to failure. In America, stated the *Herald*,

> we know no "nobility and gentry": nothing but a public which is all and everything, and in which Sam the Five Pointer is as good a man as William B. Astor or Edward Everett. Further, whatever is done by or for the public aforesaid, is done by and for Sam as much as any one else. . . . Therefore, when we open a public park, Sam will air himself in it. . . . He will enjoy himself there whether by having a muss, or a drink at the corner groggery opposite the great gate. He will run races with his new horse in the carriage way. He will knock any better dressed man down who remonstrates with him.[62]

For the first fifteen years of the park's existence, while it remained under the supervision of reform politicians, elite New Yorkers congratulated themselves, and the "public," that this exercise in aesthetic engineering had proved a success. George Templeton Strong thought that "the Central Park, the Astor Library and a developed Columbia University promise to make the city twenty years hence a real center of culture and civilization." Henry Bellows, the Unitarian minister who organized the U.S. Sanitary Commission during the Civil War, saw the Park as a "grand test of the ability of the people to know their own higher wants, of the power of their artistic instincts."[63] Yet in 1877, at the end of the national phase of Reconstruction, both the park and Olmsted fell prey to a revived Tammany Hall, emerging from the ashes of the Tweed Ring. New plans were introduced for a trotting track, for commercial restaurants, and for the independent park police to become another arena of patronage.

The competing visions of the park's uses today, and the fact that it has always—even before it existed—been an area of political negotiation, illustrate the legacy of antebellum urban culture. The period established a series of oscillations between the claims of respectability and rowdiness, between legislative control of amusements and unrestricted commercial culture, that continue to reverberate in New York City, even though they have often changed their sites and their personnel. After the Civil War the dominant mode changed. Print media and stage production were shaped by greater concentrations of capital and further integrations of entrepreneurial action. In a city that rebuilds itself every twenty years, this change was quickly registered in the geography of urban places: the imposing press buildings surrounding City Hall, the crystallization of the theater and entertainment industries in Union Square, and the "Ladies' Mile" of department stores on Sixth Avenue.

Cultural resolutions to the realities of urban inequality did not emerge out of a "consensus," however much entrepreneurs and reformers both wanted to invoke the "public" to justify their activities. Their efforts were rooted in the republican rhetoric in which the problems of American urbanization were first articulated. Though the Nabob and Five Pointer have since disappeared, at least two terms—the "public" and the "middle class"—mark the vast spaces between indigence and luxury over which they once stood guard.

Notes

1. Apart from Lindstrom's essay in this volume, see also Allan Pred, *Urban Growth and the City Systems in the United States, 1840–1860* (Cambridge: Harvard University Press, 1980), and the classic work by Robert Greenhalgh Albion, *The Rise of the New York Port* [1815–1850] (New York: Scribner, 1939).

2. There is some debate over the ideological results and timing of metropolitan industrialization. Howard Rock, in his *Artisans of the New Republic: The Tradesmen of New York City in the Age of Jefferson* (New York: New York University Press, 1979), sees the alliance of masters and mechanics fracturing in the Jeffersonian period. Sean Wilentz finds a clearer articulation of an independent journeyman's politics by the late 1820s; see his *Chants Democratic: New York City and the Rise of the American Working Class, 1788–1850* (New York: Oxford University Press, 1984).

3. Edward Pessen's many essays on the realities and myths of the Era of the Common Man are referenced and condensed in his book, *Riches, Class and Power before the Civil War* (Lexington, Mass.: Heath, 1973).

4. Among the standard accounts are Russel Blaine Nye, *Society and Culture in America, 1830–1860* (New York: Harper and Row, 1974), and Foster Rhea Dulles, *A History of Recreation: America Learns to Play* (New York: Appleton, 1965), 84–167. The democratic "stage" in urban culture is outlined in Neil Harris, "Four Stages in the Urbanization of American Culture," *Illinois Historical Society Lectures*, 1971.

5. Theater admission offers the clearest example of the lowering of relative prices for commercial amusement over the period. In 1820, the Park Theater charged twenty-five cents for the gallery and two dollars for entrance into the subscribers' boxes. By 1860, most theaters held to a general scale of fifty cents for the boxes and a "shilling" (12½ cents) for the gallery. For more on the entrance of the common man into urban commercial culture, see Peter G. Buckley, *To the Opera House: Culture and Society in Antebellum New York* (New York: Oxford University Press, forthcoming, 1989).

6. To defend Captain Mackensie against charges that he had been overzealous in his suppression of the infamous mutiny aboard the *Somers*.

7. Robert F. Lucid, ed., *The Journal of Richard Henry Dana, Jr.* (Cambridge, Mass.: Belknap Press, 1968), vol. 1, 119.

8. Lucid, *Journal*, 119.

9. Lucid, *Journal*, 120.

10. Charles Dickens, *American Notes, Pictures from Italy and Miscellaneous Papers* (London: Gresham, 1909), 85.

11. Street pigs were not new features in graphic and literary depictions of New York life; Charles Mathews, the British comic actor from whom Dickens learned much about the characterization of national types, had mentioned pigs in his play *Trip to America* (1824). It remained for Dickens to give the animal some heightened democratic qualities.

12. Philip Hone, *Diary 1828–1851*, ed. Bayard Tuckerman (New York: Dodd, Mead, 1889), vol. 2, 293–94.

13. Quoted in New York *Dispatch*, November 25, 1849. The complete run of Whitman's urban jottings in the *Dispatch* has not been identified. For a sense of the content and sequence, see Henry M. Christman, ed., *Walt Whitman's New York* (New York: Macmillan, 1963), 171–88, and Joseph Jay Rubin's comprehensive *The Historic Whitman* (University Park, Pa.: Pennsylvania State University Press, 1973), 237–43.

14. Grant Thorburn, *Fifty Years' Reminiscences of New York* (New York: 1845), 205, 208. Other popular reconstructions of the knickerbocker town were Abram C. Dayton, *Last Days of Knickerbocker Life in New York* (New York: 1882); John W. Francis, *Old New York: or, Reminiscences of the Past Sixty Years* (New York: 1858); and William Duer, *New York As It Was* (New York: 1849). The strangest and most compulsive recording of past life was Walter Barrett [Joseph A. Scoville], *The Old Merchants of New York*, 5 vols. (New York: 1885).

15. For "insatiate longings," see Abram Dayton, *Last Days of Knickerbocker Life in New York*, 10–13; Henry James, *Washington Square* (London: Penguin, 1974), 34.

16. Edward Pessen, *Riches, Class and Power*; Betsy Blackmar, "Re-walking the 'Walking City': Housing and Property Relations in New York City, 1780–1840," *Radical History Review* 21 (1979): 131–48; M. J. Heale, "From City Fathers to Social Critics: Humanitarianism and Government in New York, 1790–1860," *Journal of American History* 63 (1976): 21–41.

17. Sean Wilentz, *Chants Democratic*, 87–97.

18. Joe Cowell, *Thirty Years Passed Among the Players in England and America* (New York: 1844), 74.

19. The standard account of the handling of poverty in knickerbocker New York remains Raymond A. Mohl, *Poverty in New York, 1783–1825* (New York: Oxford University Press, 1971). On the role of sanitary reformers and the medical community in establishing the boundaries of degradation, see John

Duffy, *A History of Public Health in New York City, 1625–1866* (New York: Russell Sage, 1968), 376–540.

20. The best study of crowd disturbances in the city before 1850 is Paul O. Weinbaum, *Mobs and Demagogues: The New York Response to Collective Violence in the Early Nineteenth Century* (Ann Arbor: University of Michigan Press, 1979).

21. N. P. Willis, *Lecture on Fashion* (New York: Mirror Library no. 32, 1844), 9. See also "The Republic of Fashion," *Literary World* 3 (November 11, 1848), 811.

22. *Herald*, May 12, 1849.

23. *Herald*, November 23, 1849.

24. Allan Nevins, ed., *The Diary of Philip Hone* (New York: 1927) 2:201.

25. Hone served as president of the American Exchange Bank and the New York Bank for Savings. He also organized the American Mutual Insurance Company and was an original investor in the Delaware and Hudson Company. For similar transformations in the capital of his friends, see Edward K. Spann's wonderful synthesis of the period, *The New Metropolis: New York City, 1840–1860* (New York: Columbia University Press, 1981), 205–12.

26. Hone, *Diary*, 295.

27. Hone, *Diary*, 183; see also the full entry in the ms. Diary (New-York Historical Society) for November 11, 1835.

28. Hone, *Diary*, 837.

29. Hone was perhaps correct in judging the younger generation's different relation to the demands of luxury. The expansion of the fashion press, with Willis taking the lead, legitimated a new hierarchy of consumption between 1840 and 1860. Richard Grant White's essay, "New York Daguerreotyped," justifies the growth of luxury in the Fifteenth Ward: "The sumptuous environments of the richest merchant are by use and familiarity no greater luxuries to him, than more homely comforts are to the mechanic," in *Putnam's* 3 (1854): 237.

30. Hone, *Diary*, 644.

31. Hone, *Diary*, 518.

32. Hone, *Diary*, 141.

33. *New York American*, July 16, 1834.

34. *Evening Post*, June 17, 1826; Hone, *Diary*, 348.

35. Theodore Shank, *The Bowery Theatre, 1826–1836* (Ph.D. diss., Stanford University, 1956).

36. Walt Whitman, "The Old Bowery," in *Prose Works* (Philadelphia: David McKay), 428.

37. The most interesting undocumented guide to popular culture on the Bowery is Alvin F. Harlow's *Old Bowery Days: The Chronicles of a Famous Street* (New York: Appleton, 1931).

38. For working class housing and working conditions, see Richard Stott, *The Worker in the Metropolis: New York City 1820–1860* (Ph.D. diss., Cornell University, 1983), 329–404.

39. Many journalists and dramatists had a hand in constructing the fictional "B'hoy" who reflected the persona of the popular journalist as well as the realities of the street. See Buckley, *To the Opera House*, chap. 4, and Wilentz, *Chants Democratic*, 300–301. The typological development of the B'hoy appears to parallel the advent of "coster" literature in London.

40. *London v. New York*, "by an English Workman" (London: 1859), 51–52; quoted in Stott, *The Worker in the Metropolis*, 376.

41. Charles Haswell, *Reminiscences of an Octogenarian of the City of New York* (New York: 1897), 270.

42. George G. Foster, *New York Naked* (New York: 1851), 142.

43. Joseph Rubin, *The Historic Whitman* (University Park, Pa.: Pennsylvania State University Press, 1973), 66–84.

44. Benjamin Baker, *A Glance at New York* (New York: French and Sons, 1867).

45. John Todd, *The Young Man* (New York: 1844), 133–34; almost the exact scene is reproduced in Henry Ward Beecher's *Lectures to Young Men* (New York: 1844), 226.

46. *The Home Journal*, May 12, 1849.

47. Wilentz, *Chants Democratic*, 328.

48. The ideological origins of popular journalism and notions of "objectivity" are explored fully in Dan Schiller's *Objectivity and the News: The Public and the Rise of Commercial Journalism* (Philadelphia: University of Pennsylvania Press, 1981).

49. *Aurora*, April 6, 1842.

50. The standard account of the riot remains Richard Moody's *The Astor Place Riot* (Bloomington, Ind.: Indiana University Press, 1958). Moody overestimates the fatalities, according to the Coroner's Report (*Ms Minutes of the Court of General Sessions*, 1849, (New York: Municipal Archives and Records Office), and underestimates the class character of the cultural forces involved in the disturbance; see Buckley, *To the Opera House*, chap. 1.

51. *Philadelphia Public Ledger*, May 16, 1849.

52. Barnum's autobiography passed through seven different versions. The best coverage of his early career may be found in the *Life of P. T. Barnum Written by Himself* (New York: Redfield, 1855).

53. New York *Herald*, July 10, 1840. This puff was undoubtedly written by Barnum himself.

54. Barnum, *Life*, 34.

55. Neil Harris, *Humbug: The Art of P. T. Barnum* (Boston: Little, Brown, 1973), 105.

56. Harris, *Humbug*, 62–67.

57. See Henry Hope Reed, *Central Park: A History and a Guide* (New York: Clarkson Potter, 1967), 16; and "A Talk about Public Parks and Gardens," *The Horticulturalist* 3 (October 1848): 22.

58. *Frank Leslie's Illustrated Weekly,* August 4, 1857.

59. New York State, Board of Commissioners of Central Park, *Descriptions of Plans for Improvement of Central Park* (New York: 1858).

60. "Description of a Plan for the Improvement of the Central Park," reprinted in Frederick Law Olmsted, Jr., and Theodora Kimball, eds., *Forty Years of Landscape Architecture: Central Park, Frederick Law Olmsted, Sr.* (Cambridge: MIT Press, 1973).

61. Frederick Law Olmsted to Charles Loring Brace, December 1, 1953, in William G. McLaughlin, ed., *The Letters of Frederick Law Olmsted,* vol. 2, 123.

62. New York *Herald,* September 6, 1857; reprinted, in part, in Frederick Law Olmsted, *Public Parks: Being Two Papers Read Before the American Social Science Association in 1870 and 1880* (Brookline, Mass.: 1902), 56, 60.

63. Henry Bellows, "Cities and Parks: With Special Reference to the New York Central Park," *Atlantic Monthly* 7 (April 1861): 421. See also Clarence Cook, *A Description of New York's Central Park* (New York: 1869), 87; and Allan Nevins, ed., *The Diary of George Templeton Strong* (New York: Octagon Books), vol. 3, 30.

3

Rethinking the Origins of Machine Politics

Amy Bridges

Like Topsy, machine politics "just grew" in the United States. For nearly a century, it was the characteristic form of American city government. Although political development theorists have recently analyzed corruption, patronage, and personalistic leadership in a number of countries, machine politics was long seen to be—as indeed it was—a peculiarly American phenomenon. As a result, Americanists have sought to explain the political machine in terms of the outstanding peculiarities of the United States. Some see the purportedly nonideological style of the machine as the urban counterpart of the liberal tradition, equally grounded in absence of class consciousness. The close association of the machine and ethnic politics has led others to view the machine as a product of nineteenth century immigrant culture and ethnic conflict.

Although liberal consciousness and ethnic pluralism seem most distinctive to social scientists, nineteenth century citizens themselves had a different understanding of the exceptional character of their country. To them, the United States was special less in its ideological universe or the immigrant presence than in the broad embrace of its franchise. Across classes, ethnic groups, and political persuasions, citizens voiced the singularity and frailty of the American experiment in republican government. Advocates of mass education advised citizens that "popular intelligence and popular virtue are indispensable to the existence and continuance of a government such as ours."[1] Nativists worried lest those raised in undemocratic environments would be unable to bear the responsibilities of liberty.[2] Democrats reminded voters that in America, democratic principles guarded "the civil and religious rights of the poor man . . . as well as the rich."[3] Labor leaders argued that the workingmen had "one weapon . . . more powerful than the gun or the chain beyond the barricades of Paris. It was the ballot."[4] Finally, the organizer of the City Reform party in New York argued that the political health of the city was an index of the political health of the nation, and urged citizens "to remember the world-wide importance of the novel experiment of our Federal government, on which we believe our own and the happiness of the world to be much dependent."[5]

The great importance of white manhood suffrage early in the history of the United States should be clear to scholars as well as contemporary spokesmen. In this essay I relate the origins of machine politics to this special feature of American political development. I argue that the expansion of suffrage and the creation of the second American party system in the 1830s planted the seeds for machine politics. By 1860 they had borne fruit, and the cities of the United States exhibited central elements of machine politics. From the 1790s to the 1830s, local politics was simply a pale reflection of national debates. By 1860, however, city politics had a life of its own, relatively sheltered from national events, and quite distinctively urban. American cities exhibited intense two-party competition in the 1830s and 1840s, but by 1860 that competition had become a lopsided affair, with one party claiming the loyalty of a clear majority of the electorate. In Pittsburgh, Baltimore, New York, Boston, Providence, and Newark the second American party system gave way to one-party dominance in the 1850s. Bosses appeared in Pittsburgh, Baltimore, Philadelphia, New York, and Boston.[6] Popular clubs of various sorts provided the rudiments of ward organization, while the expanded functions of urban government provided, for the first time, significant patronage resources independent of partisan victories in state or national elections.

Machine politics was not wholly institutionalized anywhere in 1860. Discipline had yet to be imposed on party bosses who were, as Martin Shefter has written, entering an era of "rapacious individualism."[7] Nor had a modus vivendi yet been reached between bosses and urban elites. Party organization, though considerably stronger than in the heyday of the second American party system, was still a far cry from the disciplined hierarchies that would appear later in the century. Nevertheless, by 1860 the patronage, the majority, the clubs, the boss, and his reform antagonist were all in place. The origins of machine politics can thus be found in the antebellum era.

New York provides a noteworthy case of this evolution. While any number of things are special about New York, the broad outlines of its political transformation represent the antebellum experience well. New York's political transformation may be understood, first, as the local counterpart of transformations in state government and the law in the United States. A comparative perspective suggests a second understanding. In general, the themes of antebellum political life in New York and other cities paralleled the social and political conflicts in other industrializing communities in the late eighteenth and early nineteenth centuries. But the political ground on which these conflicts were fought and resolved was, by contrast, special to the United States. Here, industrialization happened simultaneously with the abolition of property barriers to suffrage. Comparing the American case with England's in the same period suggests that the exceptional context of widespread suffrage best explains the creation of machine politics as the American way of city government.

Local Politics from Jackson to Lincoln

At the election of Andrew Jackson, New York and other cities retained important aspects of eighteenth century society and politics. The merchant and the artisan were its characteristic citizens. The great waves of immigration and the disorganizing changes of industrialization still lay ahead. More generally, political life took the form that Ronald Formisano aptly named "deferential participant."[8] Wealthy men accounted for the great majority of officeholders. Their political position was based on their exercise of social leadership. "Even the most prominent citizens," Paul Weinbaum has written, "did not stand apart from the rest of society." In times of economic distress, for example, ad hoc ward committees were formed to collect funds and then distribute relief. The wealthy not only contributed money but also worked door to door distributing charity.[9] Wealthy men also provided leadership in volunteer fire companies. As partisans, wealthy men led mobs; as officeholders, patricians used the respect they commanded to control mobs. Wealthy officeholders were also generous to their constituents: for example, when Gideon Lee was an alderman he donated money for a school to be built in his ward.[10] Since personal characteristics like courage, generosity, or the capacity to exercise authority were central to both civic and political leadership, the line between public and private was indistinct. The Jacksonian city, like the eighteenth century city, might reasonably be spoken of as a "community."

In the 1830s, these relations began to unravel. The creation of the second American party system introduced the career politician and partisan competition. Population growth and abolition of property qualifications for white male suffrage created a large electorate. More subtly, increasingly diverse social and political values made the task of creating political order more difficult.

Deferential-participant politics gave way as men of substance withdrew from a variety of leadership roles. While the wealthy continued to contribute to charitable efforts, for example, the administration of charity became professionalized.[11] The fire department became the province of the working classes. Career politicians replaced patricians in office, though in taking the mantle of political office they endeavored to sustain the patrician style of civic and social leadership.

Like the patrician, the career politician provided his courage and leadership in the fire department. For him as for the patrician, the ward was the centerpiece of political life, and benefits brought to the ward served as a claim for reelection.[12] As candidates, new politicians as well as old stressed personal generosity, courage, and benevolence. Thus the friendship for the poor and the working classes that later became central to the style of the boss were part of the career politician from the beginning, even as they had been part of the patrician style.

The new and old politicians differed in two key aspects, however. Career politicians lacked the personal resources the patricians had. Lesser personal resources meant that when the politician provided for his constituents, he did so from the city budget. Expanded municipal construction, the night watch, and an effort to create paying jobs in the volunteer fire department supplemented charity as evidence of concern for voters.[13]

The second and more important difference was that career politicians were partisans. Local candidates were tied to national parties by sentiment, money, and patronage resources. While the city's wealthiest men stopped running for office, they remained active in political and party life, and local politicians depended on their contributions for party support. State and national victories by one's own party, moreover, brought plentiful patronage resources, and this further tied local politics to the national parties.[14] The short life of various local third-party insurgencies demonstrated the impossibility of sustaining a party unconnected to either Whigs or Democrats. Not long after the Whigs appeared, then, local politics everywhere was dominated by the Whig-Democrat debate.

Local politics did not fit comfortably into this mold, for citizen groups found fault with both parties. For example, organized labor in New York attacked the Democrats as hypocrites in their claim to be advocates of working men, and objected to the use of government payrolls for partisan purposes. Similarly, efforts to subject the fire companies to party control were vigorously resisted. (That some fire companies *chose* partisan allegiance was an altogether different matter.)[15] Whigs and Democrats alike opposed or refused to endorse policies for which there was significant popular sentiment. Neither party supported tenement regulation; both opposed democratization of the public school system; neither favored compensation for members of the common council; neither democratized its own organization. Indeed, party policy, government practices, and elite sensibilities were all moving away from long-standing practices for which there was popular support. In the Panic of 1837, for example, citizens petitioned the common council to restore the assize on bread. In response, the *Journal of Commerce* editorialized:

> We say, let every man look out for himself. If you weigh the loaf, you know what it weighs, but if it is stamped with the weight, you do not know. Let us have fewer laws, and we shall have less trouble. The Creator, when he made the system, gave it laws, the tendency of which is always good. Half the laws which men make, do but aggravate the evils they are intended to cure.[16]

In the same year the common council declared that "the tendency of charitable societies is . . . to diminish the industry and economy of the poor . . . and to promote a lamentable dependency," and so, in a "departure from a practice . . . long established," the city curtailed its support of alms-giving organizations.[17]

The distance between government policy and elite views on one hand, and popular sentiment on the other, endowed the actions of politicians with a schizophrenic quality. As aldermen, local politicians agreed to cut back on charity, but with campaigning in mind, they offered it. As officials, they insisted that legislation limiting the sale of alcoholic beverages be enforced, but as politicians they refrained from doing so. As officials, they denounced disorder and rowdyism by gangs and fire companies, but as politicians they offered patronage to gang leaders and joined the fire companies themselves. Both parties endorsed governmental frugality, yet both sought to enlarge the patronage payroll. The schizophrenic behavior of party politicians was symptomatic of the social tensions they attempted to manage: increasing ethnic diversity and an articulate, energetic labor movement evolved alongside an emerging stern, middle class morality. The Whig and Democratic parties dominated political life, but the coalitions they assembled were fragile and their hold on the electorate was tenuous. A more adequate political order would require politicians to accommodate the changing society of the antebellum city.

Antebellum New Yorkers experienced dramatic changes. Between

1825 and 1860 the city's population increased by 500 percent to 814,000. In the same years, three and a half million immigrants landed in the city, and though most continued on to other destinations, by 1855 more than half of the city's population was foreign born. This posed a challenge to New York's politicians: in 1855 the electorate was four and a half times larger than it had been thirty years earlier, having grown from fewer than 20,000 to 88,900 men eligible to vote. This group was almost equally divided between the native- and the foreign-born. By 1865, a full 60 percent of those eligible to vote had not been born in the United States.[18]

More profoundly, industrialization had begun to reorganize the city's social structure and the ways people got, spent, and labored. In the Jacksonian city, the characteristic worker was an artisan. Such a craftsman worked in a small shop in which a master directed journeymen; journeymen might reasonably aspire to master status; and a small number of apprentices were trained. This system had never operated in the United States with the force it had in Europe, for the opportunities of journeymen to move elsewhere to attain independence and to claim master status were great. Nevertheless, *master, journeyman,* and *apprentice* were terms that had real meaning here, in some trades until well after the Civil War. In the Jacksonian city they accounted for the largest part of the working classes.[19]

Over the next generation these workers and their patterns of work came under a variety of pressures. The crafts shop declined, and what Wilentz has called the "bastard workshop" and other forms of out-work appeared. These exhibited an increased division of labor and the abandonment of pretenses either to apprenticeship or to the possibility of rising to master status. By 1855, those who might reasonably still be termed artisans were a small proportion of the labor force (about 12 percent) and formed the elite of the working classes (about 15 percent). Another 35.5 percent of the working classes (about 19 percent of the labor force) were wage workers in trades that had once been organized as crafts, like cabinet making, printing, and shoe making. And half of the working classes (49 percent, or 39 percent of the labor force) were wage workers plain and simple, men and women whose work never had the status or style of the craft—for example, laundresses, laborers, porters, watchmen, and drivers.[20]

Native-born and immigrant workers found different places in this complex class structure. More than half of the American-born labor force was in the middle or upper classes or retained artisan status. By contrast, the most common occupations of the Ireland-born were laborer and domestic; the largest group of German-born workers, like the largest group of those from England and Scotland, were wage workers in trades that had once been organized as crafts. Despite their higher status, it would be wrong to think of the American-born workers as having been "pushed up" by the immigrants, for the number of places that opened up at the bottom of the class structure far outnumbered those at the top. If the United States–born were doing well compared to immigrants, they had nevertheless lost a great deal in wages, status, and autonomy compared to their situation a generation earlier.[21]

This social reordering posed infinitely more elaborate social and political challenges than any description of occupational changes can convey. These challenges provoked politicians to schizophrenic behavior throughout the antebellum era, and informed the long list of issues— charity, education, and municipal employment, to name just a few— that constitute the "street-fighting pluralism"[22] of local politics. For all that complexity, it still might be said that local politics was reorganized by immigration in the 1840s and by class in the 1850s.

In the 1830s and 1840s, Whigs and Democrats alike adopted a duplicitous stance toward nativists and the foreign-born. Both parties publicly courted immigrants, yet neither genuinely welcomed them. Both parties had significant nativist sentiment, but both resisted open endorsement of nativist goals. Party leaders had good reason to be reluctant to take strong positions on foreign-born citizens. Before the appearance of the nativist American Republican party in 1843, party coalitions were not nearly so ethnically differentiated as they were to become. Party competition was intense, and neither party was willing to forsake either the American-born or the (smaller) foreign-born vote.

The social tensions surrounding the immigrant presence were intimately linked to tensions around other issues. For example, New York's schools were run by the Public School Society, a closed corporation with an elite membership that dispensed public monies and administered schools. The Society was dominated by Presbyterians and Episcopalians. In 1840, Catholics, Methodists, and Baptists petitioned for a share of funds, though in order to preserve a solid Protestant front, Baptists and Methodists quickly withdrew. Although Catholics may have had little sympathy from other citizens, events also made it clear that the School Society, a most unrepublican institution, also had little popular support. Nevertheless, both parties in the city supported the Society and opposed efforts to democratize school administration. Conversely, many Baptists and Methodists voted to democratize school administration, even though it meant that in some wards control would fall into the hands of Catholics.[23] Just as issues of ethnicity and religion in the schools could not easily be segregated from the issue of a "republican" manner of administering education, so other issues might be treacherous for the parties or for party leadership. As a result, efforts to organize nativist sentiment at the polls were left to third party movements and insurgents.

The American Republican party of the 1840s and the Know Nothing organization of the 1850s served as nativist standard bearers. American Republicans claimed to be a party of "true Americanism" and a party of municipal reform. Its candidate for mayor was publisher James Harper. Harper was a child of "sturdy, upright, inflexible," teetotaling Methodists, and was himself prominently associated with temperance and moral reform. He and his brothers were craftsmen whose hard work and ingenuity had built one of the city's largest publishing firms; they managed it with a fatherly (and anti-union) concern. Harper's candidacy, then, represented paternalism, sobriety, Protestantism, hard work, and Whiggish leveling-up.[24] His presence, and party rhetoric, resonated with the aims of moral and temperance reformers on one hand, and with the waning political culture of the city's artisans on the other. Reinforcing the party's appeal in 1844 was Whig endorsement, with which the American Republicans swept the city's election. The Whigs later withdrew their approval, and the American Republicans quickly collapsed, but this episode gave the party system a stronger ethnic cast. Nativist voters were wed to the Whigs, who abandoned Irish and German immigrants to the Democrats. In the short run, this gave the Whigs the edge in local elections, but in the long run it favored the Democrats.[25]

In the 1850s, the Know Nothings briefly mobilized about a third of the city's electorate. Like the American Republicans, the Know Nothings allied with municipal reformers of the 1850s, enabling the reformers on one occasion to win a majority in the common council.[26] Though in office nativists deprived some immigrant groups of patronage appointments, they could not exclude naturalized citizens from political life, much less restrict immigration. Their lasting contribution was to give municipal reform a nativist tinge that did not shake off until well into the twentieth century.

Democrats opposed the claims of nativists, Whigs, and reformers by insisting that Democracy was the "true home of the working classes." Since the working classes were largely foreign-born, it was perhaps inevitable that, once religion and culture became politicized, the party would claim to protect their cultural interests. Democratic rhetoric fused the issues of culture, class, and liberty. Temperance legislation was denounced as "sumptuary law" and, as such, "the bane of all republics."[27] Know Nothings were denounced as "traitors to the Constitution . . . bigots and fanatics in religion."[28] In the last antebellum decade, Demo-

cratic Mayor Fernando Wood helped immigrants to organize sympathetic slates to run for ward school boards. This was especially important to Catholic parents, whose children were often the target of
Protestant proselytizing. So the party might claim that it "alone . . .
helped the working classes, was in favor of education of the children of
the poor man . . . of granting religious tolerance."[29]

The Democrats' insistence that they were the workingman's best advocate did not go without challenge from the labor movement. The
party had never been nor ever became a labor party, but workers made
an imprint on the party as their character changed with industrial
change. The Jacksonian labor movement criticized a series of gaps between party rhetoric and reality, attacking the "bold face hypocrisy of
those who are always boisterous in their professions of democracy to the
people."[30] In the 1840s, when the union movement was in disarray,
Democrats tolerated workingmen's advocates and radicals of various
sorts.

The greatly revived labor movement of the 1850s differed from its
predecessors. It was dominated by wage workers rather than craftsmen
(though a significant number of labor leaders and spokesmen from the
1830s and 1840s reappeared in leadership positions). An Industrial Congress was organized in the 1850s with a clear agenda for local politics. It
wanted to abolish the contract system for public works, arguing that
since construction was labor-intensive, low bids would come from contractors who paid low wages. They sought instead municipal employment at a minimum wage. Supervisors would be men who had served
apprenticeships rather than "political creatures"; job security would be
based on merit rather than partisan affiliation. As they had in the 1830s,
labor leaders demanded tenement regulation; the Congress called for
district surveyors to oversee landlords and rents and enforcement of a
housing code.[31]

This agenda became more pressing and more elaborate at mid-
decade, when economic collapse put thousands out of work. Each winter, beginning in 1854, there were mass meetings of the unemployed,
with as many as 20,000 attending. Though it was admitted that the
wealthy were trying to relieve suffering, private charity was declared
both inadequate and degrading. Unemployed workers demanded that
the city government take action. Again it was insisted that the city
abandon the contract system and provide public employment with a
minimum wage and without partisan bias. One suggestion was to expand work on Central Park, and this did ultimately employ as many as
1,000 men per day. Another demand was that the city build apartments
on its own land, in order to provide employment, low-income housing,

and income to the city treasury. It was demanded—as it had been a century earlier—that the export of grain be curtailed. Workers also asked for a moratorium on evictions to protect the unemployed and their families. The basic and essential demand, however, was "bread or work," the slogan on the placards of those who marched on City Hall in 1857.[32]

The Democracy could not be indifferent to these pressures. In 1857, the mayor proposed that the city issue a special construction stock to finance the purchase of foodstuffs to be used to pay those employed on public works: the improvement of Central Park; the construction of a new reservoir and some firehouses; the usual grading, paving, curbing, and cleaning of streets; and dock repairs.[33] Subsequently, and not sur- prisingly, Democratic voters were often reminded to vote for those who would, when in control of public employment, treat their employees fairly, who had provided employment in times of distress, or who had dispensed charity without respect to religion. Most often, voters were reminded that the party was best understood as "hard working Democ- racy."[34] "Democratic Workingmen's Clubs . . . permanently established in the wards" began to make their appearance early in the 1860s.[35] In 1868 the party's spokesmen asked, "Is not the pending contest preemi- nently one of capital against labor, of money against popular rights, and of political power against the struggling interest of the masses?"[36]

The reasons Democratic politicians gave voters to claim popular sup- port point to a significant feature of New York's political life in the 1850s: city government had grown even more quickly than the city itself, pro- viding plentiful resources to build party organization and to cultivate popular support. This contrasted strikingly to the 1840s, when politi- cians faced an electorate of 40,000 with perhaps 2,000 jobs.[37] Earlier, politicians had looked to state and federal employment in the city to supplement their own resources. The Customs House had the largest staff, 750. When President Jackson appointed a collector who failed to use the Customs House to reward the local party faithful, party leaders complained that he had "driven from our ward meetings a body of strong Republicans who for twenty or thirty years have been the back- bone of our party."[38] By the 1850s, however, there were seven munici- pal departments with substantial employment and elected commission- ers, including the commissioners of streets, repairs, and supplies, the almshouse, and the city inspector, whose province was public health. In addition, there were franchises, contracts, and the police force, this last initially appointed by the aldermen and later by the mayor.[39] In 1858 a local politician wrote to a friend, "It is hardly necessary . . . to tell you that city patronage is greater than the Customs House," and three years later a Tammany official declared, "No man should have power in this state if that power is to be swayed by the authorities in Washington."[40]

The rhetoric, the clubs, the charity, the patronage, and the defense of the cultural interests of the working classes are summed up in the appearance of the boss. Militant, "hard-fisted," and tough, the boss's style reflected the culture of the working classes. Aptly opposed by Sam Bass Warner to the "gentleman Democrat," the boss ostentatiously associated himself with gangs, volunteer fire companies, the places and priorities of the working classes. In some cities bosses were nativists; in others, like New York, they cultivated immigrant votes. Everywhere, they associated themselves with the many and distanced themselves from the few. As Weber wrote, "the American boss . . . deliberately relinquishes social honor."[41]

These arrangements were fraught with provocation to the city's respectable element. Some saw the association of the boss with the volunteer fire companies and gangs and with "dangerous classes" more generally as an outright endorsement of mob violence and disrespect for law. Reformers insisted that "we should rule by men instead of muscle."[42] They agreed, moreover, with newspaper editors who found the relief proposals of the late 1850s simply shocking. The *Evening Post* editorialized that state provision of work for the unemployed was "one of the most monstrous doctrines ever broached in revolutionary France,"[43] and the *Times* agreed that "the successful owe pity, and when necessary, relief, to their unfortunate brethren. The former owe it as a moral obligation, but the latter cannot demand it as a right."[44] Even some Democratic politicians denounced the mayor for "a demagogical attempt to array the poor against the rich."[45] The city's businessmen also objected to the corruption in the granting of franchises and contracts, perhaps because the common council of 1852–1853 outdid its predecessors by failing to deliver contracts to those from whom it had taken bribes.[46] Finally, the city's fiscal situation was increasingly precarious. Though the tax rate was increasing, current expenditures were increasingly covered by borrowing.[47]

These reasons moved the city's businessmen to organize a reform movement to try to regain control of city government in the 1850s. For the first time in a generation, businessmen acted as ward organizers and ran for the common council. With clandestine Know Nothing support, reformers won control of the city council in 1853. After that, reformers won only a third or so of the city's electorate, and could control the city only when some fraction of the Democracy could be persuaded to defect to the ranks of reform. Reformers were thus crippled by their lack of public appeal and consequent dependence on party. As the election of

1859 approached, the same men who had urged citizens to neglect partisanship and vote for reform in local elections desperately wanted the Democrats to win the national election. For the rest of the century, although reformers intermittently demanded that the "infamous government of the city of New York must be put down,"[48] for the most part they were condemned to futile, if valiant, opposition. By the mid-1850s, New York was a Democratic city; by 1860, overwhelmingly so. Between 1856 and 1863, Democratic factions taken together never accounted for less than half of the vote. This set the political stage for the competition of boss and reformer for generations to come.

Rethinking the Origins of Machine Politics

The origins of machine politics lie in the antebellum years, when U.S. cities lost their last resemblance to the eighteenth century municipality of merchant and artisan. In these years, the characteristic actors of nineteenth and twentieth century urban politics appeared. Perhaps most striking, the political machine was forged in an environment where no one—with the possible exception of machine politicians—wanted it. Working class leaders demanded something resembling a local welfare state, where government would hire on the basis of skill rather than politics. Catholic immigrants wanted government to stop assisting Protestant proselytizers and to assist parochial education. Reformers wanted small, efficient, honest government. Probably not a few citizens wished that things might simply be as they had been a generation before.

The fact that machine politics was not the program of either the business elite or social movements has important ramifications for explaining its creation. Most obviously, the machine did not "institutionalize" some particular set of values. Machine politics cannot be properly understood as the institutionalization of working class ethics, immigrant solidarities, or neighborhood loyalties. Nor can it be explained with reference to elite desires for social control. Rather, machine politics, like most political arrangements, was the product of inheritance and incrementalism, conflict, inadvertence, and compromise.

Satisfying explanations for the appearance of the machine must necessarily connect with the larger patterns of American political development. In particular, the close association of the machine and ethnic politics suggests to some that the machine was a product of immigrant culture and ethnic conflict. The best known of these arguments appears in *City Politics*. In that 1963 book, Edward Banfield and James Q. Wilson, following Hofstadter, argue that nineteenth century city politics was grounded in an immigrant political ethos at variance with middle class WASP values. The private-regarding values of immigrant voters led them to accept patronage, corruption, and "friendship" rather than insisting on honesty and attention to the public weal.[49] Similarly, Daniel Patrick Moynihan argues that the social norms of deference and personal dependency were lasting Irish peasant values that facilitated machine building and Irish political success.[50] More recently, in *The Private City*, Sam Bass Warner, Jr., claims that the antebellum era embraced a shift from working class to ethnic politics. This ethnic politics was based in homogeneous communities and their neighborhood associations, and paved the way for boss rule.[51]

Three empirical objections may be raised to these explanations. First, machine politics was not in any obvious way what immigrants wanted (though surely, from their point of view, bosses were preferable to reformers). Second, ethnicity was not the whole story, nor even the dominant theme of antebellum political life. Third, the hallmarks of machine politics and the persona of the boss predate an immigrant influence in the electorate. Personal loyalty and deference characterized patrician leadership; bosses hardly invented them. The partisan abuse of public employment was also not new to the antebellum era: The worst abuses may well have been committed by the Federalists in the 1790s.[52] The elements of machine politics, then, substantially predate the arrival of the immigrants and the later political ascent of the Irish.

If the antebellum reordering of urban politics does not stem from immigration, then how does it connect with larger patterns of U.S. political development? Urban political change can be better understood as one part of the transformation of the whole national political system in response to the beginnings of industrialization and the challenge of mass suffrage. The last property restrictions on white manhood suffrage had been abolished by the 1830s.[53] The first generation of the modern working class appeared at this same moment. Because the new working classes were concentrated in cities, and because urban government is more accessible to popular groups than state or national government, political reordering in the city was more chaotic, complex, and ambiguous than at higher levels of the political system. Yet economic development also provoked controversy in cities about the proper role of government and the nature of an equitable law. In this volatile setting, community was redefined, "new linkages between the particular interest of individuals and groups" organized, and "new meaning" given to "the common purpose" largely through the existing political parties.[54]

State government changed substantially in the antebellum years in response to such pressures.[55] As in cities, state government entered this period operating by eighteenth century precepts, such as regulating trade. As industrialization proceeded, the pervasive support for this stance eroded. To artisans, laborers, and farmers, the granting of such special privileges constituted "a violation of the first principles of their democratic faith."[56] To the business elite, who were losing their exclusive hold on political life, government intervention also seemed risky. As a result, by 1860 state functions like regulation and franchises, licensing, road building, and mixed enterprises had disappeared or changed their function. The rise of a powerful market system made such government activity seem "unnecessary, useless, and embarrassing restrictions" on the "inherently beneficent" operation of the economy.[57] As Hartz summarizes the new political economy, "businessmen were heroes and politicians were villains."[58] At the state level, then, the response to industrialism was marked by the appearance of a more obviously liberal political order.

These themes are not unique. "Ultimately," as Hartz writes, "for all the magical chemistry of American life, we are dealing with materials common to the Western world."[59] In England as in the United States, merchants, industrialists, and financiers rejected "what the rich owe the poor" and embraced laissez-faire ideology and moral reform. England also witnessed an organized effort to convince the working classes and the poor of the virtues of Protestantism, "self-dependence," and greater industriousness, frugality, and temperance.[60] English working classes, like the American, denounced the "industrial system" as immoral and learned political economy from Tom Paine.[61]

Although many issues were the same, the evolution of local and national politics was fought and resolved on a much narrower political ground in England than in the United States. In the United States, the ballot was added to the strike; the nominating convention to the riot; partisan insurgency to protest; and party to class. Reciprocally, electoral politics provided the contextual rules for resolving social conflicts, and so shaped the resolutions to its own logic and discipline. In England, the same social disagreements were necessarily resolved by different rules, and so produced different outcomes.

In England, the suffrage was restricted, and the range of local government responsibilities limited. Local "government" hardly existed at all, but was divided among a variety of institutions. The only potentially republican element of local governance was the vestry. Each parish chose officers to administer the poor law, and selected constable and watchmen, highway surveyors, and "improvement commissions" (which might engage in any of the housekeeping functions from lighting to street improvements to maintenance of the church). These included two issues dear to the working classes everywhere: ensuring sympathetic police and distributing charity judiciously (which also had a certain patronage component). The improvement commissions and related activities of the vestry also offered potential resources for building political organizations.[62]

John Foster also describes how a well-organized and disciplined labor movement put the vestry to the political advantage of the working classes of Oldham. Control of the police and the administration of relief are at the center of this story. Foster writes that "the basic social function of labor's organized strength was to control the police" in order to protect the illegal union movement. Vestry selection of the constable, and control of constabulary expenses, provided local officers who were passive at moments of popular protest and violence (if not active on the popular side). Control of the administration of relief had equally obvious benefits for the poor and working classes. Not only did an expanded relief budget evidence working class control of its dispensation, but paying jobs for the oversight of poor relief also provided sinecures for working people's advocates. Just as New York's earlier budget provoked controversy, the activities of Oldham's vestry invited political opposition. Rather than contest control of the vestry, this opposition successfully removed from the vestry those powers that made control worthwhile. The constabulary was made directly responsible to the magistrates, and the Poor Law of 1847 narrowed the electorate for the Board of Guardians for poor relief. That solution to the challenge of democratic politics was followed almost everywhere.[63]

Vestry politics usually exhibited less disciplined popular control than in Oldham. Nevertheless, local elites found the more moderate possibilities of democratic politics unpalatable for several reasons. First, as urban population grew, towns were also becoming both poorer and more proletarian. Second, the Municipal Reform Act of 1835 increased the potential authority of local government, and with it the potential reach of popular participation. "Before municipal reform," Derek Fraser has written, "liberal vestries counterbalanced Tory oligarchies and after it artisan and working class vestries counterbalanced bourgeois-dominated councils."[64] Municipal reform, however, joined local government to great national struggles between urban economic elites and the gentry. In this, "Victorian town halls were fortresses in the battle against country estates."[65] On one hand, urban elites needed to establish control of local government. For that purpose, denying the vestry its former prerogatives was essential. Just as state governments in the United

States had tried, in the 1850s, to remove some powers from local government jurisdiction by creating state-controlled commissions (most often for the police force), so in English cities local elites created new authorities they could control. On the other hand, bourgeois politicians worked for Liberal control of the city to balance Tory power in the countryside. As municipal government became the locus for the exercise of authority and party combat, the lower classes became "spectators to a struggle for power among their social superiors."[66] From an American point of view, what is most striking is how effectively the upper classes wrote and rewrote the rules of political life to exclude popular access: In the very same years local politics here was becoming a more contentious "street-fighting" pluralism, and the "respectable element" felt itself losing ground to the "dangerous classes."

Comparison to England is implicitly counterfactual. The argument might be phrased, "had England had manhood suffrage, the social conflicts of early industrialization would have produced machine politics there as in the United States." In London's suburbs the vitality of the vestry and popular politics provides the closest reality to this counterfactual. There at least one politician saw this opportunity and took it. Sidney and Beatrice Webb relate the career of Joseph Merceron, of Bethnal Green, "a local resident of apparently lower middle class extraction," who made his way from assistant to the Poor Rate Collector to Boss (their word) of his parish. Merceron had all the skills of mass politics. He packed meetings, failed to enforce Sunday closing laws, did favors to make friends, fixed tax assessments to avoid enemies. He was possibly as crooked as a politician can be, and was eventually found guilty of embezzling funds and was sentenced to eighteen months in prison. Having served his term, he returned to "undisputed supremacy" of his parish, which he dominated until age disabled him.[67]

The comparison with England suggests that although the social conflicts that spurred the appearance of machine politics were not special to the United States, the political settings in which they were resolved were distinctive. The machine became the American way of urban government because the first generation of industrial workers and their artisan forebears had the vote. The comparatively broad suffrage of the eighteenth century stamped the institutions of city politics that Jacksonian citizens inherited with the popular values of preindustrial society. The even broader suffrage of the nineteenth century magnified the impact of early industrialization on nineteenth century political life. This political life was the creature of neither the new business elite nor the new working classes, but was permeated by the tensions between the rules of republican government, which created gaps between social desires and public policy and between society and political order. The result was a set of urban institutions that created "community," yet were not what anyone wanted. Those institutions were the political machine and municipal reform. In the nineteenth century, for American observers and foreign students alike, New York led the way in building these characteristic forms. Tweed was the epitome of the boss; Seth Low became the archetypal reformer. New York's antebellum political transformation foreshadowed not only its own future but also the future of the other cities of the American republic.

Notes

1. *Address of the General Executive Committee of the American Republican Party of the City and County of New York to Their Fellow Citizens* (New York, 1843), 5.
2. See, for example, *The Crisis! An Appeal to Our Countrymen on the Subject of Foreign Influence in the United States* (New York: 201 Broadway, 1844).
3. *New York Herald*, April 10, 1846, 1.
4. Edward Mallon of the tailors, *New York Herald*, August 9, 1850.
5. Peter Cooper in the *New York Times*, November 3, 1854, 3.
6. The antebellum years have recently been the subject of close attention by both historians and political scientists. Among the general accounts are the following: Sam Bass Warner, Jr., *The Private City, Philadelphia in Three Periods of its Growth* (Philadelphia: University of Pennsylvania Press, 1968); Gary Lawson Browne, *Baltimore in the Nation, 1789–1861* (Chapel Hill: University of North Carolina Press, 1980); Kathleen N. Conzen, *Immigrant Milwaukee, 1836–1860: Accommodation and Community in a Frontier City* (Cambridge: Harvard University Press, 1976); Alan Dawley, *Class and Community: The Industrial Revolution in Lynn* (Cambridge: Harvard University Press, 1976); Michael A. Frisch, "The Community Elite and the Emergence of Urban Politics, Springfield, Mass., 1840–1880," in *Nineteenth Century Cities, Essays in the New Urban History*, ed. Stephan Thernstrom and Richard Sennett (New Haven: Yale University Press, 1969); Susan E. Hirsch, *Roots of the American Working Class: The Industrialization of Crafts in Newark, 1800–1860* (Philadelphia: University of Pennsylvania Press, 1978); and Michael Holt, *Forging a Majority: The Formation of the Republican Party in Pittsburgh, 1848–1860* (New Haven: Yale University Press, 1969).
7. Martin Shefter, "The Emergence of the Political Machine: An Alternative View," in *Theoretical Perspectives on Urban Politics*, ed. Willis D. Hawley and Michael Lipsky (Englewood Cliffs, N.J.: Prentice-Hall, 1976).
8. Ronald P. Formisano, "Deferential-Participant Politics: The Early Republic's

Political Culture, 1789–1840," *American Political Science Review* 68, no. 2 (June 1974): 473–87.

9. Paul O. Weinbaum, "Mobs and Demagogues" (Ph.D. diss., University of Rochester, 1974), 197–200.

10. Historians of the fire companies are unanimous in the description of company class composition changing over the antebellum period. See, for example, George W. Sheldon, *The Story of the Volunteer Fire Department in New York City* (New York: Harper Bros., 1882). For mobs and riot control, see Paul A. Gilje, "Mobocracy: Popular Disturbances in Post-Revolutionary New York City, 1783–1892" (Ph.D. diss., Brown University, 1979), and Weinbaum, "Mobs and Demagogues," passim. For Gideon Lee, see William Oland Borne, *History of the Public School Society of the City of New York* (New York: William Wood and Co., 1870), 704.

11. Weinbaum, "Mobs and Demagogues," 200, and Edward Pessen, *Riches, Class and Power Before the Civil War* (Lexington, Mass.: Heath, 1973), 265.

12. Democrats in the fifth ward, for example, were reminded to support the party's city council candidates because of their improvements and "multiplied conveniences which their influence and exertions have secured for the ward—and moreover their benevolent attentions to the poor," *Evening Post,* March 6, 1834, 2.

13. While the payroll for these was centralized, patronage was dispensed by the ward alderman. Thus the retrospective distinctions made here to differentiate the patrician from the politician—partisan rather than personal victory, municipal funds rather than personal generosity—may well have been unimportant to the beneficiary, if indeed the lucky appointee or recipient paid any attention to such things at all.

14. See Bridges, *A City in the Republic,* chap. 7.

15. For working class criticism of the Democrats, see Amy Bridges, *A City in the Republic, Antebellum New York and the Origins of Machine Politics* (Ithaca, N.Y.: Cornell University Press, 1987), 103–10. On resistance to partisan meddling with the volunteer fire department, see, for example, Lowell M. Limpus, *History of the New York Fire Department* (New York: Dutton, 1940), 161–68.

16. *Journal of Commerce,* February 1, 1838, 2.

17. New York City Board of Aldermen, *Documents,* vol. 4, doc. 57 (1838), 445–49. This was quite true. In 1807, for example, the Council had provided relief to sailors and others suffering from embargo (Gilje, "Mobocracy," 173).

18. In addition to the federal census, taken every ten years, New York State conducted a census at mid-decade. The *Census of the State of New York for 1855* provides data on place of birth of residents (117–18) and for status of voters (xliii, 8).

19. Census data for 1825 and 1835 are inadequate for constructing measures like those used below for 1855. The best description of work in Jacksonian New

York is Sean Wilentz, *Chants Democratic, New York City and the Rise of the American Working Class, 1788–1850* (New York: Oxford University Press, 1984), chap. 3.

20. The figures in the text were calculated from Robert Ernst, *Immigrant Life in New York City, 1825–1863* (New York: Columbia University Press, 1949), appendix I.

21. A more complete account is found in Bridges, *A City in the Republic*, chap. 3.

22. Douglas Yates, *The Ungovernable City, The Politics of Urban Problems and Policy Making* (Cambridge: MIT Press, 1977), 34.

23. An account of the "school war" is found in Bridges, *A City in the Republic*, 85–87; Diane Ravitch, *The Great School Wars: New York City, 1805–1973* (New York: Basic Books, 1974); and Borne, *Public School Society*.

24. On Harper, see Henry J. Harper, *The House of Harper: A Century of Publishing in Franklin Square* (New York: Harper Bros., 1912), 4–7, for childhood and family; Sheldon, *Fire Department*, 147, and *New York Herald*, November 5, 1854, for temperance activity.

25. A more complete account of activist politics in New York and its effect on the party system is found in Bridges, *A City in the Republic*, chap. 5.

26. On the Know Nothing alliance with reformers, see Bridges, *A City in the Republic*, 139.

27. *New York Herald*, November 3, 1854.

28. *New York Herald*, November 11, 1854.

29. *New York Herald*, November 5, 1859.

30. *The Union*, June 8, 1836, 2.

31. *The Union*, June 8, 1836, 2.

32. There are a number of accounts of these meetings. Carl Degler, "Labor in the Economy and Politics of New York City, 1850–1860" (Ph.D. diss., Columbia University, 1952), 161ff, provides an extensive description; Samuel Rezneck, "The Influence of Depression on American Public Opinion, 1857–1869," *Journal of Economic History* 2 (May 1942): 1–23, briefly describes the meetings and points out that other cities also witnessed "Bread or Work" meetings, 19. For contemporary coverage and commentary, see *New York Herald*, November 12, 13, 25–28, 1857.

33. Degler, "Labor," 167. New York City Board of Aldermen, *Documents*, vol. 22, doc. 1, 4–5; New York City Board of Aldermen, *Proceedings* 68:158–61.

34. *New York Herald*, November 3, 1854, 1.

35. *New York Herald*, November 22, 1863, 3; January 2, 1859, 5.

36. Gustavus Mayers, *History of Tammany Hall* (New York: Dover, 1971), 217.

37. Leo Hershkowitz estimated patronage available to the city council in 1838 as 1,200 positions, and Ira Leonard estimated the official patronage available in the 1840s as 2,000. Hershkowitz, "New York City, 1834–1840, A Study in Local Politics" (Ph.D. diss., New York University, 1960), 318. Leonard, "The

Politics of Charter Revision in New York City, 1845–1847," *New-York Historical Society Quarterly* 62 (1978): 51.

38. Jerome Mushkat, *Tammany: The Evolution of a Political Machine, 1789–1865* (Syracuse, N.Y.: Syracuse University Press, 1971), 116.

39. Leonard Chalmers, "Tammany Hall and New York City Politics, 1853–1861" (Ph.D. diss., New York University, 1967), 77, 146–48.

40. Quoted in Chalmers, "Tammany Hall," 162; Mushkat, *Tammany*, 369.

41. H. H. Gerth and C. Wright Mills, eds. and trans., *From Max Weber: Essays in Sociology* (New York: Oxford University Press, 1958), 194.

42. Opdyke Ratification Meeting, *New York Herald*, December 2, 1859.

43. *Evening Post*, November 10, 1857, quoted in Degler, "Labor," 192.

44. *New York Times*, October 10, 1857, quoted in Degler, "Labor," 192.

45. *New York Herald*, November 26, 1859, 1.

46. For example, the railroad contract for Sixth and Eighth avenues was originally awarded to John Pettigrew and his associates, on payment of a bribe. When Kipp et al. were awarded the contract, the bribe was not returned to Pettigrew and his business partners. Henry James Carman, *The Street Surface Railway Franchises of New York City* (New York: Columbia University Press, 1919), 47.

47. See Bridges, *A City in the Republic*, 134.

48. *New York Herald*, November 27, 1861, 4.

49. Edward Banfield and James Q. Wilson, *City Politics* (New York: Vintage Books, 1963), 40–41. There is no evidence that these are reasonable characterizations of WASP and immigrant political culture, or even of bosses and reformers, both of whom had selfish as well as collective interests. Like a number of other authors with whom I differ, Banfield and Wilson wrote about the benefit of studies of popular political culture provided by social historians.

50. Nathan Glazer and Daniel Patrick Moynihan, *Beyond the Melting Pot*, 2nd ed. (Cambridge: MIT Press, 1970), 221 ff.

51. Sam Bass Warner, Jr., *The Private City: Philadelphia in Three Periods of Its Growth* (Philadelphia: University of Pennsylvania Press, 1968). The argument is somewhat more complex than this summary suggests. Warner is concerned with the "culture of privatism," and argues that the limits the culture of privatism placed on government became particularly dysfunctional in the antebellum years. While Warner's exploration of the culture of privatism is very valuable, for the antebellum transformation I think greater emphasis on cultural changes provides more insight.

52. Sidney Pomerantz, *New York, an American City, 1783–1803* (New York: Columbia University Press, 1938), 37, 51, 63.

53. Chilton Williamson, *American Suffrage from Property to Democracy, 1760–1860* (Princeton: Princeton University Press, 1960).

54. Samuel P. Huntington, *Political Order in Changing Societies* (New Haven: Yale University Press, 1968), 11.

55. Oscar Handlin and Mary Flug Handlin, *Commonwealth, A Study of the Role of Government in the American Economy: Massachusetts, 1774–1861* (Cambridge: Harvard University Press, 1969); Louis Hartz, *Economic Policy and Democratic Thought, Pennsylvania, 1776–1860* (Chicago: Quadrangle Books, 1968).

56. Hartz, *Economic Policy*, 308, 177–78.

57. Handlin and Handlin, *Commonwealth*, 225. Cf. Morton Horowitz, *The Transformation of American Law, 1780–1860* (Cambridge: Harvard University Press, 1977), 253: "Law, once conceived of as protective, regulative, paternalistic, and, above all, a paramount expression of the moral sense of the community, had come to be thought of as facilitative of individual desires and simply reflective of the existing organization of economic and political power."

58. Hartz, *Economic Policy*, 314. Comparable changes were occurring in the legal world. See Horowitz, *The Transformation of American Law*.

59. Hartz, *The Liberal Tradition in America* (New York: Harcourt, Brace, and World, 1955), 17.

60. Reinhard Bendix, *Work and Authority in Industry* (Berkeley: University of California Press, 1956), 68.

61. See the sources cited in my "Becoming American: The Working Classes of the United States Before the Civil War," in *Working-Class Formations, Nineteenth Century Patterns in Western Europe and the United States*, ed. Ira Katznelson and Aristide Zolberg (Princeton: Princeton University Press, 1986).

62. For a description of the vestry and its prerogatives, see Derek Fraser, *Urban Politics in Victorian England* (Leicester, U.K.: Leicester University Press, 1976), chap. 1.

63. John Foster, *Class Struggle and the Industrial Revolution, Early Industrial Capitalism in Three English Towns* (New York: St. Martin's, 1974), chap. 3.

64. Fraser, *Urban Politics*, 30.

65. Fraser, 22.

66. Fraser, 115.

67. James Passfield, Sidney Webb, and Beatrice Webb, *English Local Government from the Revolution to the Municipal Corporations Act: The Parish and the County* (New York: Longman's, 1908), 79–90.

PART II

The Industrial Era

4

Manhattan's Business District in the Industrial Age

Emanuel Tobier

"Nothing is greater or more brilliant than commerce; it . . . fills the imagination of the multitude; all energetic passions are directed towards it." This is the way Alexis de Tocqueville characterized the *élan vital* that differentiated American society from its Old World contemporaries.[1] Its glow was nowhere more effulgent, its promises more boundless (though for most, in reality, bounded) than in nineteenth century New York. Only briefly the political capital, the city owed its undoubted and early primacy among American metropolises to its continuously demonstrated ability to attract and nurture the movers and shakers of a rising capitalist economy.[2]

Making sense of New York City's complex past requires a clear picture of the forces that shaped the evolution of its economic structure. Since its economy was at no time homogeneous, it is crucial to grapple with how its component parts interacted with and influenced the city's myriad and forever shifting political and social realms. This essay responds to this challenge by examining the expansion and changing functions of the locomotive of the city's economy—the dynamically evolving built (and continually rebuilt) physical environment constituted by Manhattan's business district—during the roughly three-quarters of a century between the Civil War and the end of the Great Depression.

At the beginning of this period, Manhattan's economy was dominated by the shipping and entrepôt activities made possible by its unrivaled deep water harbor. In this era workplaces—piers and wharves,

77

warehouses, shipyards, provisioning and support services, counting houses, and so on—were huddled in a tight band in the blocks paralleling and leading to Manhattan's waterfront, its furthest reaches extending not much above Forty-second Street. At a time when virtually all people walked to work, over 95 percent of Manhattan's 800,000-plus population lived in the nine-square-mile walking city whose northern boundary was the southernmost point of what would soon become Central Park.[3]

After the Civil War, Manhattan's growth as a manufacturing center accelerated, and, in the space of a few decades, it massively consolidated its position as the fast-industrializing nation's premier factory town. By the beginning of the twentieth century, Manhattan, capitalizing on its success during the mercantile (or port and entrepôt) era, became the command post—or front office—of the nation's rapidly expanding cohort of industrial giants. Interestingly, there was no direct link between the front offices of the capitalists and Manhattan's flourishing manufacturing sector. Physically, the buildings and districts housing the two sectors were cheek by jowl; less than half a mile separated Wall Street, the power alley of the first, from Broadway and Canal streets, the humming intersection of the second. Socially, however, they were worlds apart; as measured, say, by the differences in status and world views that separated the affluent, many-storied brownstone households of Lower Fifth Avenue from the hard-pressed families of the Lower East Side's shanty towns a short stroll away.[4] As an early center of trade and finance, Manhattan inevitably attracted an elite of enterprise, wealth, and talent, the lineal descendants, in a manner of speaking, of the overwhelmingly Protestant executive cadres that ran or supported the chief executive offices of America's end-of-the-century corporate world.[5] But those who ran its factories and built its infrastructure came from different and, on the whole, more modest backgrounds. For the most part, they were German and Irish Catholics, southern Italians, and the Jews of Eastern Europe.[6] By the turn of the present century the separate strands of Manhattan's economic existence—port, factory town, and corporate office complex—had generated socioeconomic interests and groupings whose care and feeding made major and often conflicting demands on the energies and capacities of the Greater City's civic and political cultures.

Defining the Manhattan Business District

The Manhattan business district, as a place, enjoys no autonomous political existence, or the powers that would flow from such a status. It is a mere assemblage of streets. Since 1898, it has been part of the five-borough "Greater City." Previously it had been part of New York County. Not even in these terms have its boundaries been fixed. Until quite recently, it has been useful to define it as the area below Sixty-first Street to the Battery between the East and Hudson rivers.[7] It reached this northern rim only after World War I, with the development of the Midtown office district. Though the term *business district* connotes a place to work (and play), this one includes a significant number of residential areas in its boundaries as well.[8]

Today's New York metropolitan region—with over seventeen million people[9] living in parts of three states governed by 1,400 local governments—is largely the historical outcome of economic forces that have been mediated through the business district's changing physical fabric as its economy evolved out of the compact trading post founded by the tolerant, commercially minded Dutch trading companies at the southern tip of Manhattan Island in the first quarter of the seventeenth century.[10] Then, as now, enterprises transacting business in geographically far-flung markets powered its economy. The fortunes and misfortunes of these companies and their principals are not directly tied to the ebb and flow of local conditions, though they are by no means insulated from them. They depended on opportunities and forces that originated in a much wider national and global economic sphere. When Patrick Geddes included New York City in his 1915 short list of world cities—so called because therein was conducted a disproportionate share of the world's most important business—he referred to the undertakings of the business district's firms.[11] For better or worse, the business district has always provided the city and, more recently, its surrounding metropolitan area with its chief drawing card in the ceaseless competition with other places both in the United States and abroad for employment, income, and wealth.[12]

Land and building uses in the Manhattan central business district are incredibly complex and have rarely not been in a state of flux. Its constituent elements, constantly altering in physical form and function, have exhibited extreme patterns of both competition and complementarity. As befits a commercial city built for profit and not for glory—be it of state or religion—its real estate market has exhibited little patience for nonpecuniary considerations. Yesterday's valued locational advantages of a given structure and use can never rest on their laurels in Manhattan, but must prove themselves at each new turn of the economic wheel. Failure invites the wrecker's ball and redevelopment, or worse, foreclosure for tax arrears. As a result, the history of the business district as a built environment must be understood in terms of changing market forces and their underlying technological imperatives.

The Central Business District in the Mercantile Period

Until the Civil War, urbanized Manhattan's dominant feature was its extensive waterfront. Manhattan's unique deep water harbor was easy to enter, well protected from adverse climatic conditions and linked by natural waterways, even before the building of the Erie Canal, to several rich agricultural hinterlands. Hands down, it became the eastern seaboard's leading port.[13] It was so good it was immune to bad management for a long time. One might say that a lot of ruin was built into this piece of bountiful nature.[14]

In 1815, 19 percent of all U.S. imports crossed Manhattan's docks, and by the beginning of the Civil War this figure had reached 36 percent. Manhattan's share of U.S. imports rose from 37 percent in 1821—the earliest year for which these data are available—to 69 percent by 1860.[15] At a time when foreign trade mattered a great deal to a young and fast-growing nation, Manhattan had far outdistanced all potential rivals.

At this time, the New York metropolitan region was still composed of widely scattered and very compact urban settlements. The limited means of transportation constrained growth, and Manhattan's concentrated settlement pattern reflected this fact. Within the future region, only Brooklyn, then an independent city facing lower Manhattan on the opposite shore of the East River, had experienced what could even remotely be viewed as a comparable level of development.[16]

Through the first half of the nineteenth century, most of the important wharves, piers, and port-related facilities were on the first mile of the East River extending north from the Battery. Beyond this point, near where Manhattan bulges out at Corlear's Hook, were the shipyards. The latter, a highly space-extensive activity, represented one of the chief forms of manufacturing enterprise then being carried out in Manhattan. In a walk-to-work era, its presence stimulated the initial low-density development of the Lower East Side. The East River's waterfront was first off the mark in this respect, because it was more sheltered than the Hudson River side of Manhattan, a considerable advantage when sailing craft were small and fragile.

Waterfront activity along the Hudson River was, of course, stimulated greatly by the opening of the Erie Canal in 1825 and the impetus this gave to trade with the rapidly growing American hinterland. This process, which would end with the dominance of the Hudson River piers and the virtual disappearance of their East River counterparts, was, however, basically driven by the expansion of the railroad network and the advent of ocean-going steamships. Only one of the railroads had entry for its freight into Manhattan by land. All others terminated their lines on the Jersey shore, and the bulk of railroad freight had to be transshipped by tugs and barges, giving a decided advantage to waterfront development on the island's Hudson or West Side. This tendency was further encouraged when the only line having direct access to Manhattan, the Hudson River Railroad, was opened to traffic in 1851 and attracted along its way a wider range of industrial uses.[17]

Early Days on Wall Street

In the modern world, finance and trade have always flowed together. Manhattan's pioneer office district emerged in its southernmost portions by the middle of the nineteenth century, with Wall Street as its main thoroughfare. It developed in response to the needs of a diverse group of specialist businesses engaged in foreign trade for a physically compact marketplace where the participants could meet with ease and without prior arrangement. This was a crucial consideration given that communication was costly and accurate trade information hard to come by. This initial formation—a veritable congregation of businessmen—was the seedbed of expertise and experience from which the city's extensive financial markets later flourished, attracting in turn a disproportionate number of the nation's leading corporations and organizations which arose to support them.[18]

The earliest office establishments needed only unspecialized physical facilities. Simple structures sufficed. Many of the warehouses huddling close to the piers along the East and Hudson rivers also provided office space. The homes of merchants would, in certain circumstances, hold their countinghouses as well. In Old New York, working and living accommodations, often combined in the same structure, were situated to maximize access to the waterfront.[19]

The Rise of Industrial Manhattan

While port-related activities still dominated the CBD's economy, it had acquired a significant manufacturing presence by the beginning of the Civil War. With 90,000 or so manufacturing workers spread among 5,000 establishments, Manhattan accounted for between 5 and 7 percent of the overall manufacturing activity in the United States.[20] Industrial firms infiltrated the narrow side streets leading to the East River. They were typically small workshops manufacturing largely for the local market. With the opening of the Erie Canal, city-based factories increasingly produced for the expanding hinterland trade in the western part of the United States. As a great port, Manhattan was a large local market, and high transportation costs also stimulated the growth of local manufacturing. Using this large local market as a base, the city's factories realized economies of both scale and agglomeration, enabling them to serve more efficiently the markets opened by the canal system. Limits on production technology, however, kept such economies relatively modest.[21]

After the Civil War, however, manufacturing eclipsed port activities by a substantial margin. Between 1860 and 1900, manufacturing employment in Manhattan increased by 325 percent in a period when its population rose by 127 percent.[22] As Lindstrom shows for the earlier period, Manhattan's manufacturing base expanded more rapidly than the U.S. average for the last four decades of the nineteenth century. Only a small part of this spirited climb could be explained by the growing local demand for manufactured goods. It mostly reflected an increasing ability of manufacturers to compete from a Manhattan base of operations in a rapidly growing national market whose center of gravity was moving ever westward.

The Erie Canal and other water-based means of transportation gave way to the railroad as a link to this market. However, Manhattan's increasingly off-center location with respect to this national market and its lack of raw materials made it disadvantageous as a production location for many kinds of manufactured goods. To compensate, its manufactured products had to have high sales value to shipping cost ratio, as well as to the cost of bringing in the needed raw materials. Consequently, sectors like apparel (or, on a lesser scale, millinery) soon established themselves as New York's "natural" manufacturing industries.[23]

As the nation's chief port, Manhattan was also its chief port of entry for immigrants coming to the United States. As the absolute amount of immigration tripled between 1825 and 1875 and between 1875 and 1925, the city's employers received a massive potential labor supply, a considerable advantage in a nation with rapidly growing agricultural and industrial sectors. Until the 1880s immigrants, nationally as well as locally, came from northern and western Europe—England, Ireland, Scandinavia, and Germany. But over the next forty years or so, eastern and southern Europeans dominated the flow. Jews from Russia and Poland were particularly important to the evolution of the city's economy, since this group had already acquired an urban orientation and useful industrial skills.[24]

Landing here was one thing, staying was another. Only the rapid growth of the city's industrial sector allowed so many of the newcomers to remain. The availability of work, however meager the earnings, attracted workers in an era lacking the most primitive rudiments of a welfare state. Once here, the immigrants' skills, muscle power, and entrepreneurial energies stimulated still more economic opportunities. An abundant supply of efficient, highly motivated wage labor had a significant impact on New York's industrial base. Its cost structure was inevitably highly labor-intensive. Less labor-intensive manufacturing lines would have been uneconomical because they would have been unable to compete in distant markets, given the punitive transportation costs associated with goods that need less intensive processing.

The large, easily tapped, spatially concentrated labor force made apparel, especially women's apparel, Manhattan's dominant industry. In 1869, Manhattan accounted for about 32 percent of the value of product of women's apparel in the United States. This figure rose to 74 percent by 1921.[25] Social and economic changes after the Civil War made it possible to commercialize profitably what had formerly been left to domestic production or custom tailoring arrangements. Well before the "new" turn-of-the-century immigration, Manhattan had already established itself as the nation's leading center in the production and distribution of ready-to-wear garments, though this was, at the time, a relatively small-scale activity. A significant part of this industry was run by German Jews who had arrived in limited numbers at mid-century and had moved into a logical spinoff of earlier established retail businesses. Their co-religionists from Russia and eastern Europe began to arrive in larger numbers in the 1880s, and were drawn naturally to this still small enclave.[26] Many of these men and women had the requisite tailoring skills to enter a trade that was for autonomous reasons growing by leaps and bounds. As the production process was decomposed—or deskilled—into specialized and simpler-to-perform tasks, entry became easier. Most newcomers worked in shops where the common language was Yiddish and where the boss himself was bilingual (or even monolingual in Yiddish). While German Jews may have assumed the entrepreneurial function in the early days, by the twentieth century the much more numerous Eastern European Jews had taken the helm. By and large, they had little need to interact with outsiders in an era when state-provided services were minimal.

The Growth of the Loft District

The pell-mell expansion of Manhattan's manufacturing sector after the Civil War was accompanied by locational shifts and changes in the nature of the physical facilities that firms used. Newly built multistory industrial structures (called *lofts* in the local parlance) became character-istic. Manhattan's resulting high-density environment offered a distinct competitive advantage to the typical apparel business, which was thinly capitalized, produced small runs for a highly variable fashion-fickle mar-ket, and needed to be within walking distance of a large pool of low-wage labor. Their demand for space produced block upon block of mul-tistory industrial structures in Lower Manhattan. From an economic point of view, high Manhattan land values reflect the strong demand for its sites, in turn leading to the pattern of building upward. The strong underlying demand for location comes first; high land prices are an enduring consequence.[27]

Private, profit-making interests originally built lofts for the use of small businesses. Given the unsure prospects facing these under-capitalized firms, they needed to rent. Without rental facilities, most of them would never have been able to start up. But despite a high rate of individual failure, their overall number continued to grow by leaps and bounds. Collectively, they provided a "bankable" market for the devel-opers and owners of loft buildings. As long as Manhattan's industrial sector flourished, it was lucrative to own loft buildings providing indus-trial space. During this golden age, this was the highest and best eco-nomic use of the parcels they occupied. Investors—loftlords, if you will—who risked their capital in such ventures earned competitive rates of return in the investment markets of the day.

Manhattan's industrial space market expanded extensively and inten-sively in mid-century. Initially situated along the side streets leading up to and paralleling the East River, it expanded westward along the Hud-son River shoreline and up through the middle of the island in the 1850s. This shift occurred because expansion sites were hard to come by in the East Side waterfront. More important, they needed to be close to the city's West Side freight handling facilities.[28]

The Coming of Age of the Skyscraper

Purpose-built office buildings also appeared in Manhattan in the final third of the nineteenth century. Most were occupied by their owners, but buildings also began to be put up and operated by investors on a speculative basis for rental to others. This notable instance of an agglom-eration economy also permitted new, modestly capitalized establish-ments to obtain a foothold in a prime location for a relatively small sum. Manhattan's office district expanded uptown along Broadway and its adjoining blocks. By the beginning of the twentieth century, office build-ings were being constructed as far north as Madison Square Park. However, the vast bulk of office development still occurred south of Chambers Street. At the turn of the century, this district contained an estimated 76 percent of all office space in Manhattan.[29] Nevertheless, until well into the 1960s, the streets and avenues immediately adjoining the East and Hudson rivers in Lower Manhattan, periodically expanded by landfills, were still largely given over to shipping, rail freight, and related goods-handling activities such as warehousing, as well as the drab enclaves of working class housing.

The first structures housing Manhattan's office sector tended to be small in scale. But between the 1880s and the 1920s, Lower Manhattan's appearance was radically transformed. What had been tightly developed assemblages of four-, five-, and six-story structures—still dwarfed by Trinity's and St. Paul's steeples—emerged as a compactly developed neighborhood of skyscrapers.[30] Although the elevator, skeletal steel construction, and commercially usable electric power made it technologically possible to build skyscrapers, only a specific market demand brought them into being. The advent of the skyscraper age in Lower Manhattan was the private real estate market's response to the great wave of industrial growth and empire building in the United States, which crested around the turn of the century. American industrialists at the time were challenged with developing efficient organizational structures for their newly formed multifunctional (and multifacility) businesses.[31] The freestanding central administrative office containing professional managers and other specialists who oversaw geographically dispersed facilities was the answer. This managerial revolution enabled Lower Manhattan to become the principal command post of industrial capitalism in the United States. Wall Street became the best-known geographical symbol for those who, near or far, wished to inveigh against the excesses of an unbridled capitalistic system.

Rapid expansion produced clear signs of strain. Developable sites became scarce and prohibitively expensive. The means of transportation that linked the area to its work force became overburdened, since by the beginning of the twentieth century, Lower Manhattan's white collar corps had virtually all become commuters.[32]

The attempts by Lower Manhattan's relatively well paid white collar workers and their families to escape from what they saw as the rapidly deteriorating environment for middle-income residences posed a distinct challenge to the prospects for new office building in this part of town. White collar workers journeyed to work by ferries, steam-driven railroads, elevated trains, horse-drawn railcars, and omnibuses. Significantly more journeys could not be accommodated within the narrow physical limits presented by Lower Manhattan. Something had to be done to increase the peak-hour carrying capacities of its transportation system. Measures were needed to reduce drastically the areas' up-to-then total dependence on slowly moving surface-based conveyances. The creation and subsequent elaboration of the subway system overcame this barrier. In 1904 the first line of subway opened, and this process continued throughout the first third of the century, culminating in the completion of the IND line in the 1930s. The mass transit system eventually linked the Manhattan CBD to the most distant parts of the five boroughs, permitting extensive residential development in the other boroughs and in Upper Manhattan to house the CBD's expanding white (and blue) collar work forces.[33]

The development of a comprehensive city-wide transit system with a Manhattan focal point did more than alleviate Lower Manhattan's acute problems. It opened up adjoining areas to the north to intensive commercial office and industrial development. Between 1900 and 1935, the total amount of CBD office space increased from 33 million to 138 million square feet. The amount of office space in Lower Manhattan (or south of Chambers Street) rose from 25 million to 55 million square feet. The lion's share of new office growth took place, however, in mid-Manhattan. Midtown's share of the rapidly growing supply went from 9 percent at the beginning of the century to 43 percent by 1935, when its 60 million square feet eclipsed Lower Manhattan's. Downtown's share fell from 76 percent to 40 percent. The in-between area, now known as the "Valley" because of its low-rise skyline of small factory buildings, inched up from 16 percent to 17 percent.[34]

Aside from the subway, the central fact accounting for midtown's ascendancy was its emergence, just before World War I, as the New York area's chief node for the movement of people (not goods). As a matter of conscious planning, a synergistic relationship was forged among the subway system, the newly constructed Pennsylvania Station on the West Side, opened in 1910, and the recently electrified, refurbished, and expanded Grand Central Station Terminal.[35] As a result, midtown—and Forty-second Street in particular—became the point of maximum overall accessibility not only within the city but within the region. Lower Manhattan had held this position in 1900, but by World War I the midtown office district had an unmatched ability to draw on all points of the expanding metropolis for its employees. If they lived within the city, they traveled to work primarily via the subways or the recently electrified "el" lines, or, if they resided outside its boundaries, used commuter lines terminating at Grand Central or Pennsylvania Station. This centrality loomed increasingly large as the wider availability of the auto spurred the scale of suburban development. The full impact of this linkage became apparent only after World War II. Midtown also became the focal point for business and pleasure travel at a time when nearly all such travel was by rail or ship. This function waned after World War II, when air travel conquered all, but it had left its stamp on the future by situating the CBD's tourist and business travel infrastructure—hotels, restaurants, theaters, and so on—in the midtown area.

Manufacturing at the Turn of the Century

Pratt's comprehensive survey of factory establishments showed that, as of 1906, 67 percent of Manhattan's factory workers were employed below Fourteenth Street and only 33 percent north of that line. The most intensively developed Lower Manhattan factory area, the Sixth Assembly District, was part of the Lower East Side. It had 304 factory workers per acre compared to a Lower Manhattan-wide average of 118 per acre. But even the First and Second Assembly districts, which covered the area between Canal Street and the Battery and contained the city's financial district, had more than 20 percent of the borough's overall manufacturing employment at this time.

While employment in Manhattan's manufacturing sector had grown considerably since the Civil War, it had also decentralized. In 1860, Manhattan accounted for 85 percent of all manufacturing employment in the geographic area that would eventually become the Greater City. By 1900, Manhattan's share of this total had fallen to 75 percent.[36] During the latter part of the nineteenth century, Brooklyn was the New York metropolitan region's fastest growing county. By 1900, its population of 1.2 million represented 63 percent of Manhattan's. If independent, it would have been the U.S.'s second largest city. Being so populous, it offered labor market advantages comparable to those of Manhattan, and with the construction of the subway system also provided substantially upgraded mass transit opportunities for local workers. Lower Manhattan's shoreline had, by the turn of the century, been virtually preempted by steamship and railroad piers. The vastly superior railroad facilities of the Jersey shoreline tempted manufacturers from Manhattan, but water movement of freight was still important to industrialists. Many were thus attracted to Brooklyn's superb waterfront, its virgin industrial sites, and its ample labor supply.[37] Between 1899 and 1919, Manhattan's manufacturing employment did rise by 36 percent, but manufacturing employment grew 142 percent in the other boroughs over this twenty-year period and 91 percent in the balance of the metropolitan region. Between 1899 and 1919, Manhattan's share of manufacturing fell from 73 to 61 percent in the city and from 43 to 32 percent in the region.[38]

Even before the mass use of the auto and truck began to restructure urban patterns, several developments encouraged manufacturing to decentralize out of Manhattan and New York. To begin with, large industrial firms could move to newly created large industrial complexes (like Brooklyn's Bush Terminal) and utilize railroad sidings—in effect, a private railroad—only outside crowded Manhattan.[39] The growing ability and inclination of the city's working class to move out of Manhattan operated in the same direction. Trolley lines, elevated trains, and then subways provided each borough and the region's smaller cities outside New York with a resident labor force that could be tapped by local manufacturing establishments. Reflecting such trends, the Manhattan CBD's residential population peaked in 1910 and then began a long decline.[40]

Between 1900 and 1920, Manhattan's manufacturing firms relentlessly moved uptown. While the bellwether women's garment industry had 70 percent of its employees south of Fourteenth Street in 1900, by 1922 only 10 percent remained there. Only 5 percent of Manhattan's women's clothing employment had been between Twenty-third and Forty-second streets in 1900, but this figure rose to 36 percent by 1922.[41] The floor space available in Manhattan's industrial buildings increased from 117 million to 175 million square feet between 1900 and 1920, reflecting this northward migration. The skyscraper office building defined the distant view of Manhattan CBD's physical landscape in 1920, and industrial buildings dominated the streets below. In 1920, the CBD held three times more industrial space than office space and probably twice as many factory workers as office workers.[42]

Housing the Masses

In the 1860s, Twenty-third Street separated the densely built-up city from its underdeveloped portions, except on the West Side where a well-defined industrial and transportation corridor, with interspersed factory worker housing, had emerged between Ninth Avenue and the Hudson River up through the Sixties blocks. In the span of the next half century, the inland part of Manhattan north of Chambers Street to the Thirties blocks was covered with multistory loft structures.[43] The cost of moving goods and raw materials was secondary to the ability of these firms to secure an adequate work force. The growth of this sector radically and decisively altered the nature and functioning of Manhattan's housing market.

In "Old New York" all housing classes, except the rich who could keep a horse, lived cheek by jowl, equally constrained by the need to walk to work.[44] The built-up city of this age was such a compact affair that everyone lived in the same neighborhood, so to speak, although housing circumstances obviously varied with wealth. For the ordinary worker and his usually large family, this meant living in jerry-built, poorly maintained, and desperately overcrowded tenements situated in the mean streets adjoining Manhattan's Lower East Side and West Side waterfronts.[45]

As the shifts already discussed occurred, they offered to the better off the opportunity to live at some distance from the congestion and squalor that were rapidly enveloping Lower Manhattan. For the rapidly expanding working class, moving on was simply not economically feasible. They remained bound to neighborhoods within walking distance of the business district. As the better off left for such suburbs as Brooklyn, some of their houses were haphazardly converted for reoccupancy by much larger numbers of lower-income households. But this source soon proved inadequate. Between 1850 and 1860 alone, Manhattan's population increased 58 percent, from 516,000 to 814,000. And then, after a brief Civil War-induced slowdown—because of the war's impact on European immigration—Manhattan's population resumed its rapid growth, reaching an all-time high of 2.4 million by 1910.

As a result, both sides of Manhattan were "improved," with newly built, low-cost housing, between the Civil War and World War I. On the Hudson River side arose the neighborhoods of the West Village, Chelsea, and Hell's Kitchen (today known, less ominously, as Clinton). On the East River side the sequence of intensive working class neighborhoods began with the Lower East Side, itself a complex mosaic of different ethnic villages. By World War I, all of Manhattan east of Third Avenue had, in effect, become one continuously developed tenement district.[46]

Tremendous industrial growth created a corollary intense demand for conveniently situated rental housing that working class families could afford. The range of choice available to workers and their families was exceedingly narrow at the beginning of the process. Modest and always uncertain incomes and limited means of transportation framed its limits. When the Lower East Side and the lower and middle West Side were initially developed, workers had to live within a mile, or twenty city blocks, of their centers of potential employment. For ordinary working people, this tight bond between place of work and place of residence began to be significantly loosened only when the first subway lines were placed in operation after 1900. Some, such as dockworkers, because of industry hiring practices—in the form of the infamous "shape-up"— were denied even this relaxation of constraints on where they could live.[47]

The wretched habitations erected in districts like the Lower East Side and Hell's Kitchen were financed, built, and maintained by a class of small businessmen on an unsubsidized basis. Their development was the collective product of individual actions by profit-minded businessmen, and resulted in the creation of a massive, though newly built, slum. By the beginning of World War I, virtually every available foot of land in what were working class quarters had been built over by five-, six-, and even seven-story walk-up tenement structures. As bleak as these buildings and the neighborhoods they formed were in their outward appearances, interior arrangements were still bleaker. Tiny two- and three-room apartments, lacking adequate ventilation or proper toilet facilities (collective, much less private), produced a form of multistory urban cave for hard-pressed newcomers to the city.[48]

Religiously motivated nineteenth-century reformers did ally themselves with public health officials, each concerned with some form of contagion, to institute bylaws that sought to ameliorate the housing lot of the so-called "respectable" poor. But the tide of population growth in the decades around the turn of the century swamped their modest, if well meant, efforts.[49] Advocacy by political groups, such as Manhattan's Tammany Hall, whose constituencies were increasingly drawn from the ranks of immigrants-become-voting-citizens, added some force to their efforts, bearing fruit in the 1901 "new law" Tenement House Act. This measure outlawed further construction of the building types that had virtually covered the Lower East Side as well as the lower and middle West Side. It had also initiated a process of upgrading existing tenements. However, the various provisions were neither phased in immediately nor vigorously enforced, so that between 1901 and 1910 an enormous amount of new working class construction did not greatly differ from the pre-1901 notorious "old law" phase of Manhattan's housing history.

A principal argument for gradually phasing in the new standards, and even then requiring only modest upgrading, was that the private housing sector could not otherwise meet the demands still being placed on it by the city's rapidly expanding working class population, fueled as it was by the surge in immigration which crested in the century's first decade.[50] After this decade, however, the CBD's resident population ceased to grow. Between 1910 and 1930 the Lower East Side's population fell by 54 percent, from just over 540,000 to a bit under 250,000.[51] Between 1920 and 1930 the resident population of the entire CBD fell 47 percent, from 1,280,000 to 680,000.[52] Several factors accounted for this rapid decline. For one thing, immigration into the United States and the Port of New York slowed to a trickle during World War I. High levels of immigration resumed after the war, but the enactment in 1924 of restrictive national immigration legislation sought to stem the flow of southern and eastern European newcomers who formed the principal sources of immigration into the New York area. Simultaneously, improved transportation, shifts in industrial location, and higher working class real incomes were redirecting the working class housing market, deflecting it to other ports of entry.

After 1904, the growth of rapid transit with its fixed low-fare policy made it possible for ordinary working people to commute to Manhattan from all parts of the city. Suppliers of housing vied to develop large parts of Upper Manhattan, the Bronx, and Brooklyn for working class families. The resulting housing and neighborhoods were significant improvements over such ports of first call as the Lower East Side. In part, state and local governments took a more aggressive posture in regulating the building activities in the private sector. But the private market also responded positively to the declining cost of providing working class housing and the stronger demand for it. On the cost side, land and building were simply cheaper in the areas that the expansion of the rapid transit system opened up to development. On the demand side, the real incomes of ordinary wage-earning families rose rapidly in this period and their family sizes declined. As a result, they demanded and were able to afford better housing.[53]

The massive factory exodus from lower Manhattan after 1900 also reduced its attractiveness as a working class residential area. The relocation of the clothing industry, first to the West Side between Fourteenth and Twenty-third streets and then into the area around Pennsylvania Station, had a large impact on the Lower East Side since it was a major source of employment for its residents. In addition, the Independent Division, the last component of the subway system, skirted but did not actually penetrate the area until the 1930s. After 1910 the Lower East Side began to lose some of its transportation advantages to newly developed working class neighborhoods in Brooklyn, the Bronx, and Upper Manhattan. The decline of Lower East Side real estate values, already well marked before the Great Depression, intensified after 1929. The area's population fell another 18 percent from 1920 to 1940. At the beginning of World War II, its population was barely at 38 percent of its 1910 peak.[54]

Similar trends adversely affected other long established working class residential areas on the lower and middle West Side. The erection of Pennsylvania Station and its yards and facilities in 1910 demolished an extensive working class district covering parts of Chelsea and Hell's Kitchen, and displaced a significant black population.[55] In the 1920s, new industrial construction along the West Side between Chambers Street and Fortieth Street required clearance of much low priced housing.[56] Finally, the building of the East River Drive, the West Side Highway, and the approaches to the Holland and Lincoln tunnels in the 1930s and 1940s punched additional gaping holes in the social fabrics of these compactly built working class areas.

The fate of the Lower East Side as a pioneer working class residential area was a harbinger of what befell other such communities elsewhere in Manhattan after World War II. Property abandonment and foreclosure of mortgage and tax delinquency were common events in the 1920s and 1930s. A considerable amount of demolition of vacant buildings took place, either because they were judged unfit for habitation, or in order to make way for public improvements such as road widening, or later on for the construction of units under the governmentally subsidized low-rent housing programs begun during the Depression. The events of the Depression set the stage for a significant alteration in the CBD's working class housing market. The full implications did not manifest themselves, however, until after World War II. While the CBD's residential areas remained what they had always been, a haven (of sorts) for low-income people, its old-timers yielded to later rounds of working class immigrants (Puerto Ricans, black Americans). The area's outward circumstances also changed as massive public housing projects towered above the remaining, still numerous, older walk-up tenements built before the turn of the century.[57]

Land Use Conflict in the Central Business District: The Zoning Code

Land uses in the Manhattan CBD were constantly altered in composition and intensity from 1880 to 1920. These transformations reflected market forces, an unsurprising result in a capitalist society where government was expected to do as little as possible, as cheaply as possible. New York City did not lack for radical political groups and movements, but the ruling paradigm regarding government involvement in urban development was to facilitate efforts to "release private energy," in James W. Hurst's felicitous phrase.[58] As in any market, the shifting state of

Manhattan's real estate sector reflected the interaction of supply and demand factors. It was driven over the long run by the demand side of the market equation. People demanding facilities and location within the CBD got what they wanted and could pay for. Who got what depended on the outcomes of the bidding process. Thus, if the aggregate rent that could be charged to ten working class families for a 25-by-100-foot loft exceeded what one well-to-do household would pay, then the contested site would be developed as an incredibly cramped multifamily tenement and not as a spacious upper middle class brownstone.

Local government intervention, acting under powers delegated by the state legislature, was initially confined to setting certain rules of the game such as the 1811 plotting of the streets and roads of Manhattan Island north of the then settled city. But as the city grew in size and complexity, more substantial and direct innovations were forced upon the local public sector, in terms both of regulating land and building uses and of the direct provision of public goods such as parks, transport, and public health.[59] During the great period of city building in the nineteenth century, however, there was little public restriction of or control over private development.

Prior to the enactment of the first zoning resolution in 1916, it was possible to build to almost any height for any desired use in any part of the city. Newly formed civic groups, concerned with the quality of life and urban design questions, argued that the resulting cityscape was unsatisfactory. Buildings were judged to be too big for their sites and economic uses—such as manufacturing—and were in the wrong locations. The notion that an attractive city was, above all else, an orderly city was an important source of these critics' discontent. The helter-skelter city that was being produced was decidedly not orderly. Still others, however, were affronted by the clash they apprehended between certain orders or cultures that had previously operated on separate spatial tracks. This was most apparent in the frequently expressed concern that rapidly expanding manufacturing districts would invade Manhattan's established high-quality residential, retail, and commercial office districts.[60]

To address this looming clash, New York State, in 1914, authorized a Commission on Building Districts and Restrictions to create a plan "to divide the city into districts and to regulate the height of buildings, the area of courts and open spaces, the location of trades and businesses and the erection of buildings designed for specified uses." The results of this Commission's investigations and deliberations were enacted as the zoning resolution of 1916, a first not only for New York City but for the United States. These rules remained in force until 1961, although the assumptions on which they were based had, decades earlier, been invalidated by changing technological, economic, and social forces.[61]

By 1900, a series of clearly defined subareas had evolved within the business district: the central office and financial districts in the Wall Street area, the lofts along Broadway and lower Fifth Avenue, waterfront and heavy industry along the Hudson and East rivers, and, interspersed through the remaining areas, concentrations of office and retail activity, apartment house, hotel, tenement house, and private dwelling districts (that is, brownstones typically occupied by one family). Market forces had segregated heavy industry along the waterfront and near the rail terminals. Most of the business district's industrial workers were employed, however, in light manufacturing. Such firms preferred to locate where they could easily be reached by their labor supply. In an era of cheap and abundant rapid mass transit, they had a great range of choice, which was precisely the source of the Commission's disquiet. "Strong social and economic forces," the Commission observed, "work toward a natural segregation of buildings according to use and type. In general, the maximum land values and maximum rentals are obtained where this segregation and uniformity are most complete. One purpose of districting regulations is to strengthen and supplement the natural trend towards segregation." To the Commission, "the sporadic invasion of a district by harmful or inappropriate buildings or uses," was the heart of the districting problem. "Once a district has thus been invaded, rents and property values decline, loans are called, and it is difficult ever to reclaim the district to its more appropriate use. Individual property owners are helpless to prevent the depreciation of their property. The districting plan will do for them what they cannot do for themselves— set up uniform restrictions that will protect each against his neighbor and thus be a benefit to all."[62]

In the Commission's analysis, the city's rapidly expanding light manufacturing sector was the culprit. This activity had drawn too close for comfort to the retail, hotel, and passenger terminal centers in mid-Manhattan. Manhattan's light manufacturing firms gravitated to the center of the island from Canal Street on the south to about Thirty-eighth Street on the north. And it was the perceptible quickening in the northward movement of light manufacturing and its ethnic labor force above Fourteenth Street in the decades leading up to World War I that was one of the great motivating forces behind the zoning movement in New York City.

In the 1880s, Manhattan's hotel and entertainment center was located around Twenty-third Street. Thirty years later the hotels, clubs, theaters, and better retail stores had moved to Thirty-fourth Street and beyond. The Commission, rather mechanically, interpreted their relocation as an act of flight, a response to the invasion of light manufacturing uses. The purportedly negative impact of nearby uncouth factory workers on prestigious retailing shops received particular notice. This was, after all, the heyday of American nativism. Ethnic differences and stereotypes entered strongly and explicitly into the debate on zoning. However, an alternative and more plausible explanation of this uptown exodus was that the relocating users were moving to what they regarded as a preferred location, one that put them closer to the midtown commuter cross between the subways, Pennsylvania Station, and the newly reconstructed Grand Central Station. But the Commission saw things differently. "The purely private injury incident to haphazard development has become so serious and widespread as to constitute a general public calamity. . . . The capital values of large areas have been generally impaired . . . economic depreciation due to unregulated construction and invasion have become a hazard . . . and affects not only the individual owners of real estate throughout the city, but the savings and other large institutions, the municipal finances and the general welfare and prosperity of the whole city."[63]

The Commission viewed segregation of uses, homogeneous districts, and strict control of the location of industry as appropriate responses to the location problem. Protection of public health, safety, and capital value were to be the primary aims of any districting scheme. The 1916 law provided for these three classes of districts within the CBD: (1) residential, (2) commercial, and (3) unrestricted. Regulations were prospective and did not interfere with any existing structure or use. Districts already invaded by industrial uses, such as the area west of Fifth Avenue from Fourteenth Street to Herald Square, were offered little protection against further factory intrusion.

In districts to be zoned for residences, all business and industry were excluded. Few of these districts were to be found south of Fifty-ninth Street. They covered such areas as Murray Hill, Gramercy Park, lower Fifth Avenue, portions of Chelsea, and the Fifties off Fifth Avenue, and housed what little remained of the business district resident gentry. In zoned-for-business districts, residences and businesses were permitted, but industrial uses were either prohibited or severely limited. New heavy industrial uses involving, say, the manufacture of chemicals, production of electric power, slaughterhouses, or other noxious or offensive uses were expressly forbidden in these districts no matter how small the establishment. The business district designation was meant to protect the financial district, the better residential and business areas throughout the CBD, as well as the shops, hotels, and restaurants of upper Fifth

Avenue and the entertainment district in west midtown. The catchall unrestricted districts provided no use restrictions or regulations. It was assumed, however, that the play of market forces in the unrestricted districts would largely lead to industrial development. An analysis by the Commission of the development from 1850 to 1916 showed that little change was evident in the breadth of the industrial belts extending back from the East or West Side waterfronts. Recognizing this pattern, the boundaries of the unrestricted district in Manhattan generally extended back 1,000 feet from the bulkhead line along the Hudson and East rivers. These perimeters included most of Manhattan's heavy or noxious industrial activities and much tenement housing.

The Commission's attitude toward the future location of manufacturing within the business district emerges from the zoning map that summarized the 1916 resolution. Factory development was free to continue in the sprawling low-rise loft area extending north from Chambers Street along Clinton and Chelsea, with their higgledy-piggledy mixture of factories and tenements. Greenwich Village and the northern portion of the Lower East Side were given business district designations to protect the middle class housing enclaves from further factory encroachment. By this measure, it was implicitly assumed that market forces would ultimately reshape them into predominantly middle class residential areas. As noted, even greater protection was granted to the posh areas of Murray Hill and Gramercy Park; it excluded all commercial development, even stores and offices. The business designation allowed Wall Street to grow as the financial center without fear of factory encroachment. East midtown was "saved" from factories and allowed to develop as a business and entertainment area.

Industrial Manhattan: Stability and Decline

Manufacturing activity in Manhattan boomed during World War I. It then declined sharply in the first part of the 1920s, and recovered only a portion of its lost ground toward the end of the decade, paralleling national and regional trends in this respect. As of 1929, Manhattan's manufacturing employment was 15 percent below its 1919 level. The trend was similar, though less sharply downward, for this sector in the rest of the city and the balance of the metropolitan region during the 1920s.[64] This decline did not, however, end the construction of new industrial space in Manhattan, or for that matter in the rest of the city or region. Rather, a great many of the oldest and least efficient loft structures were demolished in the 1920s to make way for considerably larger industrial buildings. New business district loft construction in this decade amounted to between 50 and 60 million square feet of gross floor space, an average yearly output of 5 to 6 million square feet. The present-day garment district buildings north of Thirty-fourth Street between Sixth and Ninth avenues (including the so-called Garment Center complex, an earlier industrial version of Rockefeller Center) were put up in this period, as were the massive structures on Varick and Hudson streets, which quickly became the strongholds of the city's printing industry. This spate of construction took place because locally based manufacturers needed more space, better designed layouts, buildings with industrial elevators, and off-street loading facilities to remain competitive.[65]

Between 1929 and 1939 manufacturing employment in Manhattan fell by another 9 percent, a similar percentage to the rest of the city but almost double the balance of the New York metropolitan region. Manhattan's manufacturing employment during the 1930s actually declined at a slower rate than in the preceding decade and by less than the nation.[66] That Manhattan did so well, relatively speaking, stemmed from the character of its industrial base. The Depression hit heavy industries like steel and machinery the hardest. Manhattan had always specialized in such areas as women's apparel, where national employment actually increased significantly during the decade. Another explanation for Manhattan's showing was absence of investment in new industrial capacity anywhere in the country during the depressed 1930s. Therefore, places with existing capacity, like Manhattan, continued to be utilized for production purposes to a greater degree than they would have in more normal circumstances. But the general economic adversity did virtually end new construction. Manhattan's stock of industrial floor space topped out in the mid-1930s at an estimated 225 million square feet. Only five loft buildings were put up in the business district over the next half century.[67]

After two decades of decline, manufacturing employment in Manhattan and New York City soared after the 1941 entry of the United States into World War II. Strictly wartime needs, such as the production of military clothing, augmented increased demand for consumer goods.[68] The return of prosperity, in a wartime situation, could most easily be satisfied from the existing capacity available in such places as Manhattan and New York City. Obviously, wartime constraints held back the construction of additional civilian capacity in other parts of the country. Between 1929 and 1947, Manhattan's share of New York City's manufacturing employment remained virtually unchanged, rising from 58 to 59 percent between 1929 and 1939, falling to only 57 percent in 1947. New

York City's share of regional employment in this sector also remained steady, as it had since 1919. Lastly, the New York region's share of U.S. manufacturing employment remained virtually unchanged between 1919 and 1947.[69]

Despite this growth and the long-term stability in its share of manufacturing activity, the basis had nevertheless been laid for the eventual significant weakening in the relative desirability of Manhattan and of New York City as the location for manufacturing activity. When rail- and water-borne transportation had been the only economical modes of moving goods over long distances, and when surface transportation for people and goods was slow and costly, manufacturing firms were literally confined to locations in the densest portions of central cities, close to the main rail and port terminals. These were the most efficient points for securing labor and access to supplies and customers. But the rapidly growing use of the automobile and the truck drastically altered this situation. In economic terms, the truck and auto liberated businesses from inner city locations. In this regard, the number of motor vehicles registered in the New York metropolitan region rose from 476,000 to 1,863,000 between 1920 and 1930. During the Depression, 574,000 more were registered. During the period from 1920 to 1940, while the New York region's population rose by 37 percent, the number of its motor vehicles rose by 412 percent.[70]

Once locational constraints were so decisively loosened, the features that had facilitated the growth of manufacturing in the CBD turned to disadvantages. When it became easy to move goods by truck, firms could choose low density locations. They could construct or rent extensive one-story plants incorporating the latest and most cost-effective industrial technologies. Comparable efficiencies could not be realized in already developed areas because of the high cost of site acquisition. By moving to less dense locations, appreciably more accessible to the evolving highway network, manufacturing firms (as well as goods handling wholesalers) greatly reduced their costs of receiving and shipping goods and materials over what they would have been in congested city locations. Eventually, these forces allowed higher paid manufacturing workers to suburbanize as well.

In addition, New York City's hitherto unmatched ability to draw upon the immigrant influx for its industrial work force had been greatly reduced. Access to large numbers of Jews and Italians had bolstered the city's labor supply and kept its wages at competitive levels with other parts of the country, despite the fact that other areas benefited more from the farm-to-city movement of native-born Americans. American blacks did come to New York, but in numbers much smaller than the immigration from Europe had been and, by and large, they took jobs in lower paid service occupations rather than in manufacturing. When the United States ended its policy of virtually unrestricted immigration in 1924, it delivered a serious blow to Manhattan's competitive position as a location for manufacturing. The adverse consequences were doubly felt by New York City since the quotas discriminated against immigration from southern and eastern Europe which had, during the preceding half century or so, dominated the ranks of newcomers to New York City.

Between these two events—the increasing use of the automobile and truck, and the curtailment of foreign immigration—New York's labor supply advantages faded dramatically. The full significance of these developments was blunted during the 1930s by the Depression. This moratorium, so to speak, continued during World War II. Afterward, however, the consequences were heavily felt in New York City.

The Office Market After the 1920s

When the Great Depression started in 1929, Manhattan was in the midst of an unprecedented office building boom. From 1920 to 1930, the amount of office space in the CBD increased from 74 million to 112 million square feet; in the next few years, before the taps were belatedly turned off, another 26 million square feet was added. This building space responded to what seemed an ever-expanding demand for office accommodations in Manhattan which, in turn, grew out of the buoyant national and world economy. During this decade, the speculative office builder, building for the occupancy of others and risking his own and other investors' capital in the process, began to play the leading role in the CBD's office market.[71]

Developers and other financial interests involved were then confronted with an economic cataclysm whose length and severity lay completely outside their historic experience. Between 1929 and 1933, the U.S.'s constant dollar gross national product fell by 31 percent and the nation's unemployment rose from 3 to 25 percent. The balance of the decade saw a substantial, if erratic, recovery from these depths, but recovery was only partial until the full-scale mobilization for the war in 1942. U.S. employment did not actually exceed its 1929 levels until 1940. Office markets everywhere were naturally deeply affected by these developments. Manhattan's office space vacancy rate climbed to a 1934 peak of 24 percent.[72] Bankruptcies and foreclosures among builders, owners, and lenders were legion. With the notable exception of the Rockefeller Center complex, little new construction was initiated after 1930. But office employment in Manhattan resumed its upward climb in the mid-1930s, and, by 1938, the vacancy rate had fallen to around 14 percent. The wartime boom and a moratorium on new commercial office building construction then reduced the vacancy rate to 1 percent, creating a standing-room-only situation.

Looking Forward (and Backward)

Between the Civil War and World War II, Manhattan's economy, its built environment, and the society it supported were primarily that of an industrial city. True, its world-famous skyline was the product of the numerous tall office buildings initially concentrated in Manhattan's financial district and then, by the 1930s, on an even larger scale in midtown. But most of Manhattan's work force through this period was still blue collar workers. Their world was located in the Valley—the area generally lying along the West Side between Chambers Street and the blocks just below Times Square. In this period, the four or five miles of piers and landings along the Hudson River were still active. Ocean-going vessels carrying freight and passengers docked there; cargo and produce to be consumed in the city or shipped inland and cargo produced in the seaboard states for export abroad was loaded and reloaded there.

By the late 1950s, this balance cf forces had greatly altered. The office sector significantly outweighed the factory sector in economic significance. It was no longer a question of whether Manhattan's industrial base would decline, but of how fast. A similar fate overtook Manhattan's port. Much was written in the early 1950s about the rampant criminality, violence, and trade union corruption on the West Side piers, but the real story was being written elsewhere. The use of the truck and the development of containerization destroyed the West Side's ability to compete.[73]

The postwar deindustrialization of New York City is another story, however much it was already evident that the pillars of the old order were crumbling in the 1930s and 1940s. Yet looking back, we can only marvel at the tremendous strength and dynamism of New York City's economy and built environment between 1860 and 1950 despite the odds against it. The disadvantages of being off-center to the growing, westward-moving national market and a dense, congested, costly production site were offset by the specialization in labor-intense goods that had a high value added relative to their shipping costs and by the accession of a vast new immigrant working class. On parallel but distinct lines, New York turned the growth of a widely diffused national economy to advantage by specializing in headquarters and corporate service activities. The degradation of vast expanses of tenement housing were, if not supplanted, then augmented through vast expanses of new working class housing outside the initial industrial core, in turn made possible by the building of the nation's largest mass transit system. While later trends undermined these achievements, they continue to be a legacy of paramount importance.

Notes

1. Alexis de Tocqueville, *Democracy in America*, quoted in James W. Hurst, *Law and the Conditions of Freedom in the Nineteenth Century United States* (Madison: University of Wisconsin Press, 1956), 18.
2. Allan R. Pred, *The Spatial Dynamics of U.S. Urban Industrial Growth 1800–1914: Interpretive and Theoretical Essays* (Cambridge: M.I.T. Press, 1966), 143–215.
3. Pred, *Spatial Dynamics*.
4. For a firsthand account of the impact of these differences on the sensibilities of a native son returning for a visit after long years abroad, see Henry James, *The American Scene* (Bloomington: Indiana University Press, 1968), 116–39.
5. Allan S. Horlick, *Country Boys and Merchant Princes: The Social Control of Young Men in New York* (Bucknell University Press, 1975), 65–144.
6. The historical transformations of the ethnic composition of New York's working class population have not been treated in a comprehensive manner as phenomena in themselves. However, studies of individual ethnic groups deal with this topic in some detail. A good place to begin is Nathan Glazer and Daniel P. Moynihan's classic work, *Beyond the Melting Pot: The Negroes, Puerto Ricans, Jews, Italians and Irish of New York City 1800–1915* (New York: Oxford University Press, 1977), 44–70, 161–77; and David C. Hammack, *Power and Society: Greater New York at the Turn of the Century* (New York: Russell Sage, 1982), 89–100.
7. Regional Plan Association, *The Region's Growth: A Report of the Second Regional Plan* (New York: Regional Plan Association, May 1967), 113–15.
8. In 1920 the business district included a resident population of slightly over one million; see Boris Pushkarev, "The Future of Manhattan," in *New York's Changing Economic Base*, ed. Benjamin Klebaner (New York: Pic Press, 1981).

9. The census-defined 17-county New York–Newark–Jersey City, N.Y.–N.J.–Conn. Standard Consolidated Statistical Area—otherwise known as the New York metropolitan region—had a population of 17.5 million as of 1983.

10. Thomas J. Archdeacon, *New York City, 1664–1710: Conquest and Change* (Ithaca: Cornell University Press, 1976), 58–79.

11. Patrick Geddes, quoted in Peter Hall, *The World Cities* (New York: McGraw-Hill, 1966), 7.

12. For a statement of its current importance, see Matthew Drennan, "Local Economy and Local Revenues," in *Setting Municipal Priorities, 1983,* ed. Charles Brecher and Raymond H. Mortor (New York: New York University Press, 1982), chap. 2, 15–45.

13. The classic account of this process is, of course, Robert Albion's *The Rise of New York Port, 1815–1860* (New York: Scribner, 1939).

14. A recent work on this neglected subject is Ann L. Buttenweiser, *Manhattan Water-Bound: Planning and Developing Manhattan's Waterfront from the Seventeenth Century to the Present* (New York: New York University Press, 1987).

15. See Diane Lindstrom's essay in this volume.

16. David Ment, *The Shaping of a City: A Brief History of Brooklyn* (New York: Brooklyn Educational and Cultural Alliance, 1979), 28–36.

17. Carl S. Condit, *The Port of New York: A History of the Rail and Terminal System from the Beginnings to Pennsylvania Station* (Chicago: University of Chicago Press, 1980), 1–24.

18. Sidney M. Robbins and Nestor E. Terleckj, *Money Metropolis* (Cambridge: Harvard University Press, 1960), 1–24.

19. Betsy Blackmar, "Re-walking the 'Walking City': Housing and Property Relations in New York City, 1780–1840," *Radical History Review* (Fall 1979): 131–48.

20. For data on trends in manufacturing employment, see Edward E. Pratt, *Industrial Causes of Congestion of Population in New York City,* vol. 43 (New York: Studies in History, Economics and Public Law, The Faculty of Political Science at Columbia University, 1911), 41. Population data from U.S. Census of Population.

21. Richard Stott, "Hinterland Development and Differences in Work Setting: The New York City Region, 1820–1870," paper given at the New York Historical Conference on Early New York City History, Spring 1984.

22. Pratt, *Industrial Causes.*

23. Robert M. Lichtenberg, *One-Tenth of a Nation* (Cambridge: Harvard University Press, 1961).

24. For one of the many accounts of the significance of the role of the Port of New York as an entry point in immigration into the United States, see Oscar Handlin, *The Newcomers* (New York: Anchor Books, 1972), chap. 2, 9–42.

25. Benjamin M. Selekman et al., *The Clothing and Textile Industries in New York and Its Environs* (New York: Regional Plan Association, 1925), 18.

26. Roger Waldinger, *Through the Eye of the Needle: Immigrants and Enterprise in New York's Garment Trades* (New York: New York University Press, 1986), chap. 3.

27. Charles R. Simpson, *Soho: The Artist in the City* (Chicago: University of Chicago Press, 1981), 111–28.

28. Lebyl Kahn, *The Loft Building in the Central Business District of Manhattan* (planning thesis, Pratt Institute, June 1963), chap. 3, 28–57.

29. Unpublished estimates for the period from 1900 to 1979 prepared by John Stern for the Tri-State Planning Commission of New York, New Jersey, and Connecticut.

30. John A. Kouwenhowen, *The Columbia Historical Portrait of New York: An Essay in Graphic History* (New York: Doubleday, 1953), 394–95.

31. Alfred D. Chandler, Jr., *The Visible Hand: The Managerial Revolution in American Business* (Cambridge: Harvard University Press, 1977), 315–39.

32. According to Pratt, only 14 percent of the male workers employed in Lower Manhattan (and 6 percent of the female workers) in the high-wage groups resided below Fourteenth Street. For the lowest wage group, the comparable figures were 54 and 61 percent, respectively; Pratt, *Industrial Causes*, 129, 131.

33. The events leading up to the completion of the first subway line are presented in Hammack, *Power and Society*, 230–58; and Charles W. Cheape, *Moving the Masses: Urban Public Transit in New York, Boston and Philadelphia, 1880–1912* (Cambridge: Harvard University Press, 1980), 20–101. Peter Derrick also provides a treatment of the subsequent development of the subway system in his 1979 New York University dissertation, "The Dual System of Rapid Transit: The Role of Politics and City Planning in the Second Stage of Subway Construction in New York City, 1902 to 1913." Despite the title, this study covers the period between the 1890s and the 1930s and is probably the most comprehensive historical treatment of New York's subway system to date.

34. John Stern, Tri-State Planning Commission.

35. Condit, *The Port of New York*, 1–9, 54–100, 239–311. See also Elliot Willensky, *Grand Central Terminal: City Within the City* (New York: Municipal Art Society of New York, 1982), 85–108.

36. Pratt, *Industrial Causes*, 26–44.

37. Benjamin Chinitz, *Freight and the Metropolis: The Impact of America's Transport Revolutions on the New York Region* (Cambridge: Harvard University Press, 1960), 133–38.

38. Regional Plan Association, *The Economic Status of the New York Metropolitan Region in 1944* (New York: Regional Plan Association, 1944).

39. Chinitz, *Freight and the Metropolis*.

40. Pushkarev, "The Future of Manhattan."

41. Selekman et al., *Clothing and Textile Industries*, 66.

42. Stern, Tri-State Planning Commission.

43. Kahn, Loft Building.

44. Blackmar, "Re-walking the 'Walking City'."

45. James Ford, Slums and Housing (With Special Reference to New York City): History, Conditions, Policy (Cambridge: Harvard University Press, 1936), vol. 1, chap. 5, 72–121.

46. Lawrence Veiller, "A Statistical Study of New York's Tenement Houses," in The Tenement House Problem, ed. Robert W. DeForest and Lawrence Veiller (New York: Macmillan, 1903), 69–118.

47. See Daniel Bell, "The Racket-Ridden Longshoremen," in his The End of Ideology, ed. Daniel Bell (New York: Collier Books, 1961), 178–81.

48. Ford, Slums and Housing.

49. Lawrence Veiller, "Tenement House Reform in New York City, 1834–1900," in The Tenement House Problem, vol. 1, 69–118; see also Allan F. Davis, Spearheads for Reform: The Social Settlements and the Progressive Movement, 1890–1914 (New York: Oxford University Press, 1967), 65–74.

50. Roy Lubove, The Progressives and the Slums: Tenement House Reform in New York City, 1890–1917 (Pittsburgh: University of Pittsburgh Press, 1962), chap. 6, 151–84.

51. Leo Grebler, Housing Market Behavior in a Declining Area: Long-Term Changes in Inventory and Utilization of Housing on New York's Lower East Side (New York: Columbia University Press, 1952), 244–53.

52. Pushkarev, "The Future of Manhattan."

53. Deborah Dash Moore, At Home in America: Second Generation New York Jews (New York: Columbia University Press, 1981), 19–58.

54. Grebler, Housing Market Behavior.

55. Gilbert Osofsky, Harlem: The Making of a Ghetto (New York: Harper & Row, 1966), 93.

56. Kahn, Loft Building.

57. Grebler, Housing Market Behavior.

58. Hurst, Law and the Conditions of Freedom, 3–22.

59. Ford, Slums and Housing.

60. Harvey A. Kantor, "Modern Urban Planning in New York City: Origins and Evolution, 1890–1933" (Ph.D. diss., New York University, 1971), 165–229, and Derrick, "The Dual System," 210–64.

61. S. J. Makielski, Jr., The Politics of Zoning: The New York Experience (New York: Columbia University Press, 1966), 23–40.

62. Commission of Building Districts and Regulations, Final Report, City Register, New York City, 1916.

63. Commission of Building Districts and Regulations, Final Report.

64. Regional Plan Association.

65. Kahn, *Loft Building*.
66. Regional Plan Association.
67. Kahn, *Loft Building*.
68. Regional Plan Association.
69. Regional Plan Association.
70. Motor vehicle registration data from the Regional Plan Association of New York (unpublished).
71. "Office Building Bonanza," *Fortune* (Jan. 1950): 84.
72. Real Estate Board of New York, *An Analysis of Competitive Office Space in Manhattan*, series 40 (Jan. 1952).
73. Bell, *The End of Ideology*.

5

The Launching of a Commercial Culture: New York City, 1860–1930

William R. Taylor

In the fifty years between 1880 and 1930, New York outdistanced other large American cities in the vigor and creativity of its commercial culture. No other American city matched the range of entertainment, theater, nightlife, and other forms of recreation that were available in New York during these years. Wealthy elites in New York, as in other cities, established cultural institutions, clubs, museums, concert halls, and opera houses that provided the usual ties with similar elites elsewhere. New York's large working population found expression for its political, ethnic, and economic concerns in union halls; ethnic, trade, and neighborhood associations; and mutual aid societies.[1] In New York, however, a system of cultural production distinct from elite culture and from the culture of working class politics flourished along Broadway and worked its way north from City Hall Park to Times Square as the period progressed. Moreover, this cultural marketplace soon began to attract the patronage of an increasingly wide spectrum of the city's population.

This essay seeks to establish the identifying features of this commercial culture, to examine how it functioned, and to suggest the needs it served. Much of what historians have written about the origins and history of mass culture detects the emerging traits of twentieth century mass culture in this entire earlier period, and therefore fails to take into account the changes occurring within it.[2] By focusing on the increasingly centralized production of cultural forms, these historical assessments neglect the complex ways in which urban audiences consumed these cultural forms. Most historians have assumed, mistakenly, that the public was sold entertainment that was sheer diversion and irrelevant to its needs, rather than being provided with cultural experiences that helped different groups within the population make sense of the new urban environment. Viewed from the perspective of its consumption, New York's new commercial culture was much more vigorous, varied, and creative than existing historical discussion of it has led us to believe.

The Rise of a Commercial Culture

The term *commercial culture* is employed rather than the more common *popular culture* in order to emphasize the distinctiveness of New York's system of cultural production and consumption before the 1930s. Commercial culture began as the culture of the nineteenth-century street, where an astonishing variety of goods and entertainment offered by itinerant peddlers and showmen was consumed in a carnival atmosphere.[3] In such a culture, the city's streets functioned as both showcase and show. What began with itinerants and storefront theatricals soon became embodied in new cultural institutions that collected and displayed entertainment just as the new department stores displayed goods. The vehicles for this new commercial culture were exhibition halls, popular museums, amusement parks, vaudeville theaters, storefront movie houses, and a new kind of newspaper that became the verbal and graphic equivalent of the new cultural bazaars. These new cultural emporiums retained the stamp of their street origin, especially in their miscellaneousness, the strident pitch of their promoters, and their emphasis on consumption as "show."

The remarkable success of these cultural forms was due to their unique capacity to provide a "reading" of the city. Each new genre of commercial culture compressed a representation of city life into its format. These new genres had in common a seemingly random, potpourri organization that continued to dramatize the discontinuity, the kaleidoscopic variety, and the quick tempo of city life, as in the vaudeville revue. Their essence was to create, out of miscellaneousness, little self-contained worlds that were perceived spatially rather than narratively and over time. Like photographs, these pastiches were susceptible to varied interpretations. They were so attractive that markets for them quickly developed in other cities, where they lost certain features of their ethnic origin and spatial particularity, as happened with minstrelsy and vaudeville.

After the 1920s, however, a quantum change took place in the degree to which New York produced commercial culture for a national rather than a local market. The reciprocal feedback from audience to producer declined correspondingly, gradually changing the character of commercial culture. Beginning in the 1920s, national network radio, theater chains, centralized motion picture distribution, and wire service journalism forever changed the previous half century's close relation among cultural producer, cultural consumer, and the city of New York, transforming them into a new mass culture.

It is hardly surprising that this kind of commercial culture developed in New York City. Nineteenth century New York's economic life descended directly from that of such Western trading cities as Venice and Amsterdam two centuries earlier.[4] It shared with these cities an extensive sea trade, a constricted land area, and the absence of the heavy hand of national government authority or official cultural institutions. This last characteristic, rare among major cities of the world, gave the mercantile and business classes in each of these cities comparatively unchecked power to shape the city, unlike their counterparts in cultural centers such as London, Paris, and Vienna, where the interests of other classes and official cultural institutions intervened. Moreover, New York was unique among major commercial cities in experiencing settlement, economic development, and urbanization as virtually simultaneous stimuli to growth.[5] A succession of disruptive changes thus shaped the culture of the city and left their mark on its spatial structure during the nineteenth century.

This spatial organization of New York reflected the growing diversity and complexity of its commercial, social, and recreational activities. The most intense cultural commerce took place in and around the major axes or squares of the city, and the central focus made its way north along Broadway from City Hall Park in the 1840s and 1850s to Times Square by World War I. By the 1890s, Madison Square had become the focus of the city's life, serving briefly as its public center. It was here, for example, that the memorial arch was constructed in 1899 to celebrate the victory of Dewey in Manila the year before, and here also that the vast parade in honor of Dewey came to a halt before the reviewing stand of the city's notables.[6]

Inter-class and Inter-gender Contact

A regionalization of class life in this period tended to lock the wealthy wage earners and the impoverished into distinct areas of the city. By the 1890s, each had acquired a name and a recognizable mythos, much as the Bowery, whose reputation lingered on, had done in the antebellum period. New neighborhoods, characterized by distinctive types of housing such as the apartment house and the purpose-built tenement, made their appearance on a massive scale during these years, and tended to set off the style of working class life from that of the middle and upper classes on Park Avenue.

Meanwhile, a new set of elite cultural institutions made its appearance after the 1870s: museums, opera houses, clubs, and other exclusive social institutions. By the end of the century, universities had withdrawn in important ways from active engagement in the city's civic life to nurture the new academic disciplines, as Thomas Bender has suggested.[7] And cultural institutions had developed to market entertainment to the lower classes: dance halls, burlesque houses, saloons, the various concessions of Coney Island, and, after the turn of the century, the new storefront movie houses.[8]

By contrast, many new institutions brought New Yorkers of different classes together in novel ways. These new forms of inter-class orchestration sometimes involved actual physical proximity; other times they were vicarious and perceptual, as in the consumption of print culture, architecture, or other shared visual experiences. The different classes in the city had always shared the principal streets and other public spaces, such as Broadway and the few unpaved, grassy areas such as Battery Park, City Hall Park, and Union and Madison squares. The developing transportation system and its stations were probably the single most important locus of inter-class mingling. Ferryboats, elevated and street railway carriages, and after 1904, subways caused different classes to rub shoulders on an altogether new scale.

Other new institutions brought different classes together on a more structured, hierarchical basis. The large hotels, theaters, and restaurants brought working class people into subservient contact with others, but the growing numbers and increasing localization of such facilities changed the scale and quality of this contact. The new large office buildings, such as the Metropolitan Insurance, brought together a working population of considerable variety. In its elevators, dining rooms, and work areas, a population varying from managers to menials daily brushed shoulders. The sheer numbers of people working in these new office spaces opened further opportunities for mutual observation up and down the social scale.[9]

Much the same can be said of the new and larger department stores that appeared during these years. They segregated employees from clientele of all classes and imposed a rigid hierarchy from the management down the power scale to buyer to floorwalker to clerk to cash boy. The customers, too, were of different classes, and consumed different grades of goods. The most important feature of this new social promiscuity lay in the large and growing numbers of working class New Yorkers who participated in, or observed, the consumption of luxury products or the new forms of commercial entertainment.[10] A large middle class population also traveled on the city's elevated transportation system through working class and ethnic neighborhoods they would not otherwise have seen. New forms of class interaction and reciprocal observation thus considerably tempered the "barrio" effect of the city's domestic regionalization.

To the people experiencing these changes at the time, the new institutions and practices that progressively brought the sexes together in the city on a radically different basis were dramatic. Distinct areas of the culture, most notably politics and management, remained male preserves, but the new presence of women was especially evident in such settings as office buildings and department stores. Men and women were both forced to improvise a decorum for these new relations in the workplace. This was especially difficult where new gender arrangements were further complicated by differences in class and in authority.[11]

Women of all classes were attracted to the new retail palladiums toward the end of the century, drawn by the alluring combination of bargains and luxury goods and by the increasingly luxurious amenities such as rest rooms, parlors, and tearooms that became available to women shoppers.[12] As a result, stores and office buildings became highly sexualized environments; each area of activity developed a distinctive folklore concerning the kinds of sexual encounters afforded by this new proximity and its new set of power relations between men and women.

During this period, the city also became a major leisure resource for middle class women.[13] In the department stores, larger hotels, and theater matinees and, after the turn of the century, in Broadway cabarets, roof gardens in summertime, and places where dancing, dining, and entertainment were offered, middle class women for the first time joined the nightlife of the city, even unescorted. A similar change took place in vaudeville and other forms of theatrical entertainment. In the 1870s, vaudeville houses like Tony Pastor's in Union Square had catered to a predominantly male audience. After the turn of the century, Florenz Ziegfeld and George White spectacles were performed to almost equal numbers of men and women. By the 1920s, men and women, in pairs or unescorted, took part in the fashionable invasion of Harlem jazz clubs and engaged in other forms of "slumming" that had by then become a regular part of middle class leisure and recreation. Prohibition further broadened the scope of permissible, if not fully acceptable, female behavior, as the elite mingled with the underworld in the speakeasies of Hell's Kitchen.[14]

The full spatial order of modern New York had emerged by the end of the 1920s, partly as a result of three other dramatic and almost simultaneous changes in the city: the rapid development of luxury apartment housing on Park Avenue after the Grand Central rail tracks were placed underground; the equally rapid concentration of office buildings in midtown, set off by the construction of Rockefeller Center; and the flowering of Broadway as a middle class theatrical mecca under the genius of Ziegfeld and his imitators.[15] The new connotation of Park Avenue as the home of the "socialite" (to use a 1920s neologism), was understood by everyone by the end of the decade. Both Condé Nast and Ziegfeld maintained establishments there, which they used for lavish entertainment. The Rockefeller decision to develop blocks of office buildings in the 1950s brought about the concentration of publishing and communications industries in the midtown area, with the new RCA Tower as its focus.

The Culture of Pastiche

The content of these new cultural forms mixed many different elements of the city's culture. New York began to develop a commercial culture of pastiche, derived from the experience of the streets, as early as 1869. In that year, publishing and printing, followed by the construction trades, were among the city's largest industries.[16] Apart from general periodicals, printers ground out publications for every trade and self-defined group, for every special occasion. The volume of this material has rarely been exceeded, but the close tie between printing and building seems particularly unique to New York. Accounts of new buildings habitually filled its newspapers, and newspapers themselves were housed in some of the city's most distinctive structures.[17] It was no accident, therefore, that two of the principal axes of the city were named after newspapers—Herald Square and Times Square (originally, Long Acre)—nor was it coincidental that the first tall building with an Italianate tower was Hunt's Tribune Building of 1877 on Newspaper Row, off Broadway at City Hall Park. These two newspaper axes eventually performed additional functions in transmitting New York's urban modernity: Herald Square as a center of department store retailing, and Times Square as the focus of theater and nightlife and as a center for large municipal celebrations.

A street derivation marks the pastiche culture after 1869. The association of popular culture with the street is, of course, very old. In the sixteenth and seventeenth centuries, streets formed the principal arteries through which the mass of Europeans received print culture: religious proclamations (often read aloud), posters, broadsides, ballads, almanacs, chapbooks, and, in France, editions of classical writers, so-called *livrets bleus* (for their cheap, colored paper), were hawked in the street by peddlers, or *colporteurs*.[18] As late as 1910, moreover, the same process continued in New York, as peddlers selling candy and seltzer dispensed editions of *David Copperfield* and *Les Misérables* (the reputed best-sellers) in Yiddish on the Lower East Side.[19] Street itinerary also continued to be a feature of popular entertainment, as pantomimists, jugglers, puppeteers, and other showmen set up shop wherever crowds could be collected.

Almost every new form of popular culture or entertainment exhibits a preoccupation with reflecting this street experience in the broadest sense. Vaudeville, the penny press, Coney Island, Tin Pan Alley, in their inclusiveness, variety, and pacing—as well as the pitch with which they were promoted—all derive from this older street-spatial tradition of entertainment. Radio, film, and television continued to exhibit some of these characteristics well after the 1930s. Whole new cultural genres have been created to give fresh expression to it. But the culture of pastiche, partly because of its street derivation, also evoked political and ideological controversy that resonated throughout the period and after, especially in a society that was energetically embracing domesticity and the values of familial order and that saw street life or anything deriving from it as representing various ugly forms of societal subversion. Getting things "off the streets" became a byword of middle class reform.[20]

Reading the City

The fact that commercial culture, despite moral and aesthetic opposition, attracted a widening clientele drawn from almost every sector of New York's diverse population testifies to the important functions it served to those who lived through these years. It interpreted the city, making a new social world intelligible in the volatile and changing urban arena of New York. Indeed, cultural forms were invented to "read" the city in one way or another. The juvenile novel and city guide of the 1860s and 1870s, the newspaper short story, the color comic, and the popular Tin Pan Alley song illustrate readings of cultural change in New York. All helped to create new markets for popular culture, and attracted a diverse clientele that crossed social or generational boundaries. Their format, their tenor, their market success, can show how and by whom they were so avidly consumed.

Juvenile Novels

Probably no aspect of popular culture or the history of journalism has been less carefully examined than the remarkable expansion of the so-called juvenile literature and magazines for "youth" in the two decades after the Civil War.[21] Something is known of the Alger and Oliver Optic novels, but the sudden mushrooming of this phenomenon is clearly ripe for further study. *Youth's Companion*, an older magazine founded in the 1820s, for example, rapidly increased its circulation under new leadership after 1869, until by the mid-1880s it surpassed the *Ledger* to achieve the largest circulation of any magazine then published—385,000—outside the cheap mail-order weeklies. This success was obtained by surprisingly modern promotional methods of offering premiums—books, pictures, tools—for subscriptions and renewals. As a result, it could raise its advertising rates to $2.25 an agate line, well above the rate of *Harper's Monthly, Leslie's Popular Monthly, Century,* and *The Police Gazette.*[22] Horatio Alger's first, and most successful, novel, *Ragged Dick*, was serialized in the competing New York-published *Student and Schoolmate* in 1868, the year before its book publication, as were the serialized versions of the first Oliver Optic novels, written by its editor, William T. Adams.[23] Such fiction provides interesting evidence about how this new popular literature was consumed.

The association between youth and the city already had a history by 1869, in the volumes of advice literature counseling young men on how to obtain a foothold in the city.[24] The circumstances under which Horatio Alger found a new and much larger audience for this kind of story—it is estimated that *Ragged Dick* sold some 300,000 copies during the century—are therefore not without precedent. The eyes of a young man were seen as a revealing perspective from which to examine the new urban industrial world. In the "reading" it gave New York, this literature prefigured the adult guidebook that would appear much later.

At the narrative level, *Ragged Dick* recounts a homeless boy's progress from the city streets to well-furnished rooms in St. Mark's Place, and from bootblack to clerk in a countinghouse on Pearl Street. Contradictions or tensions of one kind or another resonate through the story. It is, first of all, a strange combination of boy's adventure story and moral tract. Although *Ragged Dick*, like Alger's subsequent novels, is preoccupied with inducing boys to abandon the life of the streets for middle class respectability, it presents a much more attractive picture of the picaresque freedom and independence of street life than it does of the somewhat grim, confining, joyless rise to success: a life of bathing, saving, praying, ciphering, and cautious investment. Dick allows himself only the indulgence of luxurious furniture in his rooms. He spends money in this way, the book stresses, only to encourage himself to stay home.

Youthful readers, by contrast, would probably have found good entertainment in the whirlwind tour of the city that makes up the first half of the novel, even if they had to deal in some way with the moralizing of the plot. Dick's city is described as a boy's paradise in his accounts of his former street life, his colorful street argot, his various encounters with criminal types, and the heroic rescues that take place during this tour. One chapter is even entitled "Dick the Detective," in the spirit of future juvenile fiction. All of this is interspersed with moralizing and adult commentary. Similarly, although the novel officially endorses the social system that divides the city into rich and poor, there is more than a little of the irreverence of Huck Finn in Dick's bravado and his jokes about millionaires, fancy hotels, Delmonico's, or his Erie shares.

Then, too, although the novel endorses domesticity and, in the wealthy Grayson family, presents a model middle class home, *Ragged Dick* presents a gender-biased picture of contemporary domestic values. With the exception of the Grayson episode, the novel is entirely about men and boys, fathers and sons, boys and boys. The only women are Irish landladies; the only married couple is a parody of matrimonial mismatching. The downtown New York of the novel is a city of men, as no doubt it largely was, but the domesticity of the novel is also exclusively male, as thirteen-year-old Richard Hunter and his friend Henry Fosdick pair off and set up housekeeping, praying and sleeping together like husband and wife.

New York is thus seen through the eyes of boys. An adult New York almost fully equipped with contemporary moral geography emerges most forcefully in the content of the book. Early in the novel, Dick gets himself hired as a guide to a young out-of-town boy who is staying at the Astor House. For an entire day, Dick shows his young visitor the sights of the city. The New York they see, the stories Dick tells his client, and the individuals and institutions Dick singles out for description are regular guidebook fare. Only the shadowy New York of sex and sin is omitted. The tour, for obvious reasons, does not stray from Manhattan's sunny midsection into its darker parts, but in other ways it follows the content of these guides almost chapter by chapter. In guidebook fashion, Chapter 6 is entitled, "Up Broadway to Madison Square." Except for the Bowery Theatre, Barnum's Museum, and the Newsboy's Lodging House over the *New York Sun*, the tour focuses on features of the city a twelve- or thirteen-year-old would neither know nor care about, any more than such a boy would care about ward politics, matrimonial mismatching, or the dangers of illiteracy.[25]

In short, *Ragged Dick* can be construed as a kind of anthology of different genres of narrative, full of oddly different kinds of details and commentary, each with its own separate appeal, and compatible for family purchase and consumption—a species of pastiche culture characteristic of the period. No one "reading" of the city can be a universal interpretation, even during this early period. Degrees of acceptance, skepticism, and outright disbelief concerning the success ethic and the city's moral geography were probably quite compatible with enjoying *Ragged Dick* as a good boy's yarn. Conversely, the novel probably satisfied an adult reader's urge for an orderly, moral, and familial world with young boys safely off the street and put to clerical work indoors, nevertheless permitting nostalgic glimpses of cherished childhood freedom, companionship, and adventure—and even a few sly digs at the injustice of the existing economic order in the city. It also gratified middle class enviousness of the upper classes in its portrayals of the spoiled, indulged, and dishonest children of the rich.

Guidebooks

The many guides to the city published in the early part of this period were another cultural growth industry that roughly paralleled the appearance of the Alger and Oliver Optic serializations and books. They also seem to have been directed to similarly diverse audiences, attracted by different reasons. The New-York Historical Society contains between thirty and fifty such guides (depending on the criteria one employs in classifying them) published before 1900. Some of these guides went through numerous editions and obviously reached a wider audience than others.[26] Quite a number were written by clergymen or others with some definable religious or missionary intent. They form a distinct and recognizable genre with remarkably similar organization and content. They are, moreover, remarkably and interestingly different from guides to the city published in the twentieth century, such as the *WPA Guide* (1939) or W. Parker Chase's *New York, The Wonder City* (1932), though, surprisingly enough, some older moral and narrative characteristics do, in fact, linger on in Chase's book, different though it is in every other way.[27]

These guides clearly were not limited in their appeal to New York initiates, nor to visitors from out of town. The premise behind their rapid growth and apparent popularity was the desire of a wide range of readers to know about the city in a way they could not, for various reasons, from personal observation. They were, in effect, little anthologies of essays on almost every dimension of city life, characterized by the widest possible appeal to different kinds of readers. Even the order of chapters, at least compared with modern guides, seems random and miscellaneous, unrelated subjects following one upon the other. These guides, in other words, appear to present still another instance of the relationship between the city's spatial variety and a developing culture of pastiche. They underscore how far this peculiar kind of pastiche penetrated respectable, genteel literature in the nineteenth century.

These guides did, however, retain a fairly consistent point of view. The authors underscored their consistently moral evaluation of urban behaviors at every turn. A pervasive tactic was to evoke the moral geography of the city. This tactic emphasized a connection between behavior and location within the city. Not only were crime, vice, political corruption, art, commerce, and great wealth assigned their particular places, but each kind of behavior was metaphorically assigned an appropriate station in a color spectrum of light and shadow. This moral mapping of the city was, of course, nothing new to this period, and probably originated in a time when only respectable streets were illuminated.

What was new was the racy company this benevolent moralism began to keep after the Civil War. *Lights and Shadows of New York Life, or, Sights and Sensations of the Great City* is, in fact, the title of a popular guide published in 1872.[28] It mostly represents the genre, including authorship by a clergyman, the Rev. James D. McCabe, Jr. The early chapters of the guide are consistent with a surviving civic conception of the city as a subject with chapters on the harbor, city government (including the "Ring"), the major polite streets and public spaces such as Central Park, the press, the police, Wall Street, and such public facilities as hotels, restaurants, streetcars, and ferries. A chapter on Horace Greeley, one of the many biographical sketches characteristic of these guides, conforms to this civic model for the city. But after this point, a jumble of miscellaneous subjects crowds its way into McCabe's account. Chapters on "Black Mailing" and "Female Sharpers" are sandwiched between chapters on Henry Ward Beecher and Jerome Park. A sketch of Commodore Vanderbilt is followed by a chapter on "Bummers," one on James Gordon Bennett by a chapter on drunkenness, and one on Peter Cooper by "The Heathen Chinee."

This long final section communicates an overwhelming impression of exploring a *terra incognita*, an utterly new and different kind of society where older values, norms, and relationships no longer apply. This was not a society, furthermore, over which men of McCabe's stripe imagined themselves as exercising much control. On the contrary, a sense of class and moral disorientation pervades the text.

The anomalous character of this new city life frequently outruns the expressiveness of ordinary English, reducing McCabe to listing the distinctive argot that pertains to crimes and various forms of vice, just as Ragged Dick delighted in passing on to Frank Whitney bits of slang, like what was meant by a "swell," to give him the flavor of street life and the kinds of skullduggery that characterized it. At one point, McCabe included an entire glossary of criminal terms.[29] At another, he quotes Brace's observation that boys came into the Newsboys' Lodging House without real names, known only as Tickle-Me-Foot or Cranky Jim or Wandering Jew. Tenement house life is deemed sufficiently peculiar to warrant a graphic illustration of a cross-section of such a domestic novelty, showing the astonishing variety of social life that can take place simultaneously in such a structure.[30]

These guides, in other words, possessed a multifaceted interpretive character shared with other kinds of popular commercial culture, such as architecture and photography. The many contradictions in the possible significance of these culture forms thus become comprehensible. For example, the pervasive evocation of light as moral metaphor—of darkness, shadow, and vice on the one hand, and of light, brightness, and virtue on the other—displays an almost Manichaean ambivalence about the new urban world. New York was wonderful, beautiful, the Paris of America, a paradise for women (middle class, of course); yet it contained areas of unprecedented moral slime, abasement, misery, and corruption. Such contradictions seem merely confusing until we consider how they must have been read.

The superficially odd arrangement of chapter topics and illustrations, their miscellaneous substance, their format, invited casual browsing and dipping into for this or that detail or subject, rather than reading through from cover to cover, as in the seventeenth century almanacs, chapbooks, and devotional books analyzed by Chartier. Their length of 700 or 800 pages militated against such a sequential reading, as did the scores of short, choppy chapter headings. It would be a mistake, therefore, to consider the persistent moralizing in these volumes as reflecting the mentality of their readership or to assume a direct relationship between moral tone and audience response. Preachments apart, readers doubtless used these books as guides to the very vices they were being warned against. Moral rhetoric represented a threshold for entering into close scrutiny of many subjects, such as those discussed by Fowler. Moral condemnation, or at least cautionary prefacing, was the eye of the needle through which any consideration of sexual conduct was forced to pass.

The Yellow Press

By the turn of the century, new ways were rapidly extending the market for various cultural products to different groups and categories of consumers. Such products must be examined with an eye to how they were perceived and used by those who purchased them. After the 1880s, the daily newspapers, especially the evening and Sunday editions, provide the best examples of how this process worked. Without doubt, they became the single most innovative area of New York's blossoming commercial culture, far more than juvenile literature or popular guides. No single figure had a greater impact on this process of cultural innovation and market extension than Joseph Pulitzer. Despite the mythology that surrounds the so-called Yellow Press, Pulitzer perceived with great clarity that a successful newspaper must acquire a readership in every class of the city and appeal to many different kinds of readers if it was to earn its share of the advertising bonanza that became available during this period.[31] By the end of the century, Pulitzer and William Randolph Hearst, who acquired the *New York Journal* in 1896, could both boast of daily circulations of close to a million, and a Sunday circulation approaching a million and a half or more. By one estimate, one out of six New Yorkers purchased a daily paper by 1900, and almost half the population purchased one on Sunday.

Other quantitative changes in newspapers probably created an equally important context for cultural change. The size of newspapers expanded enormously, from four pages in the 1870s to sixteen pages or more by the end of the century, with Sunday papers even larger. Advertising, rather than income from sales, became the basis of profitability, and the price of daily papers dropped from three cents to one cent by 1900; the voluminous Sunday papers sold for five cents. Advertising boomed. The volume and rates of New York papers were by far the highest in the country. The actual amount spent on national newspaper advertising appears to have doubled every decade between 1870 and 1900, reaching an estimated total of $140,000,000 by the end of the century.

Equally evident changes in the content, format, and promotion accompanied these quantum changes in market and help to explain them.

The *World* institutionalized features that had appeared elsewhere by devoting specific space or departments to items of appeal to particular groups: sports reporting, fashion news, household tips for women, and other special features with wide appeal to readers. The *World* instituted polling as a basis for distinctive news reporting about changes in public opinion. In a bow to the city guides, an Episcopal minister was sent to live in Hell's Kitchen to report his experiences to the Sunday *World*. A New York shop girl was asked to review a play about a London shop girl; and Elizabeth Cochran (Nellie Bly), the *World*'s ace woman reporter, beat the record of Jules Verne's Phineas Fogg by circling the globe in 1889 in just over seventy-two days and in a blaze of *World*-sponsored publicity.[32]

Dramatic changes in newspaper format were equally significant during the 1880s and 1890s. Multicolored ads, experiments in type size and color pitch that led to banner headlines, and a front page that contained promotional stories in boldface type and other stories in boxes or in type of varying sizes were being used by both the *World* and the *Journal* by the time of the outbreak of the Spanish-American War, itself a newspaper event in New York. Like the introduction of color and the variety of new graphic illustrations, these format changes visually transformed newspapers in this period.

By the end of the nineteenth century, the private corporations that supplied large cities like New York with a new kind of journalism had become of major economic interest. The process of change could be characterized as going from community bulletin board to commercial billboard—exactly the characterization used by James Parton in the 1880s to protest the new style of illustrated, multicolor advertising. "Gentlemen," he exclaimed, "this is not advertising, this is bill-posting."[33] It was no coincidence that both Pulitzer and Hearst nursed political ambitions, since the *World* and Hearst's *Journal* had pieced together conglomerate readerships, drawn to their papers by one fact or another, that very much resembled the loose, shifting coalitions characteristic of American political parties of the period. Pulitzer, who successfully ran for Congress from New York in the late 1880s, was especially clear about the analogue between journalism and politics. "I wish to address the whole nation," he once said of the *World*, "not a select committee."[34]

The question of how the readership consumed this journalism therefore becomes paramount. It would be easy to assume, as most historians have, that this strident new form of print culture dominated the thinking of increasing numbers of the city's population, setting the tone of political discussion, even fomenting war, setting trends in dress and entertainment, and whetting the popular appetite for accounts of crime and sexual scandals. In general, such a view sees the press by the 1890s as feeding the appetites of semi- and newly literate ethnic and working class populations with a kind of integrated "culture of compensation" that robbed them of class and ethnic consciousness by pandering to their curiosity and baser interest. Such an interpretation no doubt springs in part from the difficulty of showing that it may have been otherwise and from the absence of the kinds of evidence historians are accustomed to employing. Such thinking may also be attributable to a naive assumption that consumers read these papers from cover to cover and took the contents at face value.

By the 1890s, the Sunday *World* had become a remarkable example of New York's commercial culture that offered something for almost every taste. It provided entertaining features that were subject to multiple interpretation by readers differing in class, age, and gender. As competition with Hearst heated up toward the close of the decade, the *World* added still more features and departments to hold its place in the market, and took the perilous step of reducing the price of its daily evening paper, the edition bought by the city working population, from two cents to one cent. A typical Sunday paper in this period would include a few pages of hard news; perhaps an editorial in boldface, large type, or boxed; crime stories; reports of sporting events; a society column; illustrated theatrical spreads; short fiction; a feature article on a famous literary or artistic personality; advice to working girls; household hints; and a discussion of manners. By the middle of the decade, the Sunday *World* began to include color comics in a section that rapidly grew from one or two to eight pages.

The Comics

A close look at two new Sunday features, the color comic and the newspaper short story, may help us to understand how this new kind of culture was consumed. Both genres were different from their closest antecedents and both evidently attracted a wide and expectant readership of a kind once attracted by serialized novels. Moreover, these features can best be explained by how they helped commercialize newly acquired leisure time in New York, rather than as part of a process of working class indoctrination.

In 1894, Morrill Goddard, then Sunday editor of the *World*, introduced a comic color picture by Richard Felton Outcault, part of a continuing feature involving the adventure and antics of a group of slum kids, entitled "Hogan's Alley." There had been comic pictures and even primitive comic "strips" before, but the color pictures appearing in the *World* marked the beginning of a new era in serialized caricature, one that attracted wide and enthusiastic attention. Circulation figures reflected the success of this and other Goddard innovations, rising from 266,000 in 1893 to 450,000 in 1896.[35]

The central figure in "Hogan's Alley" was an urchin of toddler age with a vacant, toothless grin, always portrayed in a bright yellow dress. He quickly captured the public imagination, eventually giving his name, The Yellow Kid, to the series and the designation *yellow* to the penny press in general. He was the first in a succession of picaresque children and childlike animal figures to enter the public domain and to take on a kind of life of their own.

"The Yellow Kid" and a succession of other comic figures, both in single pictures and, after 1897, in strip forms, provide a case study of pastiche culture and how it must have been consumed. The key to success, it would appear, lay in creating a figure that was, first of all, socially prismatic, a figure whose behavior would have comic significance to those approaching it from different social perspectives. In the American funnies or color comics, the central figures of children or animals allowed a wide range of comic responses. Ridicule of genteel middle class convention or mischievous violence against adults could be interpreted in many ways. Rudolph Dick's practical-joking "Katzenjammer Kids," which began running in 1897 in the *Journal*, delighted children for a generation with their unruly manners and were regularly used by adults to point out a moral about the fruits of bad conduct. Class interloping was another characteristic of color comics. These comics are entirely preoccupied with leisure, moreover. Almost no one works, any more than anyone goes home. Events take place in public. Leisure life is portrayed as pursued with a new kind of energy and zest. The Yellow Kid of "Hogan's Alley" and Buster Brown, as well as their English "uncle," Alley Sloper, are always portrayed as "on the town," never in the slums. They go to, or turn up at, the fashionable city places and country resorts or, indeed, in the case of Buster Brown, traveled to Europe. Despite the fact that The Yellow Kid is a toddler and Buster Brown only seven or eight, they get around the city unescorted. "Say, Tige," Buster Brown exclaims to his dog in one sequence, "meet me at Herald Square at 5 o'clock. We'll go to a French restaurant, and then we'll go to the theatre."[36]

These comics, in other words, provide still another reading of the city, one that consistently portrays it, often quite literally, as a kind of playground rather than a place of work, as it had been earlier to Ragged Dick. The attention focused on comic heroes clearly derived from their distinct individuality, even peculiarity, and their style in confronting the social world of the city (with admirable bravado, comic innocence, or foolish ignorance, depending on one's point of view). The spectacle of the individual confronting homogeneous mass society and convention underlay the appeal of comics and enabled them to feed successfully so many different kinds of appetites.[37]

The first single-page color comics were clearly designed to be read in a particular way but not in any particular order. You could start anywhere, as with a newspaper itself, and stop anywhere without a sense of incompletion. In a particular episode from "Hogan's Alley," one could begin with the signboards in the background, which parody popular ads, or with the boxed "jokes" at the foot of the page, none of which associate in any way with the picture; or, indeed, one could focus on the baseball game and the comic disregard for the widely acknowledged decorum of the diamond. Each picture contained jokes that were purely visual, others that were purely textual, thereby allowing for degrees of literacy and appetite for English and for print culture.

O. Henry

Although more transitory than the color comic, the short fiction of the period may be an even more revealing source. William Sidney Porter almost single-handedly created the form of short story that flourished briefly after the turn of the century. No one after him practiced it with the same success. For a few short years between Porter's arrival in the city in 1902 and his death there of acute alcoholism in 1910, his O. Henry stories provided a reading of the city that belongs to that historical moment in the same way that the *New Yorker* short story, created by John Cheever and others, belongs to the period surrounding World War II.

City stories were the staple of Porter's New York years, although he continued to write about the picaresque criminal types in the Southwest that had first brought him attention. In his best stories, Porter's New York is not the city of the rich and established, nor even that of the apartment-dwelling middle classes. Upper or genteel class figures pop up as narrators and sometimes set the tone and voice, but his favored terrain was the bars, dance halls, and dives of Hell's Kitchen, the Tenderloin, the Bowery, and the seedy rooming houses on the lower West Side, or what he called Brickdust Row, a world of the defeated and the transient. His central characters live on the fringe: losers, drifters, especially women locked into hopeless, humiliating, frustrating, and lonely lives.

Living semiclandestinely as a kind of outsider in the city, Porter identified in a powerful way with its oppressed, the "little people" who held menial, tedious, thankless jobs such as waitresses and laundry employees, and its large population of female clerks or "shop girls" (though he despised the term). Porter's stories are notable, furthermore, for their attention to people at work, especially women. So many stories touch on the plight of women working in department stores, for example, that Vachel Lindsay once referred to Porter as "the little shop girls' knight."[38] His city was one of hard work, fleeting pleasures, sexual vulnerability, and, for many of his characters, an ineluctable but unspecified fate. He could be seen as taking the moral geography of McCabe's guidebook and turning it upside down or inside out. His empathy for those who lived in McCabe's moral shadows and his contempt for those who victimized or exploited them produced a very different, if still ambiguous, reading of the city.

The evocative power of these stories gives them much of their present poignancy and literary interest. A succession of arresting images brings turn-of-the-century New York to life. In "The Unfinished Story," the ironic brilliance of Broadway at night looms over the weary figure of Dulcie as she walks home from The Biggest Store to her furnished room on the far West Side:

> The streets were filled with the rush-hour floods of people. The electric lights of Broadway were glowing—calling moths from miles, from leagues out of the darkness around to come in and attend the singing school. Men in accurate clothes, with faces like those carved on cherry stones by the old salts in sailor's homes, turned and stared at Dulcie as she sped, unheeding, past them. Manhattan, the night-blooming cereus, was beginning to unfold its deadly, heavy-odored petals.[39]

In a litany, Porter lists the contents of a furnished room, things that have been left behind by a succession of defeated people, a kind of literary equivalent of the blues:

> A polychromatic rug like some brilliant-flowered rectangular tropical islet lay surrounded by a billow sea of soiled matting. Upon the gay-papered wall were those pictures that pursue the homeless from house to house— The Huguenot Lovers, The First Quarrel, The Wedding Breakfast, Psyche at the Fountain. The mantel's chastely severe outline was ingloriously veiled behind some pert drapery drawn rakishly askew like the sashes of the Amazonian ballet. Upon it was some desolate flotsam cast aside by the room's marooned—a trifling vase or two, pictures of actresses, a medicine bottle, some stray cards out of a deck.[40]

This aesthetic potpourri of New York's transient working population and their fleeting moments of pleasure—Masie in "Gents' Gloves" "had twice gone to Coney Island and ridden the hobbyhorses"—gives these stories an historical authenticity.

Even Porter's best stories bring a literary manner—voice, tone, and skill in the manipulation of plot—that develops in tension with his strong empathy for his subjects.

They involve a complicated conflict between Porter's head and heart. Archness and cleverness are almost always at war with his sensibility and compassion. In many of his stories, these qualities tend to trivialize the lives of his characters by making them into marionettes dangling from the strings of his cleverness. His witticisms and mannerisms jar at times, undercutting what is humane in his vision of the city. Few modern readers will find his jokes funny, any more than they would be amused by those in color comics of the same period.

Something about the atmosphere of the time, the irritants, anomalies, and disparities that form the basis of a period's humor, has been lost to us. His cherished "little people," the working population of the city, appear instead to be at once dehumanized and sentimentalized, as in his famous "Gift of the Magi," his surprise endings, his patronizing turns of phrase. On occasion, his working class characters become the butt of upper class "in" jokes, as when a flirtatious waitress is invited by a customer "to go to Parsifal" with him, and she virtuously replies, "I don't know where Parsifal is, but not a stitch of clothing goes in the suitcase until the ring is on." On other occasions, a story exposes the terrible vulnerability of his characters like a raw nerve. In "The Brief Debut of Tildy," a homely Irish girl, unable to find an escort, takes an Italian boy to a dance, disguising him with an Irish name. Her humiliation comes when he pulls a knife in a fight on the dance floor and "everyone knew he was a dago." In another story, an unattractive waitress with whom no one has ever flirted, assumes, mistakenly, that a man has finally made a pass at her, and tells all her friends. This story, too, ends with her disappointed humiliation.

In "Brickdust Row," Porter's last story in the Sunday *World*, a young "slum lord" wanders from his club and, out of boredom and curiosity, decides to visit Coney Island. On the ferry he meets a young woman whom he accompanies through the evening. As the night progresses, his impressions of Coney Island are transformed by his feelings for her. At first, he sees it as a tasteless pandemonium: "the mob, the multitude, the proletariat . . . shrieking, struggling, hurrying, panting, hurling itself . . . into sham palaces of trumpery." Then, through his empathy, he sees it as he feels she must see it: "Here, at least, was the husk of

Romance, the empty but shining casque of Chivalry . . . the magic carpet that transports you to the realms of fairyland. . . . He no longer saw rabble, but his brother seeking the ideal."[41]

At the end of the story, he discovers that his companion of the night lives in one of his own tawdry brick row houses, "third floor back." He responds with a despairing shout the next day to his rental agent to do something about Brickdust Row: "Remodel it, burn it, raze it to the ground," he exclaims, "but, man, it is too late, I tell you, it's too late, it's too late." This story, perhaps better than most, suggests the social character of Porter's fiction. His central character begins as a rich club member with the social and aesthetic views of James Huneker, who did in fact describe Coney Island in almost the same language, but leaves him, after his sentimental holiday, just where he began. His vague, sentimental embrace of Coney Island and the girl, like his brief outburst of anger and despair, shows neither real change nor the possibility of it.

These sentimental accounts of the relations between classes in the city have a specific historical meaning: empathy without political compassion. They reduce the scale of human suffering to what atomized individuals endure as their plucky, sad lives were recounted week after week for almost a decade.

How were such stories interpreted at the time? First of all, their sentimental reading of oppression, class differences, human suffering, and affection helped create a new language for interpreting the city's complex society, a language that began to replace the threadbare moralism that New Yorkers inherited from nineteenth-century readings of the city. This language localized suffering in particular moments and confined it to particular occasions; it smoothed over differences because it could be read almost the same way from either end of the social scale. O. Henry stories demanded only a brief dispensation of emotion from their newspaper readers once a week and asked for little more. As many composers of popular songs soon learned, the sentimental was a miraculous form of social glue with a virtually unlimited national market.

Porter's stories appealed to the whole social spectrum. People like to read about themselves, just as they enjoy photography where their faces figure. The only place working people could read about themselves and find some understanding of their lives was in Porter's stories. They probably did not notice the lapses of tone or patronizing observations that we perceive. The self-conscious literary manner of these stories, their unintelligible or obscure references, must have given many readers a secure sense that they were encountering genuine literary culture. For readers in other classes, they satisfied a growing curiosity about the city's working class and underworld populations, just as the guides to the city's shadowy areas had done earlier. In short, O. Henry stories offered a gratifying, innocuous form of slumming, sprinkled with inter-class romances where millionaires marry working girls and take off into the sunset. These, too, would have appealed to either end of the social scale. The literary flaws detectable in these stories help, then, to explain the breadth of their appeal. Their focus on individuals' plights, the absence of social or political implications, their ideological neutrality, must have helped to woo a wide range of readers who would have taken flight at anything resembling political partisanship or passion.

Tin Pan Alley

The world of popular songs written, published, and promoted after 1900 is a story in itself, and requires careful separate analysis.[42] A few observations about Tin Pan Alley bring the analytical focus into final resolution because the changes Porter and others initiated in reading soon permeated the music industry. Popular songs quickly became commercially formidable on a national scale unrivaled until the flowering of radio culture in the 1930s. Between 1900 and 1950, over 300,000 songs were copyrighted, the bulk of them before World War II.

The popular song was a perfect embodiment of the culture of pastiche emerging in New York. Song content was a miscellany of trivial, personal observations—"Where do they go, those smoke rings I blow?"—and as a genre could be read in almost any way. A melodic line could simply be hummed, or whistled, without words. One could be content with a single verse, or only snatches of lyric. References were almost entirely limited to romantic love. These songs soon became the most interreferential of popular media. Songs about songs were not long in making their appearance. Popular music, therefore, spun the most secure and cocoonlike world of evocative emotion through an aura of romance and nostalgia that also limited its range.

"Bei Mir Bist Du Schoen," one of Tin Pan Alley's most legendary success stories, is a case in point. It was a Yiddish song sung and sold by Lower East Side peddlers in the mid-1930s. A bit later, it was "swung" by two appreciative black musicians, who sang it in Yiddish at the Apollo Theatre in Harlem. Two Jewish musicians who heard it in the Catskills added English lyrics and got it published despite resistance to foreign lyrics. It was introduced nationally and made a hit by the then unknown Greek-American Andrews Sisters, who became, through the song's immediate success, the first female vocal group to sell a million records. By 1938, the song climbed to the top of Your Hit Parade and had become the theme song of a popular film about marriage starring Dana Andrews.[43]

The story of "Bei Mir Bist Du Schoen" is, in other words, a microcosm of the cultural transformation that overcame New York in the succeeding quarter century. Popular music after 1910, the year of Porter's death, was the single most important ethnic group contribution to the city's commercial culture. It was the almost exclusive creation of the European Jews who had settled on the Lower East Side. An intricate network within this community recruited talent from piano-laden tenements, saloons with singing waiters, and promising young singers in local synagogues, and gave this talent a place in an expanding musical culture. What began on the Lower East Side, the Tenderloin, and Harlem became a national phenomenon. "Irving Berlin is American music," George Gershwin once remarked.[44] This culture was built on market strategies that originated in New York on "boomers" and "pluggers," whose business was to bring new songs to the attention of the public in music stores, dime stores, and on the streets. Even the exceptions to the Jewish origin of popular songs are instructive. Cole Porter, for example, was a Yale-educated Episcopalian, the son of a millionaire from Indiana, yet he once confessed to Richard Rodgers, when they met by accident in Venice, that early failures had taught him the secret of popular songs. It lay, he told the astonished Rodgers, "in writing Jewish tunes."[45] This irony has a further twist, since Cole Porter drew the melodies of such popular songs as "My Heart Belongs to Daddy" from a Yiddish musical tradition that Mark Slobin has recently shown lacked the theme of romantic love.[46]

The body of popular song created in New York by the 1930s subsequently formed part of a national culture that circulated over the radio and through Hollywood films. But it remained the product of New York culture at a particular moment, the moment when New York's immigrant Jews had little other access to recognizable forms of success; when "coon" songs, ragtime, and jazz emerged from the black ghetto; and when managerial and entrepreneurial talent arose from the Lower East Side. New technologies appearing at this moment made this cultural product generally and suddenly available, as the penny press had a generation earlier. However wide its circulation, this music never lost its New York flavor nor its roots in New York's spatial arrangements and its commercial culture of pastiche.

Conclusion

We may conclude by observing that neither commercial nor mass culture had a strong didactic function. Their orientation was broadly cultural, not pedagogical. The consumption of print, graphic, and other forms of commercial culture was only a part of the class life of New York's working population, to mention only one segment of the audience. Existing studies have emphasized the ideological intent of those who produced and distributed such culture and pointed to the narrowed options given to working class consumers. From the consumers' point of view, however, these new cultural genres provided the least oppressive component of daily life. They may even have raised expectations, and hence fired demands, for a better life among those who regularly consumed them. The hardships and oppression experienced at home and at work doubtless more strongly shaped the response to commercial culture than the consumption of such culture influenced the mentality of working class New Yorkers. The new newspapers, the popular songs, and the graphic and photographic art had an open and nonprescriptive format for consumption. The most important consideration for those who produced these cultural products was success in marketing them. Empirical research would clearly be useful, but different groups within the city's population gave multiple interpretations to these new cultural products. Within any particular group, the significance attached to them was ambiguous.

The so-called mass culture that emerged after the 1920s did not wholly transform this older commercial culture, certainly not overnight. This probably explains why commercial and mass culture are typically confused. Historians and other students have ritually criticized mass culture as formulaic, culturally rootless, and trivializing. Much the same charges have been made against commercial culture at the end of the nineteenth century, as they have about the popular culture of almost every previous era. This essay has argued to the contrary that the significance of commercial culture lies in the complex circumstances surrounding its creation, in how New York's diverse population was orchestrated to fabricate and consume it, and in how it helped consumers from across the social spectrum to decode the city.

Its vital and complex origins continued to characterize mass culture even as national markets incorporated locally created genres after the 1920s. Early films did not eclipse Broadway musical shows but drew upon and exploited their songs, dramatic materials, and New York background. The comic style developed in early films by Charlie Chaplin and Buster Keaton rose above the standards of either the English music hall or the vaudeville stage. Since these later forms were produced for different audiences with different needs and a different relationship to their production, this evolving mass culture was based on a different New York. It was no longer the city experienced by those who lived and worked in it before the 1930s, but was abstracted from history, a city frozen in time, and hence part of a national mythology about big cities. But that is a different story.

In the era before the rise of national mass media, New York's commercial culture operated not as the instrument of one class over another, but as an arena where all could find genuine, if partial, representation of their experiences. As a pastiche of such new experiences, this commercial culture was determined to be accessible and appealing to all. Its success and selectiveness in doing so, however, may well have limited the scope for a separate, politically adversarial culture rooted in New York City's new working class.

Notes

1. David Hammack, *Power and Society: Greater New York at the Turn of the Century* (New York: Russell Sage, 1982).

2. Richard W. Fox and J. Jackson Lears, eds., *The Culture of Consumption. Critical Essays in American History, 1880–1890* (New York: Pantheon Books, 1983); Stuart Ewen, *Captains of Consciousness: Advertising and the Social Roots of Consumer Culture* (New York: McGraw-Hill, 1976). The theoretical root of much of this writing lies in Gramsci and Adorno; see especially, T.W. Adorno, *Zeitschrift für Sozialforschung*, vol. II (1949): 17–48.

3. Peter Burke, "The World of Carnival," *Popular Culture in Early Modern Europe* (London: M. T. Smith, 1978), 178–205; Richard D. Altick, *The Shows of London* (Cambridge: Harvard University Press, 1978), 35–36.

4. Peter Burke, *Venice and Amsterdam. A Study of Seventeenth Century Elites* (London: Allen & Unwin, 1974).

5. See Diane Lindstrom's essay in this volume.

6. See Mark Sharman Farber, "The Conquering Hero Comes: Urban Celebrations of Public Figures in America, 1879–1910" (Ph.D. diss., New York University, 1978), 142–95.

7. Thomas Bender, "The Cultures of Intellectual Life; the City and the Professions," in *New Directions in American Intellectual History*, ed. John Higham and Paul Conkin. (Baltimore: Johns Hopkins University Press, 1979), 181–95.

8. Daniel Czitrom, *Media and the American Mind. From Morse to McLuhan* (Chapel Hill: University of North Carolina Press, 1982); John E. Kasson,

Amusing the Millions (New York: Hill and Wang, 1978); Roy Rosenweig, "The Conflict over the Saloon; Working Class Drinking and the Legal Order in Worcester, Massachusetts, 1870–1900," paper presented at the annual meeting of the American Historical Association, December 1979.

9. Marquis James, *The Metropolitan Life Insurance Company* (1935). One of the most revealing sources for examining the new office culture is the Metropolitan Company photographs in the Byron Collection of the Museum of the City of New York.

10. William R. Leach, "Transformations in a Culture of Consumption. Women and Department Stores, 1890–1935," *Journal of American History* 71:2 (September 1984), 319–42.

11. See Miriam Cohen, "From Workshop to Office: Italian-American Women in New York," *Class, Sex, and the Woman Worker*, ed. Milton Candor (Westport, Conn.: Greenwood Press, 1977); Deborah S. Gardner, " 'A Paradise of Fashion': A. T. Stewart's Department Store, 1862–1875," in *A Needle, A Bobbin, A Strike: Women Needle Workers in America* (Philadelphia: Temple University Press, 1984); Margery Davis, *Woman's Place Is at the Typewriter* (Philadelphia: Temple University Press, 1982); and Elyce Rotella, *From Home to Office* (Ann Arbor: University of Michigan Press, 1981).

12. Leach, "Culture of Consumption"; Emile Zola, *Le Bonheurs de Dames* (Paris: 1908).

13. Lewis A. Erenberg, *Steppin' Out: New York Nightlife and the Transformation of American Culture, 1890–1930* (Westport, Conn.: Greenwood Press, 1981).

14. Jervis Anderson, *This Was Harlem: A Cultural Portrayal* (New York: Farrar, Straus, Giroux, 1982). The best firsthand account of this phenomenon is that of Carl van Vechten in various articles written for *Vanity Fair* and other periodicals during the 1920s and in correspondence in the van Vechten Papers in the New York Public Library.

15. Robert C. Toll, *On with the Show: The First Century of Show Business* (New York: Oxford University Press, 1976), 295–326; and Cynthia Ward, *"Vanity Fair* and Modern Style" (Ph.D. diss., State University of New York at Stony Brook, 1983).

16. Lindstrom, in this volume.

17. Grace M. Mayer, *Once Upon a City: New York from 1890 to 1910 as Photographed by Byron* (New York: Macmillan, 1958), contains numerous citations from the daily press recording the progress of new buildings.

18. Steven L. Kaplan, ed., *Understanding Popular Culture* (Leyden, forthcoming), has especially interesting essays by Robert Chartier and Carlo Ginzburg; Roger Chartier, *Popular Culture in Early Modern Europe* (London: Oxford University Press, 1978); Carlo Ginzburg, *The Cheese and the Worm: The Cosmos of a Sixteenth-Century Miller* (Baltimore: Johns Hopkins University Press, 1980); Raymond Williams, *The Long Revolution* (New York: Random House, 1972); Peter Bailey, *Leisure and Class in Victorian England* (London: Routledge, 1978);

and Richard Hoggart, *The Uses of Literacy* (London: Peregrine Books, 1975). Important work by Americans has also been done in the area of studies in popular and folk culture in early modern Europe—most notably, Natalie Z. David, Robert Darnton, and Richard Altick.

19. Hutchins Hapgood, *The Spirit of the Ghetto: Studies of the Jewish Quarter of New York* (New York: Schocken Books, 1965), xii.

20. Christine Stansell, "Women, Children, and the Uses of the Streets: Class and Gender Conflict in New York City, 1850–1860," *Feminist Studies* 8 (Summer 1982): 309–35.

21. Joseph F. Kett, *Rites of Passage: Adolescence in America, 1790 to the Present* (New York: Basic Books, 1977), does not discuss this publishing phenomenon. The best treatment to date is still Frank L. Mott, *A History of American Magazines* (Cambridge: Harvard University Press, 1938), vol. 3, chaps. 6–8, 174–80.

22. Mott, *American Magazines*, 3.

23. Mott, *American Magazines*, 174.

24. Allan Stanley Horlick, *Country Boys and Merchant Princes: The Social Control of Young Men in New York* (Lewisburg, Penn.: Bucknell University Press, 1975). See William R. Taylor, *Cavalier and Yankee. The Old South and the American National Character* (Cambridge: Harvard University Press, 1979).

25. Horatio Alger, Jr., *Ragged Dick and Mark the Match Boy* (New York: Collier Books, 1962).

26. Three examples of this genre of writing are: James D. McCabe, Jr., *Lights and Shadows of New York Life, or, Sights and Sensations of the Great City* (New York, 1872); Junius Henri Browne, *The Great Metropolis: A Mirror of New York. A Complete History of Metropolitan Life and Society, with Sketches of Prominent Places, Persons, and Things in the City, as They Actually Exist* (Hartford: 1869); and Inspector Thomas Byrnes, *Darkness and Daylight or Lights and Shadows of New York Life* (New York: 1982).

27. See, for example, in W. Parker Chase, *New York: Wonder City* (New York: New York Bound, 1983), "Working Girls," 35, and "Chorus Girls," 41.

28. See note 26 for complete citation of the McCabe work.

29. McCabe, *Lights and Shadows*, 524.

30. McCabe, *Lights and Shadows*, 741.

31. Frank Luther Mott, *American Journalism, A History: 1690–1960* (New York: Macmillan, 1962), 440.

32. Mott, *American Journalism*, 402–04, 481, 546–47.

33. Quoted in Mott, *American Journalism*, 429.

34. Quoted in Mott, *American Journalism*, 440.

35. Mott, *American Journalism*, 525–26.

36. Richard Felton Outcault, *My Resolutions, Buster Brown* (Chicago: 1910).

37. Peter Bailey, "Alley Sloper's Half Holiday: Comic Art in the 1880s," *History Workshop* 16 (Autumn 1983): 5.

38. Quoted in Richard O'Connor, *O. Henry: The Legendary Life of William S. Porter* (New York: Doubleday, 1970), 67.

39. William Sidney Porter, "The Unfinished Story," in *The Complete Works of O. Henry* (New York: Doubleday, 1970), 71.

40. Porter, "Unfinished Story."

41. Porter, "Brickdust Row," in *Complete Works.*

42. Carol Barchas's research paper, "The American Popular Song and the Creation of a Common American Culture" (Seminar Paper, State University of New York, Stony Brook, 1983), in my seminar at State University of New York at Stony Brook started me on my own research and provided me with both insight and bibliography.

43. See John R. Williams, *This Was Your Hit Parade* (Rockland, Maine: *Courier Gazette*, 1973), 88–89. Cited by Carol Barchas, "The American Popular Song."

44. Quoted in Michael Freedland, *Irving Berlin* (New York: Stein and Day, 1974), 53.

45. Quoted in Richard Rodgers, *Musical Stages* (New York: Random House, 1975), 88. Cited by Barchas, "The American Popular Song."

46. Mark Slobin, *Tenement Song: The Popular Music of the Jewish Immigrant* (Urbana, Ill.: University of Illinois Press, 1982), chap. 1.

6

Political Incorporation and Containment: Regime Transformation in New York City

Martin Shefter

During the decades following the Civil War, Tammany Hall became the most powerful political organization in New York. From the 1890s to the 1930s, political competition in the metropolis largely took the form of periodic struggles between machine politicians belonging to or allied with Tammany, and political coalitions that rallied against them in the name of reform. By contrast, during the decades following World War II, the influence of the city's regular Democratic party organizations was considerably diminished. Wallace Sayre and Herbert Kaufman, in their authoritative study *Governing New York City*, depict politics in the metropolis during these years as being organized less around struggles between machine politicians and their opponents than around competition among interest groups within many distinct policy arenas.[1] This essay seeks to account for why the structure of political competition in New York City evolved from a machine/reform dialectic to a classic pattern of pluralism.

New York at the Turn of the Century

As the companion essays in this volume show, New York City's economy and population changed dramatically during the late nineteenth and early twentieth centuries. Regarding the economy, David Hammack has noted that as late as 1880: "Greater New York was still a mercantile city . . . engaged in the financial, commercial, and manufacturing activities appropriate to the *entrepôt* that handled the lion's share of America's trade with the Atlantic world. By 1910 the metropolis was more extensively involved in the management of American industry than in the Atlantic trade, and while its own manufacturing sector remained healthy, it produced a considerably narrower range of goods."[2] Moreover, the sectors in which New York City manufacturers increasingly specialized, particularly apparel and publishing, were linked to the city's position as a center of communication and control in the nation's economy. Clothing manufacturers had to be attuned to the latest in fashions, and publishers to the latest in ideas. In no other American city was this information more readily available than in New York.

Changes in international population flows also registered very rapidly in New York. Two-thirds of the immigrants who flooded into the United States during the late nineteenth and early twentieth centuries entered the country through Castle Garden and Ellis Island. Many settled in New York because the remarkable vitality of the city's economy during this period enabled them to find work. Consequently, the consolidated Greater New York City's population more than doubled, from 1.9 million to 4.8 million, between 1880 and 1910. In these years, Italians and Jews supplanted Germans and Irish as the largest population groups in the city. This process of ethnic succession was played out in the city's neighborhoods, many of which acquired the ethnic identity during these years they were to retain for the next half century or more. In particular, the Lower East Side and Williamsburg became predominantly Jewish at the turn of the century, and Greenwich Village and East Harlem became predominantly Italian.[3]

These developments aroused conflict among and within New York's ethnic subcommunities—conflict that was often acted out on the city's streets, to the horror of respectable opinion in the city. The Draft Riot of 1863 and the Orange Riot of 1871 were the last major disorders pitting whites against blacks and Irish Catholics against Protestants. But in 1900 a two-day riot erupted in a racially mixed section of Hell's Kitchen in which local whites fought local blacks as well as blacks from the adjacent neighborhood of San Juan Hill. The *Herald* noted in disgust that the police joined in these attacks upon blacks, contributing to the disorder rather than stopping it.[4] Two years later, the largely Irish work force at the R. H. Hoe factory stoned the funeral procession of a prominent Orthodox rabbi, Jacob Joseph, as it passed beneath the factory's windows.[5] And in 1902 and 1917, Jewish women on the Lower East Side and in Brownsville protested against rising meat prices by overturning pushcarts or pouring kerosene on the meat being offered for sale. To the editorial writers of the *New York Times*, this indicated that "they do not understand the duties or the rights of Americans."[6] Finally, according to Herbert Asbury's popular history of the gangs of New York, at the turn of the century the city's gangs—composed predominantly of either Irishmen or Jews—divided Manhattan south of Forty-second Street into exclusive territories and used force to keep out members of rival gangs.[7]

Competition among ethnic groups also emerged in the early years of the twentieth century for use of the city's poshest street, Fifth Avenue. As the city's clothing industry grew, the garment district expanded northward. During the midday hours Jewish garment workers crowded Fifth Avenue and, in the eyes of merchants, lowered its tone. To defend their control of the street, the Fifth Avenue merchants resorted not to violence but to the law, leading the drive to enact the nation's first zoning code in 1916.[8]

If immigrant Jewish garment workers threatened the Fifth Avenue shopping district from the south, some of their children encroached on it from the west. During the early years of the twentieth century the city's red-light district, the Tenderloin, migrated from north of Union Square to north of Times Square. Many gamblers operating in the Tenderloin were "East Side types," that is, Jews. For example, the victim of New York's most sensational crime of the early twentieth century was Herman Rosenthal, a gambler who was murdered in front of the Hotel Metropole on Forty-third Street between Broadway and Sixth Avenue. The street names of the gangsters convicted of murdering Rosenthal were Gyp the Blood, Lefty Louie, Dago Frank, and Whitey Lewis. Their given names, however, were Harry Horowitz, Louis Rosenberg, Frank Cirofici, and Jacob Seidenshimer.[9]

Respectable New Yorkers were concerned about the spread not only of criminal activity from the Lower East Side to other sections of the city but also of industrial strife and political radicalism. Between 1909 and 1916, workers seeking union recognition engaged in a major wave of strikes. Their parades and picket lines kept the streets of the Lower East Side and the garment district in a state of turmoil.[10] Although they had no use whatever for the socialism of the garment trades unions, many middle and upper class New Yorkers sympathized with their striking members, especially after the 1911 Triangle Shirtwaist fire that killed 146 young women.

Middle and upper class New Yorkers reacted quite differently, however, when organized strikes occurred among employees of the city's sanitation department, and among subway and streetcar workers at the (privately owned) Interborough Rapid Transit Company. And when the city's Central Federated Union called a general strike in sympathy with the striking transit workers, respectable New Yorkers became hysterical.

These strikes, unlike those in the garment trades, seriously inconvenienced the middle class and appeared to threaten the city's social and political order. Consequently, they evoked a furious and successful counterattack by the newspapers that spoke for this latter segment of the city's population and by employers.[11] These political forces reacted in the same way when quasi-radical or radical leaders or parties threatened to win a widespread following. This was evident when William Randolph Hearst, campaigning as a friend of labor and an opponent of the city's traction magnates, almost won the mayoral election of 1905. It was also evident when the Socialists ran a strong race in the 1917 mayoral election and won state assembly races in Brooklyn, the Bronx, and Manhattan districts during and after World War I.[12]

The Open City
and the Consolidation of the Tammany Machine

The conflicts produced by changes in New York's economy and population at the turn of the century had major implications for municipal government and politics. The building of the city's first subway system and the response to new immigrant groups exemplify this impact.

In the 1890s, important participants in the city's politics, particularly the Chamber of Commerce, argued that to retain its position as a center of communication and control in the national and international economy, New York must construct a rapid transit system capable of moving millions of people a day from outlying residential neighborhoods to their jobs in Manhattan. Tammany, however, reacted coolly to proposals for constructing the city's first subway line.[13] Mayors Hugh Grant, Thomas Gilroy, and Robert Van Wyck feared that supporting such a costly public works project would lead some of the machine's opponents to charge that their administrations were duplicating the excesses of the Tweed Ring. Tammany also had close ties with the Metropolitan Street Railway Company and the Third Avenue Elevated Railway Company, which would lose riders if a subway system were constructed.

In the end Tammany did turn around, in part because the subway construction contract was awarded to a firm with close ties to the machine, and the financing of the project was handled by bankers with similar ties. The Chamber of Commerce (whose members controlled the city's Rapid Transit Commission) was prepared to make these concessions to obtain a subway system it regarded as vital for the continued growth of the city's economy. Candidates nominated by the regular

Democratic organizations in New York's five boroughs thereafter sought to win the support of subway riders by pledging to maintain the five-cent fare.

By the turn of the twentieth century, machine politicians also developed a variety of techniques for coping with the political problems and taking advantage of the opportunities created by the influx of Jewish and Italian immigrants. It must be emphasized at the outset that the city's party organizations did not take the initiative in mobilizing these immigrants into politics. The members of New York's more established ethnic groups had no desire to share the rewards of power with newcomers to the city. For this reason, Italians—who had very high rates of return migration and low rates of citizenship and voter turnout—got little out of city politics. It was not until 1913 that an Italian-American was first elected to a public office (member of the state assembly) in New York, and it was not until 1929 that an Italian became a Tammany district leader.[14]

The situation regarding Jews was more complex. Because Eastern European Jews fled religious and political persecution as well as economic deprivation, return migration was rare and their stake in New York politics potentially high. Relatedly, as Moses Rischin notes, they created (or recreated in New York) a remarkably dense organizational life comprised of religious, charitable, and labor.[15] These associations were potential vehicles for participation in the city's politics. Finally, at the time of the great Eastern European migrations, a well-to-do German-Jewish community was already established in New York. These Uptown Jews, as they were called, were potentially available as political allies of their downtown counterparts.

Prior to the 1890s, however, these potentials were largely unrealized. Uptown Jews received political recognition as Germans, rather than as Jews, and that recognition came more from the Republicans than from the Democrats. Neither party made an effort to mobilize support among the new immigrants flooding into the East Side. Rather, machine politicians established ties to the Downtown Jewish community through some of its less savory members, whose function was more to control the Jewish vote than to mobilize it. These politicians also funneled profits from illicit enterprises to Tammany's district leaders. One case in point was "Silver Dollar" Smith (born either Charles Solomon or Solomon Finklestein), "a saloon keeper who had shown himself to be free of traditional Jewish scruples against the use of fists."[16] Other Jewish politicians of this ilk were Monk Eastman (born Edward Osterman), the leader of the city's largest Jewish gang, and Max Hochstim, who was involved in prostitution.

Two turn-of-the-century developments contributed to the political mobilization of Jews outside these channels. One was Henry George's race for mayor in 1886 as the candidate of the city's labor movement. George campaigned actively for Jewish votes, and Henry George clubs were organized throughout the Lower East Side. By serving as a bridge between the Jewish labor and radical traditions and American electoral politics, the George campaign encouraged thousands of East Siders to participate in electoral politics. It also convinced the city's major party organizations that there was a Jewish vote worth cultivating.[17]

An upsurge of anti-Semitism within the city's social elite also contributed to the political mobilization of New York's Jewish community. It demonstrated to members of the Uptown Jewish community that other New Yorkers regarded them as Jews more than as Germans, and therefore that their standing in the city was linked to their fellow Jews downtown. If only to defend their own position, they had a stake in defending that of the city's East European Jews. This brought the two segments of the city's Jewish community into political alliance on many occasions. For a period, as Arthur Goren has documented, this alliance was institutionalized in the New York Kehillah (Community Council).[18] The coalition of Uptown and Downtown Jews commanded more formidable resources than other new immigrant groups.

Although older patterns by no means disappeared, many politicians affiliated with Tammany, and its sister Democratic organizations responded to this upsurge in political activity by appealing for the support of Jews. John F. Ahearn and Tom Foley, for example, rose to Tammany district leaderships on the Lower East Side in this way.[19] They accomplished this partly through symbolic appeals. For example, the night after workers at the R. H. Hoe factory stoned Rabbi Joseph's funeral procession, Ahearn avenged this attack upon his constituents by having his boys break every one of the factory's windows.[20] To refugees from nations that officially sanctioned pogroms, such symbolism was not unimportant. Tammany also won support among Jews by extending to them the traditional benefits of machine politics: public services, facilities, jobs, and nominations for public office.

Democratic public officials also appealed for Jewish support in some less traditional ways. Under the leadership of Al Smith and Robert F. Wagner, Sr., both protégés of Tammany boss Charles F. Murphy, New York enacted the nation's most extensive program of social and labor legislation, as Joseph Huthmacher has documented.[21] Most of this legislation was drafted by members of Smith's predominantly Jewish kitchen cabinet. This initiated the first step in the movement of liberal and radical Jews into the Democratic party.

The actions Tammany politicians took in response to the influx of Jewish and Italian immigrants distressed many political forces. The machine's ties to the underworld, even if confined to red-light or slum districts, offended the moral sensibilities of bluestockings elsewhere in the city. It also offended many residents of poor neighborhoods. The reform crusade of 1901, for example, was sparked by a conflict over solicitation for prostitution in front of a church on the Lower East Side.[22] Many businessmen were not happy with the social and labor legislation enacted with Tammany's support. And municipal taxpayers had to pay the costs of providing the members of new ethnic groups with public services, facilities, and jobs.

Nonetheless, from the vantage point of established interests in New York, machine government could be preferable to some of its alternatives. In 1905, for example, thousands of middle and upper class New Yorkers voted for the Democratic machine's mayoral candidate, George McClellan, rather than risk the election of William Randolph Hearst.[23] And so long as New York's economy continued to grow, City Hall could increase the flow of public benefits to new claimants on the municipal treasury without driving up the local property tax rate.

The Machine/Reform Dialectic

Tammany maintained its position as the dominant political institution in New York, then, by arranging a set of accommodations among the major interests with a stake in municipal affairs that these forces regarded as preferable to the realistic alternatives.[24] As changes occurred in the environment within which the machine operated, however, Tammany's leaders did not always recognize the adjustments in municipal policies and practices that would be necessary to retain the acquiescence of these interests. Nor could top machine politicians always compel their subordinates or allies to accept such adjustments. At such points, the political forces that regarded it as imperative for the municipal government to strike out in new directions concluded that City Hall was serving the special interests of Tammany politicians, their cronies, to the detriment of the public interest. Those sharing this view could be rallied against the machine in the name of "reform."

Three times between 1901 and 1933, such reform coalitions managed to defeat the machine and take control of City Hall, electing mayors Seth Low in 1901, John Purroy Mitchel in 1913, and Fiorello La Guardia in 1933. The conditions leading to these successes were by no means identical, but there were some broad similarities in the composition of the antimachine coalition and in how the machine managed to regain power in the wake of each reform episode.

The Reform Coalition

Since the end of the nineteenth century, antimachine campaigns in New York have been initiated by what might be termed the city's reform vanguard. The founders, directors, and financial backers of the organizations through which this vanguard has operated were drawn from the city's upper classes, especially from among wealthy New Yorkers who financed organized charity. But the most numerous and active members of this vanguard were young practitioners of professions that produce, disseminate, and implement respectable opinion on political and social issues—among them, academic social scientists, social workers, clergymen, and journalists. The first two of these professions were born at the turn of the century, and the latter two were transformed by the rise of the Social Gospel and the muckraking tradition. As David Hammack says of the members of these newer professions, these "highly trained men—and women—were seeking public outlets for their newly won expertise and . . . were ready to devote a good deal of effort to local politics."[25] New York's reform vanguard was a would-be leadership class whose members sought to supplant machine politicians as the key actors in municipal government.

This reform vanguard, it should be noted, was not a mere mouthpiece for New York's business elite. Its members sought to shape, not simply to reflect, respectable opinion in New York. They believed that the machine's ties to interests with a stake in the *status quo* and its commitment to the patronage system led it to nominate candidates and appoint officials who would not and could not deal with the city's most pressing economic and social problems. Upper and middle class New Yorkers' acquiescence to machine government appalled them. They sought to convince them that the moral and financial costs of machine government were intolerable.

Exposés and investigations were a central reform strategy. The exposure of incompetence, the discovery of graft, or, best of all, the discovery of ties between machine politicians and the underworld could destroy the legitimacy of the incumbent municipal administration. For example, an investigation by the reformist Bureau of Municipal Research of waste and fraud in the Manhattan borough president's office was the first in the series of events leading to the election of John Purroy Mitchel as mayor in 1913. And Samuel Seabury's investigations of corruption in New York's judicial, county, and executive agencies contributed to Fiorello La Guardia's election as mayor in 1933. Yet neither corruption nor its discovery necessarily sparked a full-scale reform crusade. The state legislature's Meyer Committee uncovered evidence of wrongdoing by city officials in the early 1920s, for example, and investigations headed by Senator Estes Kefauver and Judge Joseph Proskauer revealed that a number of Tammany politicians were linked to organized crime in the early 1950s, but in neither decade were these revelations followed by a successful reform campaign.

If the machine was to be overturned, reform activists would have to ally with other political forces who could provide financing, mass support, and the electoral machinery necessary to mobilize voters. Opposition to the machine among important segments of the city's business community was crucial to the development of successful reform campaigns. Also important were press and public concern about the machine's ability to preserve law and order as new immigrants flooded into the city. So too were national political realignments.

Business leaders most often came to regard the continued machine rule as intolerable when, in their view, City Hall failed to manage municipal finances responsibly and to promote the growth of the city's economy. Thus municipal fiscal crises in 1907 and 1932–1933 helped trigger reform.[26]

Bankers and businessmen sought to overturn the machine because they wanted to have a direct voice in making the fundamental policy choices necessitated by fiscal crisis. To regain financial stability, the city had to pursue some combination of the following policies: (1) raise taxes, (2) cut current expenditures and services, or (3) cut capital expenditures. The last course, however, could undermine what businessmen regarded as a central responsibility of the city government: promoting the growth of the local economy. Hence in both 1907–1909 and 1932–1933 spokesmen for the downtown business community called upon the municipal government to stop financing current expenditures with borrowed funds, to balance its budget by slashing its current expenditures rather than by raising taxes, and to focus its borrowing capacity on improving transportation. They also sought to have the subway's debt service and operating costs financed with fares rather than local tax revenues. This program was not popular with New York's electorate (there were many more subway riders than property taxpayers in the city). When City Hall resisted it, bankers and businessmen regarded the incumbent administration as fiscally irresponsible. It had sacrificed New York's long-term interests for the sake of current political gains, and hence, they concluded, was fundamentally misgoverning the city.[27]

For example, in the depths of the 1933 fiscal crisis Mayor John O'Brien created a Municipal Economic Commission (MEC)—whose members included the presidents of the Chamber of Commerce, the Merchants' Association, and the Board of Trade—to advise the city on the policies it should pursue to balance its budget. The MEC proposed that the municipal government drastically cut its expenditures and reduce its property tax rate by 10 percent. Instead, the administration increased a number of taxes and fees. In protest the presidents of these business organizations resigned from the MEC three days before the election, and attacked the mayor—who was running for reelection as Tammany's candidate—for failing to adopt their proposals. The Chamber of Commerce also offered the use of its facilities to the City party, which had been organized to conduct that year's reform campaign.

Social disorder among new waves of immigrants was also conducive to reform movements. Sensational episodes that suggested corrupt dealings between Jewish gangsters and Tammany politicians sparked the reform movement that elected John Purroy Mitchel in 1913. Similar episodes suggesting that Tammany politicians had ties to Italian-American gangsters would contribute to Fiorello La Guardia's election as a reformer two decades later.[28]

The immigrant influx, however, also presented the reformers with the opportunity to extend their popular base. The ethnic groups that at any given time staffed the city's party organizations generally excluded outsiders from the fruits of power. As a rule, second-generation immigrants who sought to get ahead through politics especially resented exclusion by the machine. By nominating and appointing such individuals to visible offices, and by promising to respond to group grievances ignored by the incumbent regime, the reformers could and did extend their base of support. Theodore Lowi has shown that reform mayors, especially La Guardia, increased the number of Jews, Italians, and blacks in top appointive positions.[29]

Finally, the flux of national political alignments also aided reform movements by fostering attacks upon the city's party organizations. When the leaders of the city's party organizations opposed a candidate who won the party's presidential nomination, such as Woodrow Wilson in 1912 and Franklin D. Roosevelt in 1932, that candidate's local supporters had reason to wage war on the party bosses. Thus, after his election, Woodrow Wilson appointed anti-Tammany Democrat John Purroy Mitchel to the most important federal patronage post in the city—head of the New York Customs House. And in the municipal election following FDR's entry into the White House, many of the president's New York City supporters backed Fiorello La Guardia, the fusion mayoral candidate, or Joseph McKee, an anti-Tammany Democrat running for mayor as an independent candidate.[30]

National political alignments also influenced whether the Republicans would join forces with the reformers. When the GOP was out of power in Washington, New York City Republican politicians were more willing than at other times to make the concessions that such an alliance entails because they were especially anxious to obtain access to other levels of government. Republican participation was valuable to a fusion effort because it provided the votes of party loyalists and a ready-made campaign apparatus for turning out voters on Election Day.

Upper and middle class reform activists, prominent business leaders, spokesmen for minority ethnic or racial groups, dissident Democrats, and Republicans thus comprised the core of an antimachine "fusion" movement. Citizens' committees composed of prominent members of New York's economic and social elite, such as the Committee of 109 in 1913 and the Committee of 1,000 in 1933, organized fusion campaigns. Reformers and their business allies often sought to turn these committees into virtual countergovernments that performed public functions. They financed and conducted investigations of the municipal government and brought charges against public officials deemed guilty of corruption or incompetence. In 1932 to 1933 they also demanded, as a condition for bailing the city out of its fiscal problems, that the mayor appoint their nominees to top financial positions in the city government and implement their proposals for cutting expenditures and raising revenues. By so usurping public powers, they undermined the legitimacy of incumbent officeholders and weakened the machine.[31]

After their election reform mayors would undertake to enact new public policies and to reorganize the city government. Those allied to the machine of course resisted, opposition that at times took a violent turn. Moreover, the members of fusion coalitions had divergent interests. Reorganizing municipal agencies and reallocating their benefits in ways that pleased one reform constituency often infuriated the others. For example, efforts by the Mitchel administration to limit spending on education and social welfare programs—desired by many of its supporters within the business community—cost it the backing of many Jews who had voted for the mayor in 1913.[32] Finally, efforts to mobilize new immigrants often allowed radicals from these groups to gain positions of prominence. Reform provided openings to Jewish socialists, such as Meyer London, in the 1910s and to Italian and Jewish Communists and fellow travelers, such as Vito Marcantonio, in the 1930s and 1940s.[33] Many members of fusion coalitions viewed these radical leaders with horror. As a result of such strains, Mayor Mitchel lost his bid for renomination in the Republican primary of 1917 and Mayor La Guardia retired rather than face the same fate in 1945.

The Machine's Return to Power

New York City's Democratic machine bounced back after each reform episode not only because fusion administrations alienated important groups in the city but also because it had the capacity to reform itself. It was able to reach an accommodation with many of the political forces in the reform coalition. It placated business interests and civic associations by nominating candidates who were prepared to construct the capital projects and to pursue some of the financial policies these groups advocated. Tammany and its sister organizations also saw the wisdom of coming to terms with the forces exercising predominant influence in the national Democratic party. Finally, and most strikingly, after each episode of municipal reform, the leaders of New York's regular Democratic and Republican organizations entered into collusive arrangements that helped each maintain control over its own party and ward off the threat of third parties. This compensated Republicans with patronage for abandoning the fusion coalition.[34]

New York's machine politicians also managed to survive the various challenges confronting them because, as heirs to the party organizations constructed during the late nineteenth century, they had an independent political base. They might lose at the pinnacle of government, but they had staying power in less visible institutions such as the city council and the judiciary. This gave them leverage over everyday government activities that could be used to give groups and individuals with an immediate stake in city politics what they wanted. Machine politicians could thus continually recreate a constituency for themselves.

Once reform forcefully reminded the regular Democratic party organizations of the dangers inherent in excluding the members of new ethnic groups, ambitious lower middle class politicians from these groups had a strong incentive to work through or to seize control of the party's district organizations. Being affiliated with the regular wing of the city's majority party was personally advantageous to such politicians, providing lucrative legal fees and brokerage commissions, for example. And it was politically advantageous, providing outside assistance useful for defeating rival contenders for the political leadership of their ethnic or racial group.

Firms doing business with or regulated by the city also had strong reasons to cultivate good relations with New York's regular party organizations. Construction firms sought municipal contracts, and real estate owners and developers wanted tax abatements, zoning variances, building permits, and public facilities near their holdings. Building trade unions and mortgage bankers had similar interests. Along with contractors, developers, and realtors, they were the largest contributors to the city's regular Democratic organizations.

Finally, even independent mayors found the regular party organizations useful. The great majority of New York's city councilmen and state legislators were normally party regulars, and mayors often needed their cooperation to govern the city.

The Machine/Reform Dialectic
and the Creation of New York's Pluralist Regime

The late nineteenth and early twentieth century cyclical pattern of reform administrations followed by a return to power of the city's regular party organizations can be understood, then, as a process of *serial bargaining*. Over time, machine politicians adjusted to the efforts of (1) major downtown business interests wanting government to pursue sound financial policies and construct crucial capital projects; (2) new ethnic or racial groups seeking political recognition; and (3) middle class professionals and the local allies of newly powerful national forces reaching for greater influence in city government. Postreform administrations granted concessions to each of these groups. In return, however, these groups gave up demands that other powerful political forces in the city would not tolerate. Thus, postreform regimes put the city's finances on a sound basis and constructed the projects that downtown business interests favored. But in exchange, downtown interests tolerated the costs of some public money into the pockets of politicians. Similarly, after each reform episode, ethnic groups that had been courted by the fusionists were granted increased representation in important elective and appointive offices. In effect, however, they were required to pay for this recognition by abandoning leaders whom established interests regarded as too radical or too closely associated with criminals. Finally, postreform mayors appointed middle class professionals to new positions in city government. As Theodore Lowi notes, "this increase of upper-middle class . . . personnel is probably the most important influence of the reform movement on the political system because . . . the proportion of top political executives recruited from these upper middle business and professional strata . . . never returns to earlier levels."[35] In the wake of reform episodes party regulars also came around to endorsing candidates, such as Al Smith and Robert Wagner, Jr., committed to the newly powerful national political movements of Progressivism and New Deal liberalism. In return, middle class activists were expected to abandon their efforts to destroy the regular party organizations and to take over the *entire* municipal government.

In sum, postreform regimes in New York created new equilibriums among the major contenders for power in the city. As changes in the larger political and economic system led to the formation of new national coalitions, as new ethnic groups arrived in the city, and as the cost of financing both the machine's operation and the concessions it made to other political forces generated fiscal strains, however, new challenges to the machine were launched. This explains how machine politicians and regular party organizations remained central actors in New York City politics even while the nature of governance and the structure of political competition in the city were being transformed. The concessions machine politicians made to various political actors and organizations contracted the domain of the patronage system and increased the strength of these other interests. The aftermath of the La Guardia administration produced the greatest such changes.

The Post-La Guardia Accommodations

By establishing a close relationship with organized labor and the city's Italian and Jewish subcommunities, Fiorello La Guardia in 1937 became the first reform mayor in New York's history to win reelection, and in 1941 became the first mayor of any stripe to win a third four-year term. Tensions tore the La Guardia coalition apart in the mid-1940s, however, and the mayor decided against running for a fourth term rather than face a difficult campaign. La Guardia's reelection prospects were also bleak in 1945 because the Democrats had come to terms with many of the political forces that had formerly united behind him.

For example, the Democrats made peace with Robert Moses in their effort to regain control of City Hall. Moses, who was chairman of the Long Island State Park Commission, planned an extensive and integrated network of highways, bridges, and parks for the New York metropolitan area in the late 1920s, but because Tammany neither controlled nor needed Moses, New York City refused to construct the roads and bridges within its boundaries outlined in the Moses plan. In 1933, however, Mayor La Guardia appointed Moses to positions in the city government (parks commissioner and chairman of the Triborough Bridge Authority) that enabled him to construct the projects Tammany had blocked. These projects won Moses strong support among the city's newspapers, business leaders, construction unions, and the general public.[36]

William O'Dwyer, the Democratic mayoral candidate in 1945, sought to win the support of these constituencies by pledging to reappoint Moses to his present positions and to appoint him to some new ones—most notably, the newly created post of city construction coordinator—that would give him control of virtually all public works in New York City. O'Dwyer's two Democratic successors reappointed Moses to these numerous positions, so that from 1945 to 1960 he pretty much determined what public facilities would be constructed in New York and where they would be located. In return, Moses channeled patronage generated by his activities to business firms and individuals who had ties to New York's Democratic machine politicians. This arrangement helped finance New York's regular Democratic party organizations during the postwar period. It also won Democratic mayors the support of the newspapers, voters, and segments of the downtown business community that approved of Moses' development program.

New York's post–World War II regime also sought to assure former supporters of fusion that it was fiscally responsible. Municipal expenditure increased steadily during the period from 1945 to 1960, but the dominant bloc on the Board of Estimate kept the rate of increase low out of sensitivity to the homeowners and the small businessmen who formed the core of the Democratic machine's constituency in the city's outer boroughs. In contrast to the Tammany administrations of the early 1930s, City Hall did not finance current expenditures with borrowed funds; rather, it increased the city's sales tax and abandoned the five-cent subway fare that had been a central Tammany commitment for almost fifty years. Finally, to demonstrate to the downtown business community his determination to increase government efficiency, Mayor O'Dwyer established the Mayor's Committee on Management Survey. It recommended changes in the organization and procedures of the city government, key elements of which Mayor Wagner implemented.

The Democratic regulars also came to terms with the city's elite civic associations and charitable organizations. To a greater extent than their machine-backed predecessors, Mayors O'Dwyer, Impellitteri, and Wagner appointed commissioners who enjoyed the confidence of these organizations to agencies within the realms of health, education, and welfare.[37] These organizations were also accorded substantial influence over the formulation of new policies in these domains. The tacit quid pro quo was that they abandon the direct involvement in electoral politics that had helped defeat Tammany in 1933.

New York's postwar regime also accorded greater political influence than previous machine-backed administrations to Italians and Jews, who had supported La Guardia strongly at the polls. The Democrats regularly nominated an Italian and a Jew for citywide office beginning in 1945, and appointed increasing numbers of Italians and Jews to cabinet-level positions in the municipal government. The linkages between the city's political system and its Italian and Jewish subcommunities also changed.[38]

In the 1930s and 1940s, many Italian and Jewish Democratic machine politicians in Manhattan (and, to a lesser extent, Brooklyn) had close ties to the city's criminal underworld. Tammany's loss of municipal patronage during the La Guardia years, and its disinclination to mobilize a substantial following in Italian and Jewish neighborhoods, fostered this connection. Gangsters could provide politicians with whom they were allied sufficient manpower and money to gain and retain control of many Democratic district leaderships in Italian and Jewish neighborhoods. Tammany's ties to the underworld, however, enabled the machine's opponents to discredit it in citywide elections. To overcome this problem, Carmine De Sapio—who in 1949 became the first Italian-American leader of Tammany—moved to replace such politicians with Italian and Jewish district leaders who would not be such a liability to the party.

The American Labor party (ALP) was an equally significant link between New York's political system and its Jewish and Italian subcommunities in the 1930s and 1940s. The Democratic citywide ticket was endorsed by the ALP in 1945; numerous Democratic city councilmen, state legislators, and congressmen also ran on the ALP line; and in many predominantly Jewish districts and some Italian ones (most notably, Congressman Vito Marcantonio's), the votes cast on the ALP line provided the margin of victory to the winning candidate. During the mid- and late-1940s, however, the ALP fell increasingly under the influence of the Communist party. As the Cold War intensified, the ties between Democratic politicians and the ALP in Jewish and Italian neighborhoods became increasingly embarrassing to the Democratic party citywide. To deal with this problem, top Democratic public officials and party leaders joined with the Republicans and the Liberal party (which was organized in 1944 by the anti-Communist faction of the ALP) in a successful campaign to destroy the American Labor party. Election laws were changed to the disadvantage of the ALP, and in some districts (including Marcantonio's) the Democrats, Republicans, and Liberals nominated a common candidate to run against the ALP candidate.

After the ALP was destroyed, the Democrats and Liberals entered into a standing alliance. In return for the Democrats' nominating candidates and pursuing policies that the Liberals found acceptable (and distributing some patronage to its functionaries), the Liberals would endorse the Democrats' candidates, thereby assuring the support of tens of thousands of Jewish voters for whom the Liberal imprimatur was significant. Tammany leader Carmine De Sapio, Liberal party tactician Alex Rose, and Robert F. Wagner, Jr., negotiated and renegotiated the terms of this alliance, promoting Wagner's political career in the process. Through the De Sapio-Rose-Wagner troika, Italians and Jews gained substantial influence in New York politics. The tacit price of their inclusion was the simultaneous exclusion of those ethnic leaders whom other major participants in the city's politics found unacceptable by virtue of their criminal ties or their radical ideology.

New York's postwar regular Democratic party organizations also established a modus vivendi with the Republican party. Democrats and Republicans destroyed the ALP by changing the state's election laws and by jointly nominating candidates to run against the most prominent ALP officials. The Republicans joined the Democrats to repeal proportional representation (PR) in elections for the city council, partly because it enabled the Communists to win two seats on the council, and partly because PR greatly weakened party leaders' control over their council members. The Democrats compensated the GOP for the resulting loss of representation by endorsing Republican candidates for other offices—especially judgeships—and by channeling patronage to the regular Republican organizations.[39]

New York's postwar regime also accommodated municipal employees. Prior to La Guardia's election, the dominant organization of New York City employees, the Civil Service Forum, was essentially an adjunct of the Democratic machine.[40] The La Guardia administration had sought to weaken the machine by assisting competing municipal employee efforts to secure support from city employees, and tightening the rules and procedures that protected the autonomy of the civil service. They also extended the principle of "promotion from within" to ever higher levels of the municipal bureaucracy.[41]

Finally, the leaders of New York's postwar regime made some overtures to blacks. During the 1940s and 1950s county Democratic organizations selected some blacks to serve as party district leaders, city councilmen, state legislators, judges, and, most visibly, borough president of Manhattan. In the 1950s, the city council enacted a local law banning racial discrimination in the sale or rental of housing, and a Commission on Intergroup Relations was established to indicate the city's commitment to the goal of racial harmony. One of the more rapidly growing city agencies, the municipal hospital system, hired large numbers of blacks as orderlies and maintenance personnel.[42]

However, blacks received less than their proportionate share of municipal benefits as had been true of Italians and, to a lesser extent, Jews, prior to the La Guardia era. Racial minorities also disproportionately bore the burdens generated by municipal policies. For example, persons evicted by Robert Moses' construction projects were disproportionately nonwhite.[43] And the civil service recruitment procedures that municipal employee organizations so staunchly defended awarded a disproportionately low share of good city jobs to blacks.

Blacks received less than their due because the members of ethnic groups that had arrived—literally and figuratively—earlier in New York had no desire to sacrifice the rewards of power for their sake. Black officeholders and party politicians could not compel their white colleagues to make greater concessions, because black electoral turnout was lower than for whites and because white politicians feared that greater concessions to blacks might alienate white voters. To complete the circle, black turnout rates were low in part because Democratic machine politicians hesitated to mobilize more blacks lest they be subject to increased pressures for a more equitable distribution of municipal benefits and therefore to greater dangers of alienating white voters.

White politicians' circumspection toward racial minorities left blacks open for mobilization by leaders lacking strong ties to the regular party organizations.[44] The most prominent such politician in the 1940s and 1950s was Adam Clayton Powell. As chief spokesman for New York's black community, he played a role similar to the one that Fiorello La Guardia had played for Italian-American New Yorkers in the 1920s and early 1930s. The continuing failure of New York's postwar regime to pay greater attention to black concerns also left racial minorities open to protest leaders who mobilized their followers outside electoral channels. This ultimately contributed to the overthrow of New York's postwar regime.

The Structure of the Pluralist Regime

The concessions that Democratic politicians made to regain and retain control of City Hall after Mayor La Guardia profoundly influenced the structure of political access in the city. Prior to La Guardia's mayoralty, the machine was the major, albeit not the only, institution that "articulated" and "aggregated" disparate interests in New York City. To be sure, interest groups had participated in the city's politics prior to 1933, but during and after the La Guardia era a larger number of social forces became independently organized. These groups gained access to the municipal government through a variety of political channels or governmental institutions, and the machine's top leaders were no longer central to hammering out the accommodations among them. For these reasons, New York's political system during this period can quite aptly be termed pluralist.

The Liberal party exemplifies the first point. Prior to La Guardia, liberals in New York enjoyed access primarily through Al Smith and his kitchen cabinet. After a faction hostile to Smith gained control of Tammany in 1929, liberals consequently had no direct means of influencing the municipal government. In the post–La Guardia period, by contrast, the Liberal party institutionalized the Jewish–social democratic–trade union strain in New York's political culture. If the Democrats nominated a candidate the Liberals found unacceptable, they could threaten to defeat (or at least to endanger) the Democratic nominee by fielding their own candidate. This prospect, in turn, induced Democratic leaders to negotiate with Liberal leaders to find candidates the minor party was prepared to support. In other words, by organizing an independent party, liberals gained considerable tactical flexibility and an institutionalized means of influencing the city government.[45]

As for access points, there were a number of institutions through which social forces influenced municipal affairs in postwar New York, but the mayoralty and a nexus between the Board of Estimate and the city's Budget Bureau were particularly important.[46] The mayor was the municipal official most inclined to pick up proposals from civic associations, newspapers, or liberal political forces that wanted the city to enact new policies, to increase expenditures on existing programs, or to reorganize various municipal agencies. By contrast, the dominant bloc on the Board of Estimate was composed of officials—the city comptroller and the five borough presidents—who owed their nomination and election almost entirely to the city's regular Democratic organizations. These officials were especially responsive to the concerns of the homeowners and small businessmen who were the core constituency of those party organizations. This led the Board to resist proposals to increase expenditures on municipal programs by large amounts, or to enact new programs that might prove very costly. The Board of Estimate was also sympathetic when municipal employee organizations complained that a policy proposal would disrupt current bureaucratic routines or threaten promotion opportunities.

Finally, the mayor, the Board of Estimate, the Moses empire, and many agencies in the executive branch of the municipal government all enjoyed a substantial measure of political independence. No one of them totally controlled any of the others, and they were not subject to the control of a common master. The interests articulated through these different institutions were thus not aggregated through a centralized process presided over by a party boss, but rather through a process of pulling and hauling among these separate institutions.

During the postwar period, new policy proposals were characteristically initiated by the city's civic associations—organizations such as the Citizens Committee for Children, the Citizens Housing and Planning Council, and the Community Council. These proposals would be picked up by the mayor, but when presented to the Board of Estimate for enactment or funding, they were commonly watered down, so as not to violate vested bureaucratic interests or to alienate the city's taxpayers. The results were at once acceptable and frustrating to the city's major interests. The mere enactment of policy proposals in whatever form permitted civic association executives to report to their members that their organization was influential, and it enabled the mayor to establish a record with the city's liberal community. At the same time, the scaling down of policy proposals—often to the point of evisceration—by the Board of Estimate enabled taxpayers to avoid having to bear substantial new burdens and bureaucrats to avoid disruption of their established work routines.

Although they enjoyed access to the city government, these interests were not fully satisfied with municipal policies. Civic leaders and members of the liberal community almost certainly preferred half a loaf to nothing, but they obviously would have preferred making fewer concessions to their political opponents. The city's taxpayers did not face monumental tax increases each year, but they did face creeping budgetary inflation. City employees did not face major threats to the integrity of established procedures governing the recruitment, supervision, and promotion of civil servants, but the Board of Estimate's efforts to moderate the pace of budgetary inflation kept their salaries low.

Because these interests were independently organized, they could express their dissatisfaction through independent action in the city's electoral arena. When they did so in 1961, they upset the delicate structure of accommodations upon which New York's postwar regime had rested. And when some of these groups joined forces in the mid-1960s with the racial minorities that had occupied a subordinate position in New York's postwar pluralist regime, that regime was overthrown.

Notes

1. Wallace Sayre and Herbert Kaufman, *Governing New York City* (New York: Russell Sage, 1960).

2. David Hammack, *Power and Society: Greater New York at the Turn of the Century* (New York: Russell Sage, 1982), 33.

3. See Moses Rischin, *The Promised City: New York Jews, 1870–1914* (Cambridge: Harvard University Press, 1962), 76–81; and Caroline Ware, *Greenwich Village, 1920–1930* (Boston: Houghton Mifflin, 1935), chap. 2.

4. Herbert Asbury, *The Gangs of New York* (New York: Knopf, 1928), 251.

5. Irving Howe, *World of Our Fathers* (New York: Simon and Schuster, 1976), 123.

6. Herbert Gutman, *Work, Culture and Society in Industrializing America* (New York: Vintage Books, 1977), 61–63; William Freiburger, "War, Prosperity and Hunger: The New York Food Riots of 1917," *Labor History* 25 (Spring 1984): 217–39.

7. Asbury, *Gangs of New York*, 252–57.

8. S. J. Makielski, *The Politics of Zoning* (New York: Columbia University Press, 1966), 12.

9. Andy Logan, *Against the Evidence: The Becker-Rosenthal Affair* (New York: McCall Publishing, 1970).

10. Charles Leinenweber, "Socialists in the Streets: The New York City Socialist Party in Working Class Neighborhoods, 1908–1918," *Science and Society* 16 (1977): 154.

11. Melvyn Dubofsky, *When Workers Organize: New York City in the Progressive Era* (Amherst: University of Massachusetts Press, 1968), chaps. 6–7.

12. Irwin Yellowitz, *Labor and the Progressive Movement in New York State, 1897–1916* (Ithaca: Cornell University Press, 1965), chap. 9; and Deborah Dash Moore, *At Home in America: Second Generation New York Jews* (New York: Columbia University Press, 1981), 204.

13. Hammack, *Power and Society*, chap. 8.

14. Norman Adler, "Ethnics in Politics: Access to Office in New York City" (Ph.D. diss., University of Wisconsin, 1972), 64.

15. Rischin, *Promised City*, chap. 6.

16. Howe, *World of Our Fathers*, 100, 370.

17. Howe, *World of Our Fathers*, 366–67.

18. Arthur Goren, *New York Jews and the Quest for Community: The Kehillah Experiment, 1908–1922* (New York: Columbia University Press, 1970).

19. Thomas Henderson, "Tammany Hall and New Immigrants, 1910–1921" (Ph.D. diss., University of Virginia, 1973), chaps. 2–3.

20. Howe, *World of Our Fathers*, 375.

21. J. Joseph Huthmacher, "Urban Liberalism and the Age of Reform," *Mississippi Valley Historical Review* 49 (September 1962): 231–41.

22. Jeremy Felt, "Vice Reform as Political Technique: The Committee of Fifteen in New York, 1900–1901," *New York History* 54 (1973): 27.

23. Yellowitz, *Labor and the Progressive Movement*, 199–200. Tammany politicians were aware that they served as a bulwark against radicalism. See, for example, William Riordon, ed., *Plunkitt of Tammany Hall* (New York: Dutton, 1963), pp. 11–16; W. T. Stead, "Mr. Richard Croker and Greater New York," *Review of Reviews* 16 (October 1897): 341–55.

24. The remainder of this chapter draws upon Martin Shefter, *Political Crisis/Fiscal Crisis: The Collapse and Revival of New York City* (New York: Basic Books, 1985), 21–37.

25. Hammack, *Power and Society*, 143.

26. *New York Times*, June 29, 1907, 2; August 13, 1907, 11; August 18, 1907, sec. II, 5; Sept. 12, 1907, 5, 6; see also Martin Shefter, "Economic Crises, Social Coalitions, and Political Institutions: New York City's Little New Deal" (paper delivered at the Annual Meeting of the American Political Science Association, New York City, September 1, 1981), 16–18.

27. *New York Times*, Feb. 12, 1909, 20; Feb. 5, 1909, 20; see also Shefter, "Economic Crises," 18–35.

28. Goren, *New York Jews*, chaps. 7–8; and Charles Garrett, *The La Guardia Years, Machine and Reform Politics in New York City* (New Brunswick, N.J.: Rutgers University Press, 1961), 64–65.

29. Theodore Lowi, *At the Pleasure of the Mayor* (New York: Free Press, 1964), 198.

30. Edwin Lewinson, *John Purroy Mitchel: The Boy Mayor of New York* (New York: Astra Books, 1965), 79–80; Arthur Mann, *La Guardia Comes to Power, 1933* (Philadelphia: Lippincott, 1965), 95–96.

31. See, for example, Shefter, "Economic Crises," 25–35.

32. See, for example, Diane Ravitch, *The Great School Wars: New York City, 1805–1973* (New York: Basic Books, 1974), 224–25.

33. James Weinstein, *The Decline of Socialism in America, 1912–1925* (New York: Vintage Books, 1969), 149–54; Robert Carter, "Pressure from the Left: The American Labor Party, 1936–54" (Ph.D. diss., Syracuse University, 1965).

34. Henderson, "Tammany Hall," 191.

35. Lowi, *At the Pleasure of the Mayor*, 193–94.

36. Robert Caro, *The Power Broker: Robert Moses and the Fall of New York* (New York: Alfred A. Knopf, 1974), chaps. 32–33.

37. Lowi, *At the Pleasure of the Mayor*, chap. 5.

38. Martin Shefter, "Political Incorporation and the Extrusion of the Left: Party Politics and Social Forces in New York City," *Studies in American Political Development* 1 (1986): 50–90.

39. Shefter, "Political Incorporation," fig. 1. See also Marvin Weinbaum, "A Minority's Survival: The Republican Party of New York County, 1897–1960" (Ph.D. diss., Columbia University, 1965).

40. Ralph Jones, "City Employee Unions in New York and Chicago" (Ph.D. diss., Harvard University, 1972), 44–46.

41. Sayre and Kaufman, *Governing New York City*, chap. 11.

42. James Q. Wilson, *Negro Politics: The Search for Leadership* (New York: Free Press, 1960), chap. 1.

43. Caro, *The Power Broker*, 968.

44. James Q. Wilson, "Two Negro Politicians: An Interpretation," *Midwest Journal of Political Science* 4 (November 1960): 346–69.

45. Houston Flournoy, "The Liberal Party in New York State" (Ph.D. diss., Princeton University, 1956).

46. Sayre and Kaufman, *Governing New York City*, chaps. 17–18.

PART **III**

The Postindustrial Era

7

Governing Regimes and the Political Economy of Development in New York City, 1946–1984

Norman I. Fainstein / Susan S. Fainstein

At the end of World War II, New York City was a predominantly white industrial city.* Forty years later, almost half of all New Yorkers are either black or Hispanic and the local economy is largely service-based (Tables 7.1 and 7.2). Such massive demographic and economic alteration has inevitably triggered struggles over territory and the direction of development policy within a changing political arena. This essay analyzes the case of New York in light of a more general periodization of the politics of development in American cities during the postwar period.

Periodization of the Politics of Urban Development

Long-term tendencies and short-term policy initiatives must be distinguished in analyzing the politics of urban development. The overall tendency of local politics to favor certain interests plays out against a counterpoint of changing political regimes that respond to electoral shifts and sudden crises. National currents or local pressures may induce regimes to make significant concessions to lower income groups. In turn, these relatively progressive regimes typically lose office or are compelled by new political realities to become more conservative. By

*An earlier version of this chapter was published in the *City Almanac* 17 (April 1984). We wish to acknowledge the very helpful comments of Peter Marcuse and the able research assistance of Annemarie Uebbing.

Table 7.1 Population, 1950–1985 (in thousands)

	1950	1960	Percent Change	1970	Percent Change	1980	Percent Change	1985	Percent Change
TOTAL	7,892	7,782	−1.4	7,894	+1.4	7,072	−10.4	7,254	+2.6
White	6,890	6,053	−12.1	4,847	−20.0	3,669	−24.3	NA	
Black	756	1,116	+47.7	1,846	+65.4	1,897	+2.8	NA	
Hispanic	246	613	+148.7	1,202	+96.1	1,405	+17.0	NA	

Sources: City of New York, Department of Commerce and Industrial Development, *Statistical Guide for New York City, 1965* (9th annual edition); Real Estate Board of New York, *Fact Book 1983* (October 1982); and Regional Plan Association, *The Region's Agenda,* 16 (September 1986).

Table 7.2 Employment By Industry 1950–1983 (thousands)

	1950		1960		1970		1980		1983	
Manufacturing (including mining)	1041	(30.0%)	949	(26.8%)	768	(20.5%)	497	(15.0%)	442	(13.2%)
Contract Construction	123	(3.5)	127	(3.6)	112	(3.0)	77	(2.3)	85	(2.5)
Transportation and Utilities	332	(9.6)	318	(9.0)	323	(8.6)	257	(7.8)	240	(7.2)
Wholesale and Retail Trade	755	(21.8)	745	(21.0)	735	(19.6)	613	(18.6)	601	(18.0)
Finance, Insurance, and Real Estate	336	(9.7)	384	(10.9)	458	(12.2)	448	(13.6)	495	(14.8)
Services	508	(14.6)	607	(17.2)	786	(21.0)	894	(27.1)	968	(28.9)
Government	374	(10.8)	408	(11.5)	563	(15.1)	516	(15.6)	516	(15.4)
TOTAL	3468		3538		3745		3302		3348	

Sources: Temporary Commission on City Finances, *The Effects of Taxation on Manufacturing in New York City* (December 1976), Table 1; Real Estate Board of New York, Inc., *Fact Book 1983* (October 1982), Table 56; and *Fact Book 1985* (March 1985), Table 56.

recognizing that local regimes can change rather quickly, we can analyze abrupt transformations in urban programs and politics, yet accept the broader context of constraints imposed by the drive for capital accumulation and the interests of property owners.

Since World War II, we detect a succession of three types of local regimes and three stages in the politics of urban development that are fairly uniform across American cities.[1] From the late 1940s until 1965, local regimes planned and implemented large-scale development projects. These "directive regimes," as we call them, operated with little effective opposition. They were succeeded by "concessionary regimes," which urban unrest and federal policy forced to be more responsive to lower class interests than before or afterward. The third period, dating from 1975 to at least 1984, was marked by the resumption of business influence and the muting of popular demands. Its "conserving regimes" tried to preserve social control at minimal cost without wholly jettisoning the policies and institutions devised in the previous period.

We assume that a common location in the American national political economy explains the similarity across cities in the pattern of political development. Therefore, while such factors as the rise of militant minority groups or the power of corporate leaders within the city determine local politics, we view these forces as at least partially exogenously generated. Likewise, local policy shifts can be traced to national sources; indeed, major pieces of federal legislation tend to demarcate typical periods for many cities. While the New York case is generally consistent with this periodization, the essay concludes by analyzing two unusual traits: New York's unique business stratum and its atypically liberal politics.

Elite-Dominated Development in New York: The Directive Period (1946–1966)

The stage for the directive period in New York was set well before the inception of the federal urban renewal program in 1949. During the Great Depression, the La Guardia administration sponsored slum clearance, public housing, and major public works. By 1940, the nascent City Planning Commission had laid out ambitious plans for rebuilding residential neighborhoods and the city's transportation infrastructure. After the war, New York started urban renewal programs and highway programs years ahead of other big cities.

Two early postwar projects, Stuyvesant Town and the United Nations, were mounted without federal involvement and set the pattern followed throughout the directive period. In the former, under the leadership of Robert Moses, the city condemned eighteen blocks of tenements housing 12,000 people, then resold the buildings and land to the Metropolitan Life Insurance Company, which was given complete control of site planning and tenant selection.[2] In the UN project, Moses worked with the Rockefeller family and developer William Zeckendorf to attract the UN to the old East Side slaughterhouse district.[3] Contributions from the Rockefellers and the city permitted purchase of Zeckendorf's options on the property. This combination of actions, later termed a "public-private partnership," laid the groundwork for the development of east midtown as a center of commercial and upper-income residential development.

For a decade after the inception of the federal urban renewal program (Title I of the 1949 Housing Act), Moses coordinated the actors and put together the financial packages enabling redevelopment of cleared land.[4] Moses had lobbied vigorously for the program and worked closely with Senator Taft in formulating the 1949 act. He was ready to move the day President Harry Truman signed the bill. He pushed legislation through Albany to establish the Committee on Slum Clearance Projects (CSC) as the city's official urban renewal agency with himself as the head. He made sure that the CSC did not become an autonomous professional bureaucracy by headquartering it in the offices of the Triborough Bridge and Tunnel Authority (TBTA), which he controlled.

Through this administrative mechanism, Moses implemented the "New York method" he had developed with Stuyvesant Town.[5] He privatized urban renewal by giving developers immediate title to occupied parcels of land and then allowing them to clear sites, relocate occupants, arrange financing, and erect new structures. He guaranteed them a 10 percent return on the preclearance assessed value of the property. This system allowed Moses to line up sites and prospective developers quickly, thereby getting earlier commitments of federal money. As it showed in Title I results, New York became the U.S. Urban Renewal Administration's favorite funding recipient.

The CSC's urban renewal projects reflected the "New York method's" emphasis on market and political rationality. Three-quarters of the projects were located in Manhattan (see Table 7.3), because it was here that powerful institutions and private investors wanted to reshape an already built-up territory to realize its potential for other uses. Expansion-minded universities sponsored Title I projects: New York University (NYU) in Washington Square, NYU Medical School in Kips Bay, Fordham University in Lincoln Square, and Pratt Institute in one of three Brooklyn projects. In Morningside Heights, a David Rockefeller-

Table 7.3 Urban Renewal Projects and Programs, 1949–1974

	Borough	Planned Reuse: Percent of Area Resid.[a]	Orig. Pop. Percent Non-White[b]	Fed. Expnd. (thous. dol.)[c]
Committee on Slum Clearance Projects (1949–1959)				
Fort Greene	Bk	48	62	5,990
Corlears Hook	Mn	84	24	3,396
Morningside	Mn	93	65	2,793
Columbus Circle	Mn	49	54	6,019
North Harlem	Mn	72	100	4,658
Pratt Institute	Bk	80	36	5,181
West Park (Manhattantown)	Mn	75	52	8,863
Washington Square S.E.	Mn	66	00	14,111
Seward Park	Mn	41	09	5,316
Kips Bay (NYU-Bellevue)	Mn	75	01	4,275
Lincoln Square	Mn	38	07	30,899
Seaside-Rockaway	Qu	60	00	2,379
Hammels-Rockaway	Qu	61	67	5,668
Penn Station S.	Mn	51	03	17,946
Park Row	Mn	29	08	2,634
Cadman Plaza	Mn	25	08	3,960
Park Row Extension	Mn	5	08	2,634
Lindsay Park	Bk	46	46	8,100
SUBTOTAL				137,657
West Side (1958)	Mn	99	NA	37,538
Washington St. (1960)	Mn	00	00	15,219
Other Projects (1960–1966)				129,355
Community Renewal Program (1960–1973)				7,744
Code Enforcement Programs (1967–1974)				13,400
Neighborhood Development Program (1968–1974)				207,166
TOTAL				548,079

Sources: Derived from J. Anthony Panuch, *Mayor's Independent Survey on Housing and Urban Renewal, Building a Better New York, Final Report to Mayor Robert F. Wagner,* March 1, 1960; U.S. Housing and Home Finance Agency, *Urban Renewal Project Characteristics,* June 30, 1962; and U.S. Department of Housing and Urban Development, *Urban Renewal Directory,* June 30, 1974.

[a] Indicates residential functions are predominant use. Acres planned for residential use divided by total acres.

[b] These data are at best suggestive. They are based on families, not individuals, who were officially counted as requiring relocation assistance. While the actual numbers of families counted is ridiculously low, the racial composition is probably more accurate. It is this percentage that we calculate.

[c] Dollar amounts authorized and reserved. Actual expenditures are virtually identical except for programs that were not completed by 1975, when CDBG replaced these categoricals.

backed organization joined Columbia University in financing middle income housing to buffer the Heights campus from Harlem. Other sponsors included TBTA itself, which built the Coliseum in Columbus Circle, and Lincoln Center, Inc., another Rockefeller enterprise, which anchored the adjacent Lincoln Square Project. The labor-sponsored United Housing Foundation (UHF) built many middle income units at Penn Station South and other sites. Private developers, often with Tammany connections, were involved with Park West, Washington Square, Kips Bay, and Lincoln Square. When a number of these ventures failed financially (after long years during which the developers profited from tenement ownership), William Zeckendorf took over the projects.

During the period when he directed the city's slum clearance program, Robert Moses also controlled the Housing Authority. He refused to build public housing in sparsely developed peripheral areas, feeling that new low income housing should be contained in the old working class neighborhoods.[6] Moreover, Moses saw slum clearance as the only justification for Title I. He considered redevelopment of mainly commercial areas to be socialistic, but if government used its powers to raze a slum, then intervention was appropriate. In Moses' hands, the Slum Clearance Committee and the New York City Housing Authority (NYCHA) were both redevelopment agencies. Each cleared slums. The difference lay only in reuse: the Slum Clearance Committee encouraged development of middle income, publicly subsidized housing and market rate upper class housing; and the NYCHA, acting in neighborhoods that private investors would not enter, built new public housing afterward. In the process of erecting about 135,000 new housing units through 1965,[7] the Authority eliminated a similar number of existing units. Moses thus used housing to redevelop large areas of the city, thereby upgrading the lower income housing stock, although he did not expand the supply of lower income housing. Whatever the criticisms of public housing's aesthetic and social deficiencies, lower income families perceived it as an improvement. From the 1930s on, the waiting list for Housing Authority units always exceeded 100,000 people.[8]

Highways and Transportation

Closely tied to urban renewal was the vision of a modern transportation system linking the city with the region. Two powerful actors, TBTA and the Port Authority (PA), defined and implemented such a system for the metropolitan area. For years, the bitter rivalry between the authorities for revenue sources had been reflected in a personal antagonism between Robert Moses and Austin Tobin, the long-lived executive director of the PA.[9] The two agencies could agree only on their commitment to the automobile and their desire to protect their surpluses and large borrowing capacities—together, about $1.2 billion in 1953—from being diverted to mass transit subsidies.[10] During the 1950s, however, a rapprochement served the interests of both organizations and permitted the implementation of a master highway plan.

The TBTA-PA Joint Arterial Facilities program, announced in 1955, resulted in the construction of the Throgs Neck, George Washington lower deck, and Verrazano Narrows bridges and dozens of miles of expressways during the next ten years at the cost of perhaps $1.7 billion, $500 million of which was financed by the city.[11] Moses and Tobin agreed that the PA would defer its plan to build a bridge across the Hudson at 125th Street and would instead finance the construction of the Narrows Bridge, which would be entirely controlled by the TBTA, first through a leasehold and eventually through ownership. Moses was thus able to build the bridge without having to divert funds from his Throgs Neck project. Tobin got the road links that would turn around the PA's money-losing crossings from Staten Island into New Jersey.[12]

Of all the projects, the Verrazano Narrows Bridge probably had the biggest impact on the city. Its Brooklyn access highways displaced thousands of people. Bay Ridge residents and Brooklyn's elected officials vehemently opposed the bridge.[13] But Moses overcame the opposition by threatening to resign as construction coordinator and to kill the entire arterial plan if the mayor and the Board of Estimate would not agree. Moses was backed by a constellation of construction industry interests that saw huge payoffs in the bridge, its supporting highways, and the opening of Staten Island to real estate development. The Board finally gave the go-ahead in 1958. The bridge cost more than $300 million; with its completion in 1964, the value of undeveloped land in Staten Island increased thirteenfold from its 1959 level.[14]

In retrospect, the Joint Program appears to have sought an efficient interconnection of the authorities' present and proposed toll-producing facilities. Autos and trucks would be able to circulate around and through the region without being bottled up in Manhattan. With no plans for strengthened mass transit facilities, the Joint Program assumed commuters would increasingly drive into Manhattan. They would be provided with new means of access: Manhattan was to be trisected by elevated highways at 125th Street, 30th Street, and Grand Street. In effect, the TBTA-PA envisioned the core as a network of superhighways, interchanges, and parking garages (a common idea of planners in the 1950s for redeveloping downtowns). Community and liberal opposition in the 1960s to key elements of this highway plan—along with the razing in 1956 of the Third Avenue el—permitted the development of the city's central business district (CBD) along rather different, but still highly profitable, lines.

Moses' Downfall

Urban renewal and highway building displaced at least half a million New Yorkers from their homes between 1945 and 1960.[15] Unlike Europe, New York took on an increasingly bombed-out aspect as the war receded into the past. Development politics in the city was pluralistic only in that it had many powerful players, certainly not in the sense that ordinary communities or working class and minority groups influenced the process. Looking back from 1960, Sayre and Kaufman could hardly have been more mistaken when they claimed: "No part of the city's large and varied population is alienated from participation in the system. All diverse elements in the city, in competition with each other, can and do partake of the stakes of politics; if none gets all it wants, neither is any excluded. Consequently, no group is helpless to defend itself, powerless to prevent others from riding roughshod over it, or unable to assert its claim and protect its rights."[16]

Even the plurality of elites was largely illusory. Actors and institutions were locked in just a few circuits of power and money. At the center stood Robert Moses, the power broker. Thus William Zeckendorf, the nation's biggest Title I developer, noted that whereas most cities required a strong mayor or a cohesive business elite to overcome community mobilization against urban renewal, New York only "had Bob Moses [who] all by himself [was] worth two-dozen blue-ribbon citizens' commissions."[17]

From 1945 through the 1950s, a material, closed, and corrupt politics interlocked the formal electoral system with centers of development power. Two influential journalists lamented in a special issue of *The Nation* entitled "The Shame of New York":

In today's New York, . . . power speaks only to power, and no further. The power is of many kinds and degrees, but its varying forms have one thing in common. It is derived from the top, not the bottom. The men who control the $2 billion-a-year city government deal only with their counterparts—with the men who wield millions in private finance, with the men whose fortunes control all the large media of public opinion. The rule by power has rendered sterile and useless one of the key figures of old-line city politics, the district leader. Even in the worst days of Tammany Hall . . . the political machine had liaison with its people through the district leader. The machine might be totally corrupt, but it had its finger on the pulse of block and ward. . . . Today, this essential chain has been broken, this vital communication has been lost.[18]

In fact, the "essential chain" of party organization had broken long before. After the war, city politics shifted to the right with the breakup of the American Labor Party and La Guardia's progressive coalition. Concurrently huge public and private resources for development were marshaled by Moses and the other elites with whom he worked. Working class residents resisted the urban renewal and highway projects displacing them. But only an attack from the liberal intelligentsia and the press, along with several public scandals, eventually forced Mayor Wagner to redirect the city's efforts and to dismiss Moses.

Investigative journalists disclosed that Moses sold land to politically connected developers at unjustifiably low prices, then subsidized them while they allowed their tenements to decay. Legitimate developers were frequently excluded from the secret allocation process. When those who were chosen could not implement projects, the CSC bought out their original investment without penalties (in flagrant violation of federal regulations). Moses defended himself with his usual vigor. But his power was seriously reduced when, in 1958, the administration bypassed the CSC and gave control over the big West Side urban renewal project to a new entity, the Urban Renewal Board. In 1960, Moses resigned his TBTA post (apparently in exchange for running the 1964 World's Fair), and Wagner abolished the CSC.

Moses frequently proclaimed his opposition to planning, yet the phase of postwar urban redevelopment that he dominated revealed a consistent pattern of operations:

a. Sites were always cleared in their entirety. Although the 1954 Housing Act permitted rehabilitation, Moses did not believe that approach was economically feasible.

b. Areas selected for redevelopment were residential, mainly working class, but with potential for private investment. While some were in poor condition, they certainly did not comprise the worst slums in the city.[19]

c. Reuse was mainly residential. In contrast, Friedland found that during this period only 19 percent of renewed land in larger cities (population more than 150,000) was devoted to residential reuse.[20] As Table 7.3 shows, the New York figure exceeded 25 percent in every instance, and frequently was much higher.

d. Territorial redistribution was regressive. New housing in Title I areas was mainly occupied by middle and upper income, predominantly white populations. As of 1960, apartments on cleared land had rental levels about 2.5 times those of the original units.[21] This was the typical national pattern. Moses noted correctly that "Title I was never designed to produce housing for people of low income . . . [it] aimed solely at the elimination of slums and substandard areas."[22]

e. Lower income households were displaced in large numbers. According to Davies, 15,000 people were removed to make way for Park West Village (97th to 100th streets and Columbus Avenue).[23] Spillover effects undoubtedly contributed to the deterioration of other areas. Blacks displaced from various Manhattan sites were forced by a racist housing market into instant ghettos. Some potential new ghetto areas (for example, Morningside Heights, and Penn Station) were eliminated in the process. Overall, the effect was to increase racial segregation.

f. Several projects contributed to the class and economic restructuring of Manhattan. Columbus Circle, Lincoln Square, and Kips Bay effectively removed large tracts of working class housing and facilitated commercial and institutional development.

Nevertheless, development politics in New York was more liberal than elsewhere. Public housing and rent control received strong political support throughout the directive period. Moreover, during Robert Wagner's second term (1958–1961), minority groups, Democratic party reformers, and critics of urban renewal united against Moses and his practices. By 1960, the redevelopment approaches characteristic of the directive years were coming to a halt in New York, even as they continued unabated in other big cities. But New York had started the period earlier. After fifteen years, it bore the enormous impact, for better or for worse, of the biggest urban renewal, housing, and highway programs in the country.

After Moses

The second phase of urban renewal reflected a different philosophy. Urban renewal could no longer involve massive clearance. Instead, it would facilitate neighborhood preservation and rehabilitation. Projects would be redistributed citywide to areas of greatest need. In addition, small-scale efforts would be launched in many neighborhoods through a

Community Renewal program. Finally, there would be better mechanisms for both central planning and neighborhood representation.[24]

The West Side urban renewal project, in many ways the city's most ambitious undertaking during the directive period, illustrates changing attitudes toward redevelopment of residential neighborhoods. The project covered a socially heterogeneous twenty-square-block area from Eighty-seventh to Ninety-seventh streets. The Urban Renewal Board (URB), under the direction of James Felt, chairman of the City Planning Commission, published a preliminary plan in 1959 that reflected its "progressive" approach to urban renewal. The plan called for rehabilitating the area's architecturally distinguished brownstones, widening Columbus and Amsterdam avenues, phased public relocation of 4,300 families and 1,500 individuals, and construction of 7,800 new housing units—5 percent of them low income, 30 percent middle income, and 65 percent upper income.[25] The URB also helped establish a citizen participation organization and expected the community to support its activities.

Despite avoiding large-scale clearance, the West Side plan provoked stronger and more negative community reaction than any of the CSC projects. The citizen participation process got out of the URB's control with the formation of the Strycker's Bay Neighborhood Council, which strongly criticized the project. Puerto Ricans organized a citizens' housing committee. The National Association for the Advancement of Colored People (NAACP) became actively involved, as did the FDR–Woodrow Wilson Reform Democratic Club. Each actor had its own constituency and objectives. But all agreed that the plan provided too little lower income housing and involved too much displacement. The result was continuous conflict.

By 1962, the city was forced to make substantial concessions to community demands. Mayor Wagner had just been reelected on a reform ticket. Minority group political activity had been aroused. The city finally agreed to triple the number of low and middle income units in the West Side Project. Implementation began during 1963, in the first of three stages, so as to minimize displacement. As Wagner left office in 1965, however, little had been built on the West Side and new conflicts erupted, now played out along racial and class lines between those who wanted more low income housing and those who wanted an "integrated" balance.

Meanwhile, as public housing occupancy became increasingly nonwhite, the earlier brisk rate of construction declined precipitously. Until as late as 1950, public housing in New York had been mainly a white program with some racial integration, an outcome in part of the close connection between housing construction and slum clearance. The oldest and worst slums were in Lower Manhattan, and that was where public housing was first constructed. These areas were remote from black ghettos, having retained their white populations as a result of the acute postwar housing shortage. But during the 1950s, fast growth of the minority population, increased white prosperity, and government placement of welfare families in the projects changed the racial composition of tenants. Thus the projects, which had been about 88 percent white in 1945,[26] became racially mixed in the early 1950s,[27] and mostly black and Hispanic by the mid-1960s.[28]

Consequently, public housing lost much of its earlier popular support. Whites equated public housing construction with minority group penetration of their neighborhoods, and were increasingly effective in vetoing locations in part because of the new mechanisms for citizen participation. Smaller projects also meant more sites, multiplying the opportunities for veto. After 1954, no public housing bond referendum won a majority upstate, and the margin of positive city votes dropped so sharply in successive referenda in 1964 and 1965 that they were defeated statewide.[29] Combined with the changed local political situation—and the arrival of Richard Nixon a few years later—the elimination of the state program brought new public housing to a virtual halt in the city. Only 41,000 units were constructed during the 1960s, 27,000 of which went up during the Wagner administration.[30]

The decline of the public housing program meant an increased reliance throughout the city on projects aimed at moderate and middle income households. After 1960, construction of publicly subsidized, privately developed housing accelerated (see Table 7.4). An extremely active and competent sponsor, the United Housing Foundation (UHF), played a major role. UHF was established in 1951 by a consortium of trade unions to build publicly subsidized housing for moderate income families. Through the 1950s and 1960s, the UHF accounted for half of all publicly subsidized construction. Many UHF projects were on land cleared by Title I (though two of the biggest, the 5,900-unit Rochedale Village in Queens and the 15,372-unit Co-op City, were not). Other for-profit developers were able to use hundreds of acres of land previously cleared by Moses' slum clearance efforts for middle income projects.

Simultaneously, improved state finances provided larger subsidies. The 1955 Mitchell-Lama program greatly increased public support for moderate income housing; but state bond issues to finance the projects were not approved until 1958, and then at inadequate levels.[31] As a

Table 7.4   New Dwelling Units Completed, 1921–1983 (in thousands)

	Total	Public[a]	Publicly Assisted[b]	Private
1921–1930	762	00	01	761
1931–1940	207	10	05	192
1941–1950	166	26	12	128
1951–1960	323	72	17	234
1961–1970	348	41	75	232
1971–1980	166		111	49
1981–1983	25		NA	NA

Sources: Elizabeth Roistacher and Emanuel Tobier, "Housing Policy," in Setting Municipal Priorities, 1981, ed. Charles Brecher and Raymond Horton (Montclair, N.J.: Allenheld, Osmun, 1980), Table 6.1; George Sternlieb and David Listokin, "Housing," in Setting Municipal Priorities, 1986, ed. Charles Brecher and Raymond Horton (New York: New York University Press, 1985), Table 12.4; New York City Housing Authority, Project Data, January 1, 1982, 43; and New York City Housing Authority, Research and Statistics Division, "Special Tabulation of Tenant Characteristics," January 1, 1983, 1.

[a]Units built or operated by the New York City Housing Authority. As of 1982, there were about 169,000 public units in 247 projects housing a population of about 491,000. The racial breakdown of occupants was about 10 percent white, 58 percent black, 28 percent Puerto Rican, and 4 percent "other."

[b]Units insured, subsidized, and in other ways aided by the municipal, state, or local government.

result, only 11,002 Mitchell-Lama units were under way when Governor Nelson Rockefeller greatly invigorated the program in 1960. That year, he established the Housing Finance Agency (HFA) and instituted moral-obligation revenue bonds, which do not require public approval since they are not backed by the full faith and credit of the state. By 1965, HFA had borrowed almost $1 billion, most of which went to Mitchell-Lama housing in New York City,[32] significantly expanding publicly subsidized housing. More than 75,000 units were constructed in New York City after 1960.

In summary, the alliance of a strong labor movement with liberal social reformers produced large-scale production of subsidized housing during the directive period, mainly in desirable parts of Manhattan. This coalition achieved state legislation for subsidized housing and created the UHF as a vehicle to sponsor it. Thus, while working class neighborhoods were unable to block centrally determined decisions for Title I clearance, through labor union influence they could press for new units that would shelter middle income households.

Redevelopment of Lower Manhattan

Although the redevelopment of Lower Manhattan began during the earlier phase of urban renewal, it was largely consummated after Robert Moses left the scene. The Rockefellers, from the mid-1950s on, were dominant figures. They pursued a fourfold strategy: intervening directly in the financial district real estate market; sponsoring a growth-oriented coalition through a business planning group; mobilizing the Port Authority's investment capacity; and encouraging the city to undertake supportive projects.

Lower Manhattan went into decline after World War II. Since the area was primarily nonresidential, its problems, from the perspective of the businesses located there, did not stem from lower class occupancy or potential minority influx. Rather, they resulted from antiquated structures that could not easily support modern business functions. More than 80 percent of its office space had been constructed prior to 1920, and no new buildings had gone up since the war.[33] Neighborhoods to the north and west were filled with manufacturing lots and wholesale food markets, whose occupants were either going out of business or seeking more suitable quarters elsewhere. Unless action were taken, the postwar movement of banks, insurance companies, and law firms to midtown would accelerate, with the eventual total decay of the Wall Street area.[34]

Although there was no shortage of development capital, each potential investor viewed the area as risky. David Rockefeller and his Chase Bank promoted concerted action. Chase announced construction of its own new headquarters building and helped finance several other structures. William Zeckendorf arranged for five large banks to move into new quarters in a game of musical chairs which he termed his Wall Street Maneuver. Within a decade of Chase's decision, private capital had erected thirty buildings and added more than 11 million square feet downtown.[35]

While Zeckendorf maneuvered real estate, David Rockefeller helped unite and define business interests. After experimenting with a subcommittee of the New York State Chamber of Commerce, he established in 1957 his more narrowly focused Downtown–Lower Manhattan Association (DLMA). Its objective, according to Rockefeller's aide Warren Lindquist, was to assure that downtown continued to be "the heart pump of the capital blood that sustains the free world."[36] He claimed DLMA sought to sustain a physical environment that would permit downtown business institutions "to enjoy their share of the expanding commerce of the city—excuse me—of the country and of the world."[37]

DLMA commissioned studies that culminated in a plan for Lower Manhattan and proposals for government action. DLMA wanted urban renewal of the commercial slums along the East River, relocation of the West Side markets, widening of streets, construction of the proposed Lower Manhattan Expressway to act as a barrier to the incursion of manufacturing uses from the north, development of a Second Avenue subway, and, most important, the creation of a world trade center under the auspices of the Port Authority.[38]

The city began a series of projects around 1960 to implement the elements of the DLMA master plan. A wholesale food market was built at Hunts Point in the Bronx to house firms previously located in Lower Manhattan.[39] The Washington Street urban renewal project condemned the old markets and compensated their owners with federal funds.[40] The Housing and Redevelopment Board refashioned previous plans for waterfront housing south of the Brooklyn Bridge. After a series of alterations, the board eventually permitted private capital to redevelop part of the area, while it established additional urban renewal projects which culminated, over the ensuing decade, in the Civic Center, Pace University, and Beekman Hospital. Under Governor Nelson Rockefeller's guidance, the Port Authority reshaped and expanded DLMA's proposal for a trade center; by the time the facility opened in the early 1970s it had cost more than $1 billion.[41]

The Wagner regime also supported construction of the Lower Manhattan Expressway, which the Board of Estimate approved in 1962.[42] But the project provoked tremendous political opposition. Residents of Little Italy protested vehemently and were backed by the regular Democrats representing the area. Reform Democrats joined forces, and Wagner was forced to pull back. Other city capital projects for Lower Manhattan moved ahead, but the expressway was never built.

The forces against the highway typified the new, more effective community response to redevelopment programs after 1960. By the end of Wagner's administration in 1965, residential renewal was politically much more difficult. Thus, neighborhood residents defeated two proposed projects. In the East Village, the Cooper Square Development Committee, with help from professional planners, successfully prevented redevelopment.[43] In the West Village, Jane Jacobs led a group that stopped urban renewal of the mixed industrial area near the Hudson River. Her West Village Committee brought together historic preservationists, reform Democrats, and residents who feared that the proposed middle income housing might bring blacks into the neighborhood.[44]

The Concessionary Period (1966–1974): Conflict and Response

During the late 1960s and early 1970s, ethnic strife and conflict between urban bureaucracies and their clients permeated development politics in New York City. As racial consciousness peaked, black and Hispanic community groups fought to control the administration of schools, hospitals, housing projects, and poverty programs. They used the tactics of sit-ins, marches, boycotts, rent strikes, and inflammatory rhetoric, as well as the more mundane devices of petitions and lobbying. Black protest groups began organizing communities and using neighborhood issues as a basis for attracting members. Interestingly, earlier reforms of the program turned the focus of radical activism away from urban renewal, whereas in many other cities it was a principal area of conflict. The most important development controversy was not over displacement of low income inhabitants but the effort to build public housing in white, middle class Forest Hills.[45] Here white neighborhood groups mobilized to oppose the project.

John V. Lindsay's 1966 victory as mayor inaugurated a political alliance between part of the business elite and restive minority groups. Minority group pressure had become increasingly intense during Wagner's last term. Lindsay wished to transcend the broker role of his predecessor. He was among the group of mayors who represented "the new convergence of power" in American cities.[46] No longer caretakers of routine municipal functions, these glamorous chief executives sought to modernize city government through emulating private sector management techniques, attracting private development capital and upper middle class residents to the central city, and increasing the urban poor's share in the affluent society. Perhaps more than most other mayors, Lindsay stressed this third objective.[47]

By vastly expanding the scope of government, Lindsay incorporated new constituencies into the governmental process.[48] He was therefore widely credited with averting the civil disorders that ravaged other cities.[49] At the same time, his initiatives were also blamed for subsequent fiscal crisis and political backlash. The mayor's symbolic identification with the plight of low income minorities gave the popular impression that resources were pouring into the hands of the undeserving poor at the direct expense of the hard-working middle class. This perception eventually created the climate for the quite different coalition developed by Edward Koch.

Development Efforts

Although social welfare and capital expenditures expanded in poor neighborhoods during Lindsay's mayoralty, money also continued to flow into expensive economic development projects. Thus, while avoiding bulldozer renewal, the Lindsay administration did sponsor development for the benefit of relatively well-off sectors.

Robert Moses' departure in 1960 meant that, by mid-decade, New York lacked a unified program under a powerful renewal "czar."[50] Authority over the urban renewal program resided in City Hall, not in a semi-autonomous agency with bonding authority and its own lines to Washington. Consequently Lindsay could control the scope and locations of development investment better than could his counterparts elsewhere. But because it had few resources for overcoming community resistance and attracting private sector participation, the city had difficulty implementing projects. This led Governor Nelson Rockefeller to press for a state-level agency with extraordinary powers—the Urban Development Corporation (UDC)—which began operations in 1968.

Given its unique ability to issue moral-obligation bonds, the UDC was envisioned as attracting considerable private investment.[51] Administrative autonomy and immunity to local regulation meant that the UDC could negotiate with private developers without the restrictions facing the city. The Lindsay administration initially opposed the creation of the UDC as an encroachment upon home rule and a barrier to citizen participation. But the agency could funnel public subsidies into areas outside the priority poverty neighborhoods and support commercial projects as well as middle and upper income housing.[52]

Commercial construction boomed during the Lindsay years, peaking in 1972 with the completion of 15.6 million square feet of office space in eleven new buildings, including the two towers of the World Trade Center. This increased supply, and a downturn in employment resulted in a 1972 vacancy rate of about 12 percent.[53] Thirty-five million square feet were added in midtown alone between 1960 and 1973. Zoning incentives for such amenities as plazas and street-level shopping and the transfer of development rights from underutilized properties to the new office towers encouraged this growth. Additions to downtown rentable space also increased enormously, from 5.4 million square feet in 1960–1964 to 22 million in 1969–1973.

Downtown development proceeded within the context of an overall strategy that did not exist for the remainder of the Manhattan CBD. When Lindsay took office in 1966, planning by the DLMA had established the character of the area's future. The Lindsay administration's commitment to improving low income residential areas did not preclude it from supporting these plans.

> The [city's] Lower Manhattan Plan stated ideas about what the city and city-dwellers are in design terms. The city, for the Lower Manhattan planners, was intensive interaction among members of an educated, well-off, chic upper and upper middle class. Their work consisted mainly of decision making and communication with other members of the same group. Their time was so valuable in economic terms that great saving could be achieved by their working in areas that were densely developed to allow very ready face-to-face communication. At play, this elite enjoyed theaters, galleries, specialty shops and a wide variety of restaurants. Again they wanted these things readily at hand.[54]

Port Authority and Battery Park City Authority development of this part of the city for upper class uses proved convenient for Lindsay, who therefore did not have to become directly involved in questions of job and residential mix.

The administration and its elite business allies did, however, try to foster community-based economic development as an alternative to welfare dependency. For example, the New York Urban Coalition, founded in 1967, sought to mobilize corporate resources to support minority businesses and employment.[55] The Bedford-Stuyvesant Restoration, founded in 1967 by Senator Robert Kennedy, enlisted numerous corporate sponsors as well as federal and city assistance.[56] It developed a shopping center; backed local minority-owned businesses; attracted an IBM branch plant; and provided health care, employment placement, and other social services. While its achievements were substantial, it was also a product of the unique circumstances surrounding the Kennedy commitment and dwarfed other efforts at community economic development in the city.

Housing and Neighborhood Programs

New York was among the first municipalities to participate in the federal Model Cities Program.[57] Begun in 1966, this program sought to coordinate physical redevelopment and social services within designated poverty neighborhoods. By targeting governmental assistance to a few extremely disadvantaged areas, it fit well with Lindsay's development objectives. The city administration directed most of its housing construction and rehabilitation funds to the Model Cities neighborhoods and mounted ancillary programs of job training, day care, health service, recreation, education, code enforcement, and housing maintenance. New construction was much less than under Title I, and local groups were actively involved from the start. The termination of federal Model Cities funding in 1974 marked the end of this concentrated strategy in the city, although the Model Cities agencies lived on for several years thereafter.

The 1972 federal moratorium on housing subsidies threw the city back on its own resources for low income housing and caused a shift almost entirely to rehabilitation. The Neighborhood Preservation Program, established in 1973, relied on low interest loans to not-for-profit community-based institutions to stimulate rehabilitation activity.[58] This effort and the Model Cities program both suffered from administrative confusion, competition among local groups, financial difficulties, the inexperience of sponsors, and maintenance problems in renovated housing. Building-by-building difficulties prevented rehabilitation on a wholesale basis comparable to the construction of large new projects.

New York State subsidized housing construction for better-off segments of the population. Development of moderate and middle income housing on Welfare Island, renamed Roosevelt Island, was an expensive proposition, which, if carried out by the city, would have subjected it to accusations of subsidizing well-to-do residents. Sponsorship by the state's UDC permitted it to support the project without taking a leadership role.[59]

Co-op City also developed a large, isolated community on land that did not require clearance. Plans for moderate income units financed under Mitchell-Lama at Co-op City far exceeded the scope of UDC's Roosevelt Island project. Built by the United Housing Foundation and opened for initial occupancy in 1968, the project ultimately contained 15,372 housing units in a 300-acre tract, as well as schools, community centers, a shopping center, and other amenities.[60] But while its 50,000 occupants found affordable housing in a reasonably secure if rather sterile environment, many analysts blamed the rapid deterioration of housing conditions in the South Bronx on the sudden exodus of many Co-op City residents from other parts of the borough.[61]

The volume of new residential construction dropped precipitously during the Lindsay administration. State subsidies for low income housing ended in 1965, and federal funds declined. It became increasingly difficult to find acceptable sites in which to locate public housing projects even when financing existed. Private investment in new residential construction simultaneously diminished sharply, as investors, deterred by rent controls, the high cost of building in the city, a more stringent zoning code, and fears of urban instability, shifted their funds elsewhere.[62] Between 1966 and 1971, 104,212 new units of housing were built, only 43 percent of the number put up in the preceding five-year period. Of this amount, 39,105 were subsidized units, approximately one-half the number of the earlier period.[63] Between 1965 and 1975, total housing units increased only 1.6 percent, compared to 10 percent during the decade of the 1950s.[64] Abandonment—amounting to an estimated 71,000 units between 1970 and 1975—reduced the net increment to the housing stock.[65] Political opposition and high cost meant that neither market forces nor public action contributed much despite the extremely low vacancy rate of 1.5 percent in 1965.[66]

Movements for Community Power: Conflict and Retrenchment

Lindsay's political orientation and the election of a black, Percy Sutton, and a Hispanic, Herman Badillo, to the borough presidencies of Manhattan and the Bronx reflected an increase in the power of minority groups within the regime. Organizations representing minority constituencies sought to increase their power by controlling service delivery. The Wagner administration's strong opposition to neighborhood participation in decision making within the federal antipoverty program produced a highly conflict-laden situation.[67] Lindsay, who actively broadened participation and ensured direct representation of low income people, succeeded in mitigating the tensions that beset the program.[68]

Community participation raised minority expectations about the Lindsay administration's stand in the battle over community control of public schools. But Lindsay's initial support for community school boards estranged many white communities and the civil service unions. Symbolically framed in terms of politics versus education and played out against a backdrop of accusations of racism and anti-Semitism, the conflict broke apart the liberal coalition of Jewish and racial minority groups.

Minority group demands for power over the structures that affected their lives provoked countermovements and policy reversals. The Forest Hills public housing project was reduced in size and other proposed, scattered-site projects were dropped. The state legislature's 1969 school decentralization act essentially ended the potential of local school boards to act as radical advocates for community-based interests. The increasingly influential civil service unions decried the threat of client activism and promoted state legislation protecting their authority within the workplace.

Racial polarization combined with growing fiscal difficulties caused Mayor Lindsay to change direction during his second term. The new mood of caution did not mean the end of earlier commitments but did cause the administration to curtail spending, improve service delivery, and dampen its rhetoric about minority empowerment.[69] The final year of Lindsay's reign produced a noticeable drop in the level of tension that had characterized municipal politics during his time in office.[70]

Changes in the national and local political scene made this shift possible. Richard Nixon and Gerald Ford interpreted the 1968 presidential election as a mandate to dismantle federal programs that had increased spending on low income communities. The freezing of federal housing programs and reduction in urban renewal appropriations decreased the city government's role in shaping urban development. The national political climate no longer sustained local protest movements, and militant groups within the city declined in number and salience. Locally the integration of minorities into the civil service, and increased responsiveness of city bureaucracies to the needs of low income clients, reduced antagonisms. But many who played active roles in New York's citizen politics were also weary. The 1973 election of Abraham Beame, Democratic party regular, former comptroller, and low-keyed representative of the white middle class, marked a "return to normalcy."

The Conserving Period (1974–1984): Emergence of a New Political Coalition

When Abraham Beame took office in 1974, fiscal stress and economic decline had become the focus of those concerned with America's urban problems. The plight of low income minorities had lost political significance; insolvency, not riot, became the principal threat to civic stability. Many saw government intervention as cause rather than cure for the difficulties of big cities, and stabilization replaced renewal as the ambition of development programs.[71]

This shift was embodied nationally in the Housing and Community Development Act of 1974, which terminated the urban renewal and Model Cities programs and established the Community Development Block Grant (CDBG) program. The CDBG program distributed federal subsidies by formula, gave cities broad latitude in how to spend their money, and reduced the possibility of mounting major projects. Locally, Roger Starr's appointment to head the Housing and Development Administration signaled the introduction of a "triage strategy." Rather than concentrate on the worst-off areas of the city, as had been the Lindsay policy, Starr proposed to direct governmental attention to salvageable districts: "We must recognize that every city has had a permanent slum, and we could simply withdraw all housing construction effort from certain sections where the disorderly and disorganized families concentrate, where there is a critical mass of very, very difficult people. It's a mistake not to focus new housing resources in areas where they can accomplish something for the people who are living there."[72]

Beame's restraint contrasted sharply with Lindsay's first term self-confidence. Beame did not dismantle the programs established in the preceding period, but dramatically slowed the rate of expenditure increase.[73] Thus, the conserving period did not begin with counterrevolution. Economic recession, increased need, and diminished resources, however, quickly culminated in the fiscal crisis of 1975, followed by a period of corporatist rule by private business through the Municipal Assistance Corporation (MAC) and the Emergency Financial Control Board (EFCB).[74] The election of Edward Koch and the improvement of the city's financial status ultimately produced a new governing coalition and a changed pattern of urban development, but with various elements remaining from the concessionary period.

Development Activity

The city's fiscal crisis severely curtailed governmental involvement in development projects. The collapse of UDC preceded the city's own near default and terminated the UDC's subsidized housing programs. The city's capital budget dropped drastically, aborting such major construction projects as the third water tunnel, the Second Avenue subway, and the expansion of the City University. Simultaneously, private real estate activity almost ceased. Investment in residential construction fell from $725 million in 1972 to a mere $80 million in 1975.[75] Even more precipitous was the plunge in office construction from over twenty-five million square feet in 1972 to under two million in 1975.[76]

Private residential rehabilitation became the most important real estate activity of the middle 1970s. The rehabilitation and conversion of rental buildings into co-ops and condominiums and of industrial space into loft apartments presented new opportunities for profit in the context of little new construction. The state's J-51 tax abatement law, originally enacted in 1955 to facilitate the upgrading of "cold water" tenements, reduced the risk of such projects. Amendments in 1975 broadened eligible expenditures and extended benefits to privately financed condominiums and cooperatives, as well as to commercial or industrial space converted into residential units.[77] With indirect governmental assistance, banks became much more willing to advance mortgages for conversions. As a result, the number of units underwritten by J-51 doubled between 1974 and 1975.[78] The annual amount of taxes forgone totaled $37.7 million by 1978 and over $100 million by 1983.[79]

The J-51 program contributed to the gentrification movement, which was reversing the trend toward neighborhood decay in the better located, more architecturally interesting parts of the city and removing units from the low income housing stock.[80] About 75 percent of the value of the subsidy went to Manhattan, with the benefits mainly enjoyed by upper income occupants.[81] At the same time, shrinking subsidy programs and housing abandonment worsened the always difficult situation for low and moderate income households.

Once the city ceased to target its worst neighborhoods for special attention, it proceeded to disperse resources scatter-shot. The CDBG program particularly reflected this pattern. Because CDBG was not tied to specific projects or neighborhoods, it could be used in discrete sums throughout the city. The fragmented nature of the program caused the watchdog group formerly headed by Roger Starr to comment that "planning for Community Development has largely been a matter of how to offend the smallest number of people, and so the money has been sprinkled about like pepper and salt."[82]

The *in rem* program, in which the city manages housing units acquired as a consequence of property tax delinquency, became the fastest growing form of government housing assistance. By 1981, the Department of Housing Preservation and Development (HPD) was directly operating 23,000 units of in rem housing. It was also subsidizing an additional 12,000 units under its alternative management program, whereby other entities, most often community organizations or tenant associations, managed properties.[83] Uniquely among U.S. cities, New York allocated more than 50 percent of its $289 million CDBG budget to rehabilitating and managing the in rem housing stock.[84] Because in rem units were not concentrated in any particular area, CDBG funds continued to be geographically dispersed; but they were also strongly targeted to low income people, virtually the only occupants of in rem housing.

Changing Fortunes

With economic recovery, private development activities burgeoned during the late 1970s. After 1977, vacant office space became absorbed and housing starts accelerated.[85] By 1980, office construction shot rapidly upward, rivaling the pace of the early 1970s.[86] In 1981, New York City first achieved a genuinely balanced budget.[87]

The city's economic and financial revival allowed it once again to embark on major capital projects. Following past patterns, the largest commitment of funds was in Manhattan. In contrast to urban renewal's focus on large housing projects, these projects mainly fostered economic development. Chief among them were South Street Seaport, the West

Side Convention Center, Battery Park City, and the Times Square Marriott Hotel. In addition, plans had been approved for massive redevelopment of the entire Forty-second Street–Times Square area.[88]

Battery Park City, originally planned during the directive period, did not involve a land use change because it was built on vacant landfill that had been generated by the excavation for the World Trade Center. Originally intended as an integrated project of office and luxury residential megastructures arrayed around superblocks, it was a large-scale version of Roosevelt Island. However, when developers failed to materialize and default on the revenue bonds seemed imminent, a plan for phased development on extensions of the regular Manhattan street grid was generated. Downtown Manhattan's recent office boom and residential potential encouraged the giant Canadian firm of Olympia and York to implement the first commercial phase, and residential construction rapidly followed.[89]

UDC, revived by new state financing, managed three of these efforts—the Convention Center, Battery Park City, and Times Square—and the federal Urban Development Action Grant (UDAG) program helped finance the Seaport and the Marriott Hotel.[90] UDC's legal powers exercised through subsidiaries for each project meant that development could avoid local oversight better than if the city managed the endeavors itself. Their vast scope restricted business participation to the largest development firms on the continent.

Besides these major, multistructure projects, private developers began many buildings using tax subsidy programs for new construction to lower their costs. In 1979, $150 million in tax exemptions subsidized the construction of approximately 5,500 units under the 421a program for residential construction.[91] The Industrial and Commercial Incentives Board (ICIB), which administered a tax incentive program for commercial and industrial construction, had, in 1982, participated in twenty-eight office building projects in Manhattan, accounting for over 90 percent of an estimated $47 million in tax expenditures that year.[92]

These activities resembled development efforts in other cities, but on a grander scale. They depended on private funds and utilized indirect public subsidies in the form of tax exemptions. Aside from the relatively small federal UDAG program, direct governmental contributions were raised through New York State-sponsored, tax-free bonds. With the exception of Battery Park City, the projects were heavily oriented toward tourism and included such characteristic structures as a recycled, waterfront marketplace managed by the Rouse Corporation (South Street Seaport); the geographically isolated Convention Center; and the Portman-designed hotel with giant atrium (the Times Square Marriott).

Community Participation, Representation, and Opposition

Many community organizations dating from more militant times continued to be active in the conserving period, and new ones formed. The tide of neighborhood organizing had swept the city in the 1960s and 1970s and left behind an estimated 15,000 block associations, three dozen community development corporations, at least two dozen direct action groups, and over 1,000 housing groups.[93] Neighborhood Housing Services (NHS), which opened six offices in 1982 to provide reduced-interest loans and technical assistance to low income homeowners, attempted to act as a community advocate and to provide a publicly funded base for the low income housing movement.[94] Various community housing development corporations used public funds and private sector loans to build or to substantially rehabilitate housing for moderate income homeowners.[95] Tenant organizations, formed in response to the failure of landlords to provide adequate services, were able to collect rent monies withheld from landlords and use them on needed services and repairs.[96] But the involvement of formerly militant community groups in operating housing, usually under the auspices of the in rem alternative management program, caused them to moderate their demands and to devote their energy to making the buildings economically viable.

THE COMMUNITY BOARDS   Community boards constituted the principal institutionalized mode of citizen participation in the development process. Under the revised City Charter, implemented in 1977, the city's fifty-nine community boards, appointed by the borough presidents, were given three principal tasks: to monitor the delivery of services, to advise on budget priorities, and to review land use and development proposals.[97] Their offices, staffed by a full-time district manager, increasingly took on the role of "little city halls," receiving service complaints and requests for assistance with various projects.

The effectiveness and representativeness of the boards were open to debate. The boards clearly varied on both dimensions from district to district. The most effective, drawn primarily from more stable, middle class neighborhoods, had highly committed members with well-developed political contacts. In poor neighborhoods, relatively few members commanded the intricacies of planning issues, and the boards were less strong advocates and more often factionalized.[98]

Their charter status made the community boards—along with the thirty-two community school boards—the most permanent legacy of the decentralizing efforts of the concessionary period. Their continued existence and limited authority indicate the way in which the decade after

1974 could be called conserving. The boards were not radical advocates of community interests and did not promote urban political movements, as had some Community Action Programs. They insulated City Hall from neighborhood concerns while offering a limited platform for constituencies that were formerly not heard. To some extent, developers took them into account when shaping their development proposals: "When a developer starts to talk up a project," says Howard Rubenstein, whose public relations firm represents many New York developers, including Helmsley and the backers of 500 Park Avenue (a skyscraper rejected by the local community board), "the first question is, 'What will the community board say?' "[99]

ENDURING CONFLICTS   A number of conflicts continued through the four decades after World War II. Rent regulation, landlord responsibility, neighborhood impacts of development, preservation of existing land uses, and the distribution of assisted housing to various income groups continually provoked passion. Proponents of rent control, led by middle class tenants, most successfully combatted organized real estate interests. In 1974, at the beginning of the conserving period, the State Emergency Tenant Protection Action revoked vacancy decontrol, which had been put in place only three years earlier.[100] Rent controlled apartments were placed under rent stabilization as they became vacant, and rent stabilization regulations were extended to buildings built between 1969 and 1974. In 1983, the Omnibus Housing Act transferred rent regulation of 1.2 million rent controlled and rent stabilized units from the city to the state and provided new protections for tenants, albeit with some concessions to landlords. State takeover meant that landlords would have to obtain state approval for virtually any act, including any change in the level or method of delivering building services.[101]

Community elements criticized the South Street Seaport for changing the character of one of the few remnants of nineteenth century New York; construction of the Convention Center was delayed for years by controversy over its location; representatives of low income groups demanded, and got, subsidized units financed by Battery Park City; theater personnel mobilized loudly but unsuccessfully against the demolition of three theaters on the site of the Marriott; the Times Square development plan generated considerable antagonism even among those opposed to present uses.[102] By and large, however, this opposition at most slightly modified the plans for these major endeavors.

Opposition was more effective in halting construction of Westway, the superhighway along the Hudson.[103] The original 1971 proposal for the project, to be 90 percent federally funded, involved massive landfill and construction of a deck over the road, which would provide 93 acres of waterfront park and 101 acres for housing development. A consortium of community boards, using city funds to hire consultants, argued that Westway would only increase traffic congestion and air pollution. The Army Corps of Engineers' environmental impact statement was found to be flawed, and procedural delays caused the city to cancel the project in order to meet the deadline for exchanging the highway for mass transit aid. Although he initially opposed Westway, Mayor Koch subsequently supported it and continued to press for various nonhighway aspects of the project.

Another long-standing controversy centered on how much low income housing would be built in the West Side Urban Renewal Area (WSURA).[104] The Stryckers Bay Neighborhood Council represented low income groups; as the official urban renewal project area committee, it received government funding for its advocacy activities. An organization of middle class homeowners and tenants contended that more subsidized housing would drive out the middle class. It joined with the exclusive Trinity School in a lawsuit to stop a public housing project on one site. Although the plaintiffs ultimately lost, the site remained vacant and the city apparently lost interest in building low income housing on it. The compromise forged in the concessionary era called for 6,700 units of low and middle income housing in WSURA, yet only 2,070 had been built by 1982. Termination of federal Section 8 appropriations for new construction made it doubtful that even the reduced commitment of 220 additional low income units would be met. The Stryckers Bay Neighborhood Council estimated that although 60 percent of the area's residents were low income at the project's inception, only 17 percent would be so when completed.[105]

Overall, then, public controversy about major projects continued in the conserving period, and projects were tailored to minimize predictable negative reactions. But though government-sponsored projects no longer produced the wholesale displacement that characterized the directive period, they nevertheless continued to be large, oriented toward major capital interests, and unresponsive to the housing needs of low income residents.

THE KOCH REGIME   While community groups did retain some funding, neighborhood leaders, especially those from the black and Hispanic communities, remained largely outside the Koch coalition. The mayor's rhetoric, and the racial composition of the Board of Estimate and the high-level mayoral staff, particularly those working on development issues, did not reflect the interests of New York's lower classes.

The mayor still claimed that these groups received the lion's share of public benefits. In his autobiography he gave his response to a black teenager's complaint:

> You see no progress. Well let me tell you what we're doing, okay? We have a budget of thirteen billion six hundred million dollars. Regrettably, the poorest people in the city happen to be black and Hispanic. . . . And what you should know is that fifty-six percent of our budget goes to twenty-six percent of the people who live in this City. They are the twenty-six percent who are below the poverty line, okay? They are overwhelmingly black and Hispanic. . . . What I am trying to convey is that our budget, as big as it is, overwhelmingly, our budget goes to black and Hispanic people. And it should. We've got to provide for the poorest of the poor, and we're going to, but I want to tell you what you have to know is: there are demagogues and idealogues who don't give a damn about the middle class. I speak out for the middle class. You know why? Because they pay the taxes; they provide jobs for the poor people, and we're not going to be able to do as much for them economically as I would like, but at the very least, I'm gonna recognize the sacrifices they make.[106]

The Mayor's rhetoric glued together a new electoral coalition: "Manhattan may not like it but it plays in the outer boroughs, where people rejoice in the admiring self-portrait of their irrepressible mayor, fighting for their interests in a scurvy world of wackos, nuts, elitists and anti-Semites."[107]

This white middle and working class coalition belied Shefter's prediction that a program appealing to the relatively liberal Jewish population would antagonize the city's Catholic homeowners.[108] As it turned out, Koch united these seemingly hostile elements while maintaining at least the tolerance of business leaders.

The mayor's governing coalition incorporated financial capital, as represented by the Municipal Assistance Corporation (MAC), and the civil service. He worked closely with the New York Partnership, an elite business group concerned with physical and economic development, chaired by the ubiquitous David Rockefeller. Major developers like Donald Trump increasingly determined the character of midtown.[109]

A final assessment of the character of the conserving period is not yet possible. Community representation weakened; the city made extensive use of the UDC, which is bound by no citizen participation requirements. While not as freewheeling as Robert Moses, neither did it have his reluctance to involve government in commercial enterprises. Although a number of small housing rehabilitation and commercial revitalization projects operated around the city, development planning was once again largely a top-down, major-project-oriented activity, focused on Manhattan.

New York in Comparative Perspective

Most of the development patterns discussed in this essay parallel those of other large cities throughout the country. Since New York is a world capital, it necessarily diverges from other American cities in some respects. But at least three dimensions of New York's distinctiveness deserve comment: (1) the character of its business elite, (2) the liberalism of its political culture, and (3) the organization of its public intervention in the built environment.

The Business Elite

New York's business leaders are the most powerful in the world. Perhaps because of the global scope of their interests, they have shown less concern with developing their urban environment than have their counterparts elsewhere. Since midtown Manhattan never suffered the decay characteristic of CBD's in other cities, the need for a business-sponsored citywide strategy was less apparent. Office construction surged during the 1950s without the use of eminent domain or public subsidy. In contrast, no new buildings went up in Boston for a decade after the war, and only after the Boston Redevelopment Authority began its Government Center enterprise in the 1960s did momentum develop. In Lower Manhattan alone New York displayed a corporate presence and planning comparable to many other cities.

The business elite's fragmentation into divergent sectors also worked against the kind of organized effort for redevelopment that characterized Pittsburgh and San Francisco. While Rockefeller influence paralleled that of the Mellons in Pittsburgh, the Rockefellers did not press for a plan for the future development of the entire CBD. Nor did they put together a group comparable to the Allegheny Conference in its continued surveillance of the city's growth.[110] In San Francisco "big" and "little" capital, led by the hotel industry, united behind a common scheme for a drastic restructuring of land use.[111] But in New York, despite the importance of tourism to its economy, representatives of that industry have been surprisingly inactive in encouraging redevelopment.

New York's big businesses were more concerned with the city's failing services and financial condition. The decrepitude of the public transportation system, the shortage of housing, fear of crime, and unsatisfactory education of the clerical labor force make efficient operation difficult. But a physical development program could not address these problems. By seriously threatening the stability of key financial institutions, the fiscal crisis mobilized the business community far more actively and concertedly than had deterioration of the physical environment or the condition of the "other half."

In the directive period, when business elites intervened most forcefully in the development policies of other cities, they played a less important role in New York. In the succeeding periods, however, the city conformed more closely to national patterns. Business supported Lindsay's social melioration efforts during the concessionary years and engaged in a number of public/private ventures to improve the situation of minorities. During the conserving period it participated directly in managing the fiscal crisis, strongly advocating the decrease of social spending. Capitalists actively sought and were gladly given public subsidies for economic development.

Liberal Political Climate

New York strongly resembles other cities in the pattern of popular demands that are placed on government. During the directive period, communities did not organize effectively against the threats of highway building and urban renewal. Traditional parties and interest group leaders failed to protect working class constituencies from demolition and displacement. Ward-level party organizations had greatly weakened in much of the city, and the party system had failed to incorporate black and Hispanic residents. The labor movement, however, was much stronger in New York than in almost all other places. The involvement of labor, as lobbyist and sponsor, in providing social housing was particularly unusual. Consequently, although working class neighborhood resistance to government-sponsored community destruction was ineffectual, workers' organizations obtained what for the United States was a uniquely large amount of new low and moderate income housing.

New York entered the concessionary period relatively early. Agitation to block highways and urban renewal, rent strikes, demonstrations against school segregation, and the movement for a civilian police review board all preceded the passage of the 1965 federal poverty legislation. The city's urban renewal program exhibited a new responsiveness to community input by 1962, and the Ford Foundation's gray areas program started shortly thereafter. Once Lindsay was elected, however, New York's politics underwent a qualitative discontinuity: the governing regime actually incorporated minority interests, as opposed to simply granting the concessions that the last Wagner administration and most other mayors had made after 1965. Nonetheless, as New York moved into the conserving period, these interests were once more excluded.

The Organization of Intervention

New York's initial administrative unity in the directive period emanated not from a mayoral coalition but from Robert Moses' unique role. His aggressive use of New York State resources launched the directive period earlier in New York than elsewhere, since development activity preceded the 1949 federal Housing and Urban Renewal Act. Once that act was passed, New York took advantage of it much faster than other cities, because Moses already had the necessary apparatus in place.

Moses, however, did not believe in citywide planning except for highways, and he killed the master plan and zoning ordinance of 1950.[112] Thus, during the heyday of urban planning elsewhere in the United States, New York's redevelopment effort ran on a piecemeal, project-oriented basis. But, although no written plan guided it, Moses had a vision of an integrated arterial system and a city cleared of slums. This end point was not to be reached through a programmed set of stages; it was simply assumed that massive road building and land-clearance operations would enable the private sector to rebuild the city. If profit-making enterprises would not provide low and moderate income housing, government would either build the housing itself or subsidize developers.

In New York as in other cities, economic development and social service functions became vested in different agencies, with those carrying out the former effectively insulated from popular control.[113] Highway planners, working within self-financing and self-governing state authorities, were largely oblivious to mass transit needs, a common pattern. But the particular structure that operated Title I in New York was unique. Here the tension between redevelopment and social housing was not as great as elsewhere, initially because Robert Moses controlled both and built a great deal of social housing; later because the mayor controlled both redevelopment and housing provision.

The 1974 federal Housing and Community Redevelopment Act did not halt urban renewal in New York as in most cities, because the program had already been greatly modified. The only major project under way in 1974 was the West Side, and it already stressed community participation, rehabilitation, and staged, scattered-site demolition and new construction. The 1974 act did end the concentrated neighborhood strategy of the Model Cities program and led to the dispersal of development funds throughout the city. Deconcentration characterized other cities too, but not typically as an assault against a significant Model Cities effort.

New York also differed from other cities because independent authorities such as the UDC, its subsidiary, the Battery Park City Authority, and the Port Authority played such central roles. In most states, state agencies raising capital through revenue bonds only passed the money on to municipalities, as had been true for New York's Mitchell-Lama program. But long before most other states even financed local development with bond funds, New York State agencies energetically spearheaded the construction of office complexes and housing projects. Accordingly, while federal Title I expenditures were not applied primarily to commercial development and luxury housing complexes in New York, as was common elsewhere, bond revenues were used for this purpose.

The financial power of these public authorities permitted New York to frame an unusually large development program. Where other cities were using CDBG and UDAG funds for relatively modest projects, New York embarked on monumental projects reminiscent of the old days of Title I. But while these projects deviated in size and in the prominent role played by public agencies in their formulation from those mounted elsewhere, they fit the larger national pattern of economic development subordinated to private investment. New York was therefore singular in the exact timing of particular types of political demands and programs, the specific objectives of its business elite, the greater liberality of some of its phases, and the active presence of state agencies. But, despite these variations, New York fit the national trend that evolved since 1945. Its development politics moved on the same general course as in other American cities and for the same reasons.

If the experience of the four postwar decades provides any guide, the city's future development will be shaped by larger forces. Its prosperity depends on the maintenance of Manhattan's dominance in world financial markets and on the continued political and economic attractiveness of U.S. real estate to foreign capital. Under the Reagan administration, federal policy advanced business interests and discouraged political participation by lower income groups. The conserving period thus continued nationally, as it did in New York.

Notes

1. Susan S. Fainstein et al., *Restructuring the City*, 2nd ed. (New York: Longman, 1986), chap. 7.

2. Arthur Simon, *Stuyvesant Town, U.S.A.* (New York: New York University Press, 1970), 22ff.; Robert Moses, *Public Works: A Dangerous Trade* (New York: McGraw-Hill, 1970), 433; and Charles Abrams, *Forbidden Neighbors* (New York: Harper & Row, 1955), 253.

3. Moses, *Public Works*, 485ff.; William Zeckendorf, *Zeckendorf* (New York: Holt, Rinehart, and Winston, 1970), chap. 6; Robert Caro, *The Power Broker: Robert Moses and the Fall of New York* (New York: Knopf, 1974), 771ff.; and Peter Collier and David Horowitz, *The Rockefellers* (New York: Holt, Rinehart and Winston, 1976), 244–47.

4. Title I of the 1949 Housing Act created the urban renewal program, under which the federal government subsidized the taking of land, demolition of structures, and writedown costs by a municipality for resale to a developer.

5. Jean Lowe, *Cities in a Race with Time* (New York: Random House, 1967), 68; see also J. Clarence Davies III, *Neighborhood Groups and Urban Renewal* (New York: Columbia University Press, 1966).

6. Moses, *Public Works*, 438.

7. Elizabeth Roistacher and Emanuel Tobier, "Housing Policy," in *Setting Municipal Priorities, 1983*, ed. Charles Brecher and Raymond Horton (New York: New York University Press, 1982), table 6.1.

8. Roger Starr, "Housing: Projects for New Construction," in *Agenda for a City*, ed. Lyle Fitch and Annemarie Walsh (Beverly Hills: Sage, 1970), 349–75.

9. Jameson Doig, *Metropolitan Transportation Politics and the New York Region* (New York: Columbia University Press, 1966); and Michael Danielson and Jameson Doig, *New York: The Politics of Urban Regional Development* (Berkeley: University of California Press, 1982), 197.

10. Caro, *The Power Broker*, 922.

11. Caro, *The Power Broker*, 930.

12. Danielson and Doig, *New York*, 202.

13. Moses, *Public Works*, 226ff.

14. Danielson and Doig, *New York*, 202–3.

15. Caro, *The Power Broker*, 20.

16. Wallace Sayre and Herbert Kaufman, *Governing New York City* (New York: Norton, 1965), 720–21.

17. Zeckendorf, *Zeckendorf*, 235.

18. Fred J. Cooke and Gene Gleason, "The Shame of New York," *The Nation* 189 (Oct. 31, 1959): 262.

19. Cf. City-Wide Council for Better Housing, *New York's Slum Clearance Committee: A Critical Study* (1957); and Charles Abrams, *The City Is the Frontier* (New York: Harper & Row, 1965).

20. Roger Friedland, *Power and Crisis in the City* (New York: Schocken Books, 1983), table 4.1.

21. Calculated from data in J. Anthony Panuch, *Mayor's Independent Survey on Housing and Urban Renewal, Building a Better New York, Final Report to Mayor Robert F. Wagner*, 1960.

22. Moses, *Public Works*, 454.

23. Davies, *Neighborhood Groups*, 113.

24. New York City, *New York's Renewal Strategy*, (1965), 6–8.
25. Davies, *Neighborhood Groups*, 121.
26. Anthony Jackson, *A Place Called Home: A History of Low Cost Housing in Manhattan* (Cambridge: MIT Press, 1976), 226.
27. Abrams, *Forbidden Neighbors*, 273.
28. Starr, "Housing," 355; see also note b, table 7.4, this essay.
29. John Clapp, "The Formation of Housing Policy in New York City, 1960–1970," *Policy Sciences* 7 (1976): 77–91.
30. Roistacher and Tobier, "Housing Policy," table 6.1.
31. Peter McClelland and Alan Magdowitz, *Crisis in the Making: The Political Economy of New York State Since 1945* (New York: Cambridge University Press, 1981), 156ff.
32. McClelland and Magdowitz, *Crisis in the Making*, table 6.3; and New York State, Division of Housing and Community Renewal, *1980–81 Annual Report to the Legislature on Mitchell-Lama Housing Companies in New York State* (Albany, 1982).
33. Derived from the Real Estate Board of New York, *Office Building Construction Manhattan 1901–1953* (New York, 1952), table 4.
34. See Maynard Robison, "Rebuilding Lower Manhattan; 1955–74" (Ph.D. diss., City University of New York, 1976).
35. Calculated from Robison, "Rebuilding," 37.
36. Quoted in Collier and Horowitz, *The Rockefellers*, 315.
37. Quoted in Robison, "Rebuilding," 37.
38. See Robison, "Rebuilding"; and Abraham Stein, "The Port Authority of New York and New Jersey and the 1962 PATH–World Trade Center Project" (Ph.D. diss., New York University, 1980).
39. New York City, *The Administration of Robert Wagner* (1960, mimeo), 38.
40. Robison, "Rebuilding," 137ff.
41. McClelland and Magdowitz, *Crisis in the Making*, 250.
42. Robison, "Rebuilding," 272ff.
43. Norman I. Fainstein and Susan S. Fainstein, *Urban Political Movements* (Englewood Cliffs, N.J.: Prentice-Hall, 1974), 43–45.
44. See Davies, *Neighborhood Groups*; and Lowe, *Cities in a Race with Time*, 103.
45. Jewel Bellush, "Housing: The Scattered-Site Controversy," in *Race and Politics in New York City*, ed. Jewel Bellush and Stephen David (New York: Praeger, 1971), 98–133; and Mario Cuomo, *Forest Hills Diary* (New York: Random House, 1974).
46. Robert Salisbury, "Urban Politics: The New Convergence of Power," *Journal of Politics* 26 (November 1964): 775–97.
47. Douglas Yates, "The Urban Jigsaw Puzzle: New York Under Lindsay," *New York Affairs* 2 (Winter 1974): 3–19.

48. Martin Shefter, "New York City's Fiscal Crisis: The Politics of Inflation and Retrenchment," *The Public Interest* 48 (Summer 1977): 98–127.

49. Charles Morris, *The Cost of Good Intentions* (New York: Norton, 1980).

50. In 1966 M. Justin Herman, the West Coast version of Moses, headed the powerful San Francisco Redevelopment Agency, and Edward J. Logue played a similar role with the Boston Redevelopment Agency.

51. Eleanor Brilliant, *The Urban Development Corporation* (Lexington, Mass.: Heath, 1975), 16.

52. Brilliant, *The Urban Development Corporation*, 3.

53. Brilliant, *The Urban Development Corporation*, 77.

54. Robison, "Rebuilding," 152.

55. Arthur Reiger, "The Corporate Response to the Urban Crisis: A Study of the New York Urban Coalition" (Ph.D. diss., Cornell University, 1972).

56. Fred Powledge, "New York's Bedford-Stuyvesant: A Rare Urban Success Story," *AIA Journal* 65 (May 1976): 45–59.

57. Clara Fox, "Public Programs for Housing in New York," *City Almanac* 8 (February 1974): 5–6.

58. Peter Roggemann, "Community Organizations and Neighborhood Preservation: Housing Initiatives and Agency Response in New York City" (Ph.D. diss., Rutgers University, 1976).

59. Brilliant, *The Urban Development Corporation*, 79.

60. Frank Kristof, "Housing and People in New York City," *City Almanac* 10 (February 1976): 5.

61. Herbert Meyer, "How Government Helped Ruin the South Bronx," *Fortune* 92 (November 1975): 146.

62. See Roistacher and Tobier, "Housing Policy," 157–58.

63. Clapp, "Formation of Housing Policy," 78.

64. George Sternlieb and James Hughes, *Housing and Economic Reality: New York 1976* (New Brunswick, N.J.: Center for Urban Policy Research, Rutgers University, 1976), 36.

65. Kristof, "Housing and People," 5.

66. Kristof, "Housing and People," 5.

67. Stephen David, "Welfare: The Community Action Program Community," in *Race and Politics in New York City*, ed. Jewel Bellush and Stephen David (New York: Praeger, 1971), 30–40; and David Greenstone and Paul Peterson, *Race and Authority in Urban Politics* (New York: Russell Sage, 1973), 274–75.

68. David, "Welfare," 40–53.

69. See Morris, *The Cost of Good Intentions*, chap. 7; Norman I. Fainstein and Susan S. Fainstein, "From the Folks Who Brought You Ocean Hill–Brownsville," *New York Affairs* 2 (Winter 1974): 105–15; and Barry Gottehrer, *The Mayor's Man* (Garden City, N.Y.: Doubleday, 1975).

70. Morris, *The Cost of Good Intentions*, 169.

71. Norman I. Fainstein and Susan S. Fainstein, "Restoration and Struggle: Urban Policy and Social Forces," in *Urban Policy Under Capitalism* ed. Norman I. Fainstein and Susan S. Fainstein (Beverly Hills: Sage, 1982), 9–20; and Peter Marcuse, "The Targeted Crisis: On the Ideology of the Urban Fiscal Crisis and its Uses," *International Journal of Urban and Regional Research* 5 (September 1981): 330–55.

72. Roger Starr, "Effluents and Successes in Declining Metropolitan Areas," in *Post-Industrial America*, ed. George Sternlieb and James Hughes (New Brunswick, N.J.: Center for Urban Policy Research, Rutgers University, 1975), 262.

73. Shefter, "New York City's Fiscal Crisis," 110.

74. William Tabb, *The Long Default* (New York: Monthly Review Press, 1982); and Maarten de Kadt, Joan Hoffman, and Matthew Edel, "Business's Plans for New York," *Social Policy* 12 (May–June 1981): 7–15.

75. Real Estate Board of New York, *Fact Book*, table 144.

76. Real Estate Board of New York, *Fact Book*, table 154.

77. George Sternlieb, Elizabeth Roistacher, and James Hughes, *Tax Subsidies and Housing Investment* (New Brunswick, N.J.: Center for Urban Policy Research, Rutgers University, 1976), 12; and Sharon Zukin, *Loft Living* (Baltimore: Johns Hopkins University Press, 1982), 13.

78. Real Estate Board, *Fact Book*, table 144.

79. Andrew Parker, "Local Tax Subsidies as a Stimulus for Development," *City Almanac* 16 (February–April 1982), 11.

80. See Peter Marcuse, "Gentrification, Abandonment and Displacement in New York City," PIP 24, Graduate School of Architecture and Planning, Columbia University; Jim Sleeper, "Neighborhood Gentrification," *Dissent* 29 (Spring 1982), 169–75; Emanuel Tobier, "Gentrification: The Manhattan Story," *New York Affairs* 5 (Summer 1979): 13–25; and Zukin, *Loft Living*.

81. Parker, "Local Tax Subsidies," 12.

82. Quoted in Citizens Housing and Planning Council of New York (CHPC), *Progress, Programs and Projects* (January–March 1977, mimeo), 1.

83. New York City, Department of Housing Preservation and Development, *The In Rem Housing Program, Third Annual Report*, 1981, 33.

84. New York City, Department of City Planning, *Eighth Year Community Development Program: Statement of Objectives and Budget*, 1982, 5–9.

85. See Matthew Drennan, "Local Economy and Local Revenues," in *Setting Municipal Priorities, 1983*, ed. Charles Brecher and Raymond Horton (New York: New York University Press, 1982), 15–45.

86. Real Estate Board, *Fact Book*, tables 55, 128, 153, 154.

87. New York City, Office of the Mayor, *The City of New York Financial Plan, Fiscal Years 1981–1985*.

88. Susan S. Fainstein, ed., *The Redevelopment of Forty-Second Street*, special issue of *City Almanac* 18 (Summer 1985).

89. Robert Ponte, "Building Battery Park City," *Urban Design International* 3 (March/April 1982): 27–34.

90. See John Mollenkopf, "Economic Development," in *Setting Municipal Priorities, 1984*, ed. Charles Brecher and Raymond Horton (New York: New York University Press, 1983), 131–57.

91. Sternlieb, Roistacher, and Hughes, *Tax Subsidies*, 90–112; and Real Estate Board, *Fact Book*, table 142–43.

92. Mollenkopf, "Economic Development," 147.

93. Janice Perlman, "New York From the Bottom Up," *New York Affairs* 7 (Winter/Spring 1982): 28.

94. Tom Robbins, "Banking the Unbankable," *City Limits* 8 (March 1983): 12–15.

95. See, for example, Andrea Olstein, "Park Slope: The Warren Street Balancing Act," *New York Affairs* 7 (Winter/Spring 1982): 59–64.

96. Ronald Lawson, "Origins and Evolution of a Social Movement Strategy: The Rent Strike in New York City, 1904–1980," *Urban Affairs Quarterly* 18 (March 1983): 371–95.

97. Susan Baldwin, "Community Board in the Buffer Zone," *City Limits* 12 (June–July 1982): 13–16; David Lebenstein, "A Report Card," *New York Affairs* 6 (Winter 1980): 10–18; and New York State Charter Revision Commission, "A Charter Revision Guide for Community Board Members," 1976.

98. See Baldwin, "Community Board"; and Lebenstein, "Report Card."

99. Carter Wiseman, "Power to the People," *New York* 14 (October 1981): 62–63.

100. Michael Hinds, "For Rent Regulation, A New Beginning," *New York Times*, sec. 8 (March 25, 1984).

101. Alan Oser, "Drafting New Code Poses Thorny Issues," *New York Times*, sec. 8 (March 25, 1984).

102. See Wiseman, "Power to the People."

103. Regina Herzlinger, "Costs, Benefits, and the West Side Highway," *The Public Interest* 55 (Spring 1979): 77–98; and Ann L. Buttenwieser, "Relining New York City's Shore: A Call for a Vision of the Waterfront," *New York Affairs* 8, no. 2 (1984): 117–28.

104. Susan Baldwin, "West Side Renewal Story," *City Limits* 12 (December 1982): 27–29.

105. Hank Perlin, "Feds Step Out of West Side Renewal," *City Limits* (January 1982): 15.

106. Edward Koch, *Mayor* (New York: Simon and Schuster, 1984), 220–21.

107. Arthur Schlesinger, Jr., "I'm the Greatest!" *New York Review of Books* 31 (April 12, 1984): 16.

108. Shefter, "New York City's Fiscal Crisis," 122–23.

109. See William Geist, "The Expanding Empire of Donald Trump," *New York Times Magazine* (April 8, 1984).

110. See Lowe, *Cities in a Race with Time,* chap. 3.

111. See Frederick Wirt, *Power in the City* (Berkeley: University of California Press, 1974); Fainstein et al., *Restructuring the City,* chap. 6.

112. Caro, *The Power Broker,* 792.

113. See Roger Friedland, Frances Piven, and Robert Alford, "Political Conflict, Urban Structure and the Fiscal Crisis," in *Comparing Public Policies,* ed. Douglas Ashford (Beverly Hills: Sage, 1978).

8

White Ethnicity: Ecological Dimensions

William Kornblum / James Beshers

This essay deals with people and cultures at the city's rim. The people we describe live mainly along the shore in the boroughs of Queens, Brooklyn, and Staten Island, but we will focus specifically on communities along Jamaica Bay. The residents of these communities are sometimes lumped together as middle class "white ethnics" since they are predominantly white New Yorkers of Italian, Irish, and Jewish ethnic heritage. But this label assumes more than is actually known about their cultures, their communities, and their class identifications. In this essay, therefore, we will look first at the ecological ordering of white ethnic New Yorkers in one major borough of the city. We will then explore some of the meanings of "white ethnicity," and its dubious value in explaining recent outbreaks of white violence against blacks in the areas we describe. Our emphasis will be on how features of the natural environment and the cultures that different groups bring to that environment interact to sustain "knowable communities" with particular attachments and predictable patterns of intergroup conflict and accommodation.

New York City's edge is an ecological zone, both in human and natural terms. We refer to New York City's ocean and wetland borderlands on the one hand, and the patterns of settlement and commercial uses that have come to be located there on the other. Unlike other suburban edges of the city, the beaches and tidal lagoons of south shore Long Island—which actually begin at Brooklyn's Coney Island—are not the rolling hills of glacial moraine that extend down to the rocky coves and narrow beaches of the sound shores. The south shore habitats of

New York City are broad, marshy lowlands. For much of the city's history these lowlands have been treated as urban wasteland, best suited for dumping garbage and construction fill. As newly created lands, they became convenient terrain for commercial recreation, suburban housing tracts, public housing, harbor forts, and airports.

When historians Peter Buckley and William R. Taylor trace the emergence of popular culture in New York City in the nineteenth and early twentieth centuries, they find evidence of a commercial blending of class tastes and ethnic cultures in cultural institutions like the amusement park, Tin Pan Alley, and the musical stage, where demands for cultural products like comic strips, popular songs, and the musical "brought New Yorkers of different classes together in novel ways."[1] In this essay we also deal with places and institutions that bring New Yorkers together in novel ways, but that togetherness is our problematic. We seek to know how attachments of ethnicity, community, and class help to explain the kinds of intergroup conflicts and local institutions that we find now along the shores of Jamaica Bay and New York's Atlantic beaches.

The American commercial culture that produced Coney Island in the pre–World War II decades was undeniably vibrant, but after midcentury popular culture began more typically to be produced for a national audience, consumed at home and in suburban shopping malls. Commercial culture has become a more segmented marketplace. Many of the urban places that once melded classes and ethnicities have declined and almost disappeared. Entertainment areas like the Broadway theater district remain, but cater primarily to a middle and upper middle class audience. Mass culture continues to sell themes of American pluralism, but its consumers are typically gathered in private, family groups in the rec room or the backyard. Mass events draw huge and diverse audiences, but fans are not expected to create the kind of participatory leisure culture that was typical of life on the boardwalks of Coney Island and Atlantic City in their heydays or in the restaurants and streets of Times Square before World War II.

Towering over the remains of Coney Island stands the gaunt structure of the abandoned Parachute Jump. Steeplechase is defunct; but the Wonder Wheel, the last of the great Ferris wheels, spins along season after season. Today the vast majority of its riders are black and brown, as are the bathers who continue to make Coney Island the most heavily used beach in the United States. And along Surf Avenue, the former sites of bath houses and beer gardens are now housing projects that dominate Coney Island's older ethnic ghettos. Elsewhere along the Brooklyn and Queens shorefront, newer tract communities have become neighborhoods whose residents often feel embattled by the growth of nearby minority communities. The ideal of a communal culture of leisure at the shore has floundered on racial and class obstacles.

"Is not industrialism, by its own momentum," Raymond Williams asks, "producing a culture that is best described as classless?"[2] Williams answers his question in the negative. Cultures, as "whole ways of life," do differ in working class and bourgeois communities. Bourgeois cultures are organized around values that are highly individualistic and consumerist; "that is to say an idea of society as a natural area within which each individual is free to pursue his own development and his own advantage."[3] The core concept of working class culture, by contrast, is socialist in the broadest sense: it regards society as neither neutral nor protective, "but as the positive means for all kinds of development, including individual development. Development and advantage are not individually but communally interpreted."

In the communities described below, the interactions of individualism and communalism are not easily located in one class or another. Rather, they are attributes expressed in cultural forms in different communities, each with a history of ethnic and class settlement and each contributing in particular ways to the overall ethos of the New York shore. The limits of communalism are often territorial; they are evident in conflict over access to natural values and in the persistent and sometimes violent defense of turf. But along this urban strand, once a fantasyland of American cultural pluralism, one still finds some important evidence of communal sharing. It exists around old and new forms of mass recreation and through communal efforts to shape the natural and urban environment to facilitate both the sharing and the defense of space.

Gravesend, Coney Island, Sheepshead Bay, Manhattan Beach, Breezy Point, Plum Beach, Canarsie Pier, Broad Channel, Riis Park, Belle Harbor, the Rockaways—to millions of New Yorkers these are places that evoke the sensations of summer and the pleasures of the city's cooler shores. To Joseph Heller's anxious and assimilating intellectual, Julius Gold, "the smell of the sea at Sheepshead Bay was a powerful call to clams on the half shell, shrimp, lobster or broiled flounder or bass. 'Let's go to Lundy's,' he suggested, 'We'll have a good piece of fish.' " Although the legendary eating arena of the Irish Lundy brothers was defunct even as Gold spoke, others run by Italian, Irish, Greek, and Jewish managers continue to do battle with the burger franchises. Along this strand the volunteer fire and police companies are as likely to be manned by Jews and Italians as by the Irish. In this region within the city a yenta can be of any ethnicity. And who knows anything about the heritage of the parents who shout, "Help, our son the doctor is drowning!"?

In his study of culture and politics in Brooklyn's Canarsie community, Jonathan Rieder presents the best portrait we have of solidarity and cleavage in an embattled, middle class community on New York's outer edge.[4] Rieder shows that Jewish and Italian Canarsians tend to maintain distinct Jewish and Italian subcultures. As neighbors on a block, they may become friendly and share mah jong games, street life, and membership in civic voluntary clubs. They also come together in the political clubs from which the community's leadership develops. But the Italians and Jews are culturally separate as well. Each group has its particular vernacular, personality types, religious institutions, and political styles. Thus Rieder observes that "ethnicity continued to shape Canarsie sensibilities and acquaintanceships. Defying those theorists who direly predict the atomization of American life, countless Americans remain joined to one another by bracing ties of kinship, ethnicity, territory, religion, and status."[5] These differences of affiliation in a community like Canarsie are often bridged by a common fear of racial invasion. The Canarsians Rieder came to know resent deeply the lifeways of some ghetto blacks, who they feel drove them from the Brooklyn neighborhoods of their youth. When they identify themselves as "white middle class ethnic Americans," it is usually because they feel caught between the encroaching pressures of lower class blacks and Hispanics on the one hand and the demands of maintaining a middle class lifestyle on the other. But Rieder also shows that backlash against minorities and their liberal champions becomes a dominant theme only when political leaders seem totally to ignore their own needs. He concludes that "ultimately, whether communities like Canarsie realize their capacities for avarice or for generosity will turn significantly on the acts of the leaders who either court them or mock them."[6] This essay will show, however, that territorial defense can block the creation of a pluralist communal culture. We can understand the origins of white ethnic defensiveness and still show that this reaction bars minorities from their rightful access to the urban commons.

The limits of this pluralism do not begin only with race. That is the most evident barrier and, confounded with class cleavages as it almost always is in our cities, it explains much of the conflict along these shores. But there is also much latent ethnic and class conflict only hinted at by patterns of residential segregation. Reference to case material drawn from field notes on the Gateway National Recreation Area will provide a basis for analyzing these conflicts.[7]

The main, somewhat counterintuitive, finding of the demographic-ecological data we present is that the city's older white ethnic groups maintain patterns of residential segregation even in higher class neighborhoods of second or third settlement.[8] It is increasingly expensive (economically and politically) to maintain the ethnic enclave. It is a luxury not all members of a group can afford or would care to pay for. Meanwhile, the communities of first settlement, closer to the city's factory and warehouse zones, are forever under pressure from newcomers of other nationalities and other races. White ethnic and other nationality groups in the borough of Queens illustrate this pattern.

Residential Segregation: Problems of Measurement

Three major categories in the 1980 U.S. census may expand the study of race and ethnic residential patterns in cities. These categories are defined in Standard Tape File 1, Tables 7 and 8, and Standard Table File 3, Tables 27 and 28. They include six new Asian categories in Table 7, four new Hispanic origin categories in Table 8, and ancestry categories that are presented as single ancestries in Table 27 and as multiple ancestries in Table 28. Both tables can be constructed for census tracts or for block groups (but not for blocks).

Perhaps the most important addition to the census's array of ethnic data is to be found in The Census of Population STF3 Tables 28 and 29, on ancestry. For the first time in its history of ethnic data collection, the Bureau of the Census asked what was in fact an attitude question. Respondents were asked not the "country of origin of their parents," as had previously been the practice for every decennial census since 1880, but what ancestry or ancestries they claimed. The question was phrased in terms of national origin with no reference to parents' place of birth. There is another question on country of origin for foreign-born respondents, which is essential for studying immigrant demographic patterns, but no comparable data exist in the 1980 census on parents' nativity of native-born respondents.

The new "ancestry" item promises to increase the number of self-identified white ethnics in the population, but without the older parents nativity item it is difficult to determine anything about respondent's ethnic generation. And in New York City, or any other place with significant numbers of Jewish residents, ancestry in terms of national origin loses a great deal of meaning. Since religion is never included in the census this has always been a serious problem, but the present array of items makes the situation even worse. With the old item it was somewhat safer to assume that Jewish respondents would give the country of origin of their parents. But now, when faced with a more vague heritage question that does not include "Jewish," it is even less clear what the pattern of Jewish responses would be. In consequence, there remains the decennial problem of inability to separate out those who truly iden-

Table 8.1   Race and Ethnicity in Queens and New York City, 1980

	Queens	NYC	Queens Percent of NYC
Total Population	1,891,805	7,071,639	26.7
White	1,335,805	4,294,075	31.1
Black	354,129	1,784,331	19.8
Asian	93,456	231,504	40.4
Hispanic	262,422	1,406,074	18.7

Source: U.S. Bureau of the Census, 1980.

tify themselves as Polish Americans, for example, from the Jewish Americans who may give Poland as their ancestry but have little in common with actual Polish ethnics. Despite these severe shortcomings, there is as usual a wealth of important comparative data available on ethnicity and small urban areas.

Tables 8.1 to 8.3 merely confirm what most New Yorkers already know about the population of Queens. It is predominantly white with significant minority populations of blacks (primarily in Jamaica), Hispanics (especially in the older apartment house areas of inner Queens and along Roosevelt Avenue), and Asians (in Elmhurst and Flushing and small neighborhoods of first settlement elsewhere). Indeed, al-

Table 8.2   Major White Ethnic Categories in Queens, 1980

Ancestry	Total	Percent of Total Population	Percent of Major White Ethnics
Italian	235,081	12.4	38.0
Irish	106,982	6.0	17.3
German	83,963	4.4	13.6
Polish	59,131	3.1	9.6
Russian	56,715	3.0	9.2
Greek	48,374	2.6	7.8
Hungarian	17,986	1.0	2.9
Ukrainian	9,662	0.6	1.4
Multiple	292,479	15.5	41.9

Source: U.S. Bureau of the Census, STF 3, Table 28.

Table 8.3   Asian Ethnicity in Queens, 1980

Ethnic Group	Total	Percent of Total Population	Percent of Total Asian
Chinese	39,135	2.1	42.0
Indian	21,736	1.2	23.3
Korean	14,486	0.8	15.5
Filipino	11,195	0.6	12.0
Japanese	5,487	0.3	5.9
Vietnamese	1,418	0.1	1.5

Source: U.S. Bureau of the Census, 1980.

though it is not shown in these summary tables, the settlement patterns of Hispanics and Asians in Queens closely mirror those of older white ethnic groups earlier in the century. They tend to settle in small neighborhood clusters, due in part to the effects of "chain migration."

Such first settlements often grow into larger communities (e.g., the diverse Hispanic community centered at Junction Boulevard and Roosevelt Avenue), but rarely concentrate all their members in one contiguous community area. The latter pattern of residential segregation is far more characteristic of Afro-American and West Indian settlement. In their case, voluntary neighborhood formation is usually outweighed in influence by the effects of neighborhood defense tactics and racial exclusion in white ethnic communities.[9]

Tables 8.4 through 8.7 bring us further toward an analysis of white ethnic ecological patterns in the borough. Table 8.4 is a simple measure of residential concentration constructed by ranking each of the major white ethnic groups' census tracts in descending order. The highest 10 percent of that group's tracts are then selected for analysis. There are 674 census tracts in the borough, but only Italians, the largest identifiable white ethnic population, are represented in every tract.

At first glance the figures in Table 8.4 may seem somewhat unusual. In most American cities, Greeks are highly suburbanized and dispersed. Their occupational specialization often requires this dispersion, and the Greek Orthodox churches typically serve as the focal institution in their far-flung community.[10] Italians, on the other hand, are reputed to be the most prone to ethnic self-segregation. They are often described as a people who "make the city livable" by investing heavily in the local neighborhood and defending it vigorously. Jews (represented indirectly

Table 8.4   Percent of White Ethnic Group's Population
Residing in Top 10 Percent of Its Tracts, 1980

Ethnic Group	Population in Top 10 Percent	Total Population	Percent in Top 10 Percent
Italian	65,957	235,081	28
Irish	39,460	106,182	36
German	24,906	85,963	29
Polish	23,133	59,133	39
Russian	32,491	56,715	57
Greek	25,675	48,374	53
Hungarian	7,847	17,986	44
Ukrainian	3,495	9,662	36

Source: U.S. Bureau of the Census, STF 3, Table 28, 1980.

and, with a few important exceptions, by the clustering of Hungarian, Polish, Russian, and even German ancestry groups in these tables) are typically seen as less parochial than Italians and more prone to choose neighborhoods on class and status criteria, while counting on the easy availability of a congenial synagogue.

But these patterns are not confirmed by the figures in Table 8.4. Greeks in Queens are the most concentrated group, followed by Jews. The Italians, Irish, and Germans are the most dispersed. It should be noted, however, that the safest comparisons within this and the other tables are for the Greeks, Irish, and Italians. Observations about the Jews on the basis of the ancestry variables are often interesting but may well be artifacts of the self-selective nature of the ancestry question. It is likely that Jewish residents of Queens who chose to give a foreign ancestry may be recent immigrants (the relatively low numbers bear this out), who would be more expected to live in neighborhoods of first settlement than Jews in general.

The situation with regard to the Greek and Italian comparison seems more clear-cut and is further clarified by the information presented in Table 8.5. Greeks in New York City have a special occupational niche in the Manhattan restaurant industry (although this is by no means their only occupational base), and they are, in this city, a group with relatively high rates of family-based immigration. Their settlement in Astoria is an ideal location for access to Manhattan. Those of Italian ancestry, on the other hand, are so numerous in the borough that they are able to sustain ethnic enclaves at the same time that an increasing proportion of their members live in neighborhoods lacking a definite Italian identity.

Table 8.5 sorts the borough's white ethnic population by census tract and community area. Here we list only those tracts that have two or more ethnic groups represented in above average numbers. Thus the table allows one to note who lives where, with whom (at least for other white groups), and what proportion of the total tract population their combined numbers represent. The numbers reveal some important relationships, but are most comprehensible to one familiar with Queens communities.

In general, it appears that Italians are most nearly the "universal neighbors." They live with the Greeks in Astoria, with the Germans in Linden Hill (a community area in the "Necropolis" section of the Queens-Brooklyn border, in this case hard by the Lutheran Cemetery), with the Irish in Howard Beach, and with the Jews in the most suburban sections of the borough on the Nassau line (Douglaston, Bayside, etc.). The table indicates that Forest Hills and Rego Park remain clearly dominated by Jewish ethnics but, again, the figures tell us little about actual identification or real numbers of Jewish residents there. The Irish are well dispersed in the borough, although not well represented in Jewish neighborhoods. They are no longer a strong presence in the inner-city sections of the borough (with the exception of the old, blue collar community of Maspeth). The Irish presence in the Jamaica Bay area, however, is one of the most instructive highlights that emerge from ecological analysis of these census data. But before turning to a more detailed discussion of the Jamaica Bay communities, consider the issue of ethnic neighborhood homogeneity, as evidenced in the Table 8.5 column that lists the total proportion that the combined white ethnic groups in each row account for.

For the most part, the self-identified white ethnics account for less than 50 percent of the population of the tracts in which they are numerically strong. This raises questions about what constitutes ethnic identity in an urban neighborhood. Reliance on numerical data alone suggests where to look for patterns of ethnic affiliation, but leaves open many questions about the actual character and local cultures of neighborhoods that only actual observation and interviews can answer.

Tables 8.6 and 8.7 indicate the most concentrated ethnic community areas for those of Irish and Italian ancestry. Here the results of white ethnic enclave formation beyond the old inner city of "ethnic villages"

Table 8.5   Queens Tracts with Two or More White Ethnic Groups Present in Above-Average Proportion, 1980

Tract #	Pop.	German	Greek	Hung.	Irish	Polish	Ital.	Russ.	% Loc.
65	7,611		1,497		522		1,145		42 Astoria
69	3,656		588				1,014		44 Astoria
97	3,740		895				1,134		54 Astoria
113	4,763		902		578		564		43 Astoria
117	4,143		1,025				1,165		53 Astoria
131	7,508			179	935				15 Maspeth
309.01	7,104		584				1,490		29 Elmhurst
309.02	7,006		861				1,170		29 Elmhurst
317	5,818		607				1,963		44 Corona
591	4,379	973					1,407		50 Linden Hill
613	4,807	978					1,080		43 Linden Hill
664	8,195				499		2,131	463	38 Broad Channel
697.02	4,502			268		495			17 Rego Park
713.01	11,414	501		426		1,252		1,708	34 Forest Hills
721	5,201					402		734	22 Forest Hills
739	6,186			191		410		887	24 Forest Hills

Tract									
757	8,205			266		579		985	22 Forest Hills
709.02	4,906			168		588		407	24 Forest Hills
809	6,542					493		538	16 Richmond Hill
884	8,087			1,062			3,094		44 Howard Beach
892	9,527						4,085	438	48 Howard Beach
934	7,629		157	1,987		577	524	536	42 Rockaway
997	7,085		257				1,383	482	29 Beachurst
997.02	12,734		383	276		983		1,664	23 Bayside
1,010	11,758					813		1,048	18 Far Rockaway
1,017	6,508					405	1,321	445	33 North Flushing
1,047	6,917	460		151			1,636	445	39 Mitchell Gardens
1,227.01	8,087				587	574		637	22 Richmond Hill
1,291.01	9,072			241		665	766	1,071	30 North Jamaica
1,347	8,693				584		545	931	24 Fresh Meadows
1,367	5,058					475		747	24 Creedmore
1,479	4,099			591		735			32 Douglaston
1,529.01	5,347			164		451		777	26 Douglaston
1,551	11,239				522		1,306	1,220	34 Douglaston
1,621	5,120				735	617	1,055		35 Bellerose

Source: U.S. Bureau of the Census, STF 3, Table 28, 1980.

211

Table 8.6   Location and Proportional Representation of Italians
in First Ten Most Italian Tracts, Queens, 1980

Tract #	Location	Total	Italian	Other White Ethnics	Other
892	Howard Beach	9527	4085	1578	183
884	Howard Beach	8087	3094	3384	183
62	South Ozone Park	11254	2304	5385	297
58	South Ozone Park	4645	2238	774	184
664	Rosedale	8195	2131	1433	780
54	South Ozone Park	4111	1980	1898	162
317	Corona	5818	1963	1467	598
1039	Whitestone	5744	1923	1355	633
1047	Whitestone	6916	1636	1997	981
44.01	South Ozone Park	2532	1600	400	129

may be clearly seen. With the exception of Maspeth and Sunnyside for the Irish and Corona for the Italians, these "most" Irish and Italian areas are single home neighborhoods located in the borough's most desirable sections. In the main, these are relatively affluent, highly familistic neighborhoods which have only low ethnic identity outside the groups

Table 8.7   Location and Representation of Irish
in First Ten Most Irish Census Tracts, Queens, 1980

Tract #	Location	Total	Irish	Other White Ethnics	Other
934	Rockaway	7629	1987	2163	457
916.01	Breezy Point	3618	1310	619	60
938	Rockaway	4607	1221	1204	446
884	Howard Beach	8087	1062	3839	183
283	Jackson Heights	6443	949	1440	2220
181	Maspeth	7508	935	1499	2982
253	Maspeth	6423	934	988	2639
928	Belle Harbor	3691	906	977	287
185	Maspeth	6697	894	1288	2457
295	Sunnyside	3588	860	647	67

Source: U.S. Census, STF 3, Table 28, NYC.

themselves. These are not the stereotypical ethnic villages whose restaurants and shops specialize in the commercialization of ethnicity for suburban ethnics and cultural outsiders.

Settled largely after World War II, these communities were, and still are, good examples of the American Dream realized for first and second and even later generations of ethnic New Yorkers. They are residential neighborhoods of single family homes with backyards, neighborhood schools, and churches and synagogues nearby. From door to door, the neighbors will very likely differ in white ethnic heritage, and from block to block there will also be some important differences in socioeconomic standing. Yet despite the large numbers of Irish and Italian residents, there are neighbors of other ethnicities and religions as well.

The dominant groups do make their presence visible in the local commercial districts with a few specialty shops and an ethnic association or two. Each has a share of the annual calendar of community events. So ethnicity is shared (to varying degrees, but always in some part); public feasts and festivals mark the communal sharing of ethnic experience. Although there can also be fierce ethnic rivalries among the adolescents under some local conditions, the schools and churches tend to bring them together, as does their fear and hostility toward nearby racial minorities.

Does it come down then to sharing a "white ethnic" lifestyle, an expensive and often insecure amalgam of working class, ethnic, and middle class American cultural ways, lived out on the edge of the city, as far away from the status-contaminating threat of minority people as possible? Can most of the people in these communities be lumped together as "white ethnics"? Their quest for social mobility, waged in large part through the agencies of their ethnic and family affiliations, brought them (and they are among the fortunate) to these suburban neighborhoods they share. But have they now merged their identities?

It may make some sense when selling beer or automobiles or national candidates to assume that there is a white ethnic culture and consciousness, but there is only spotty social scientific evidence to support that assumption. Aside from the numbers we have in these tables, not much is known about intermarriage, or the actual distribution of ethnic solidarities, or the cultural mobility of children, or much else that one would need to know to gain a whole picture of the changing nature of ethnic consciousness and ethnic social structures in the white neighborhoods of second settlement. Thus even a necessarily brief description of some patterns of community formation and conflict around Jamaica Bay fills in a few of the gaps.

Class and Ethnicity at the Shore:
Jamaica Bay and the Rockaways

Tables 8.6 and 8.7 group quite different types of places as Italian and Irish enclaves. There is, for example, a world of difference between Whitestone and Howard Beach, even though both have high concentrations of Italian Americans. Although both communities are at the water's edge—Whitestone on the Long Island Sound near the Whitestone Bridge, and Howard Beach below the Belt Parkway along Jamaica Bay—Whitestone is older and its houses are set rather far apart. Howard Beach was built largely after World War II. Its houses are closer, some are clustered around canals that lead into the bay, and all are located directly under one of the most heavily used flight paths to nearby Kennedy Airport. On the west, Howard Beach is bordered by the city's second largest garbage dump site. In this beleaguered community, the SST roars over breakfast, and flights of gulls from the nearby dumps can darken the afternoon sky. With all these environmental problems bearing down on them, it is not surprising that the residents of Howard Beach are usually embroiled in bitter controversies with city agencies of every description.

In these controversies, ethnicity and class issues are far less important than struggles within the community to preserve or to enhance property values and values that contribute to perceived quality of life. Ethnic and class affiliations are usually experienced within family and peer networks, rather than in the public life of the entire community. Each of the white ethnic communities along Jamaica Bay has churches and synagogues and organized social groups which maintain traditional ethnic cultures to varying degrees—depending, for example, on whether the Jewish congregation is Orthodox, Conservative, or Reform, or on how ethnically homogeneous a given Roman Catholic congregation is at particular Masses—but none of them is as heavily dominated by a single ethnic group. Thus the broader community institutions represent a plurality of cultural backgrounds. Belle Harbor, for example, an affluent community East of Riis Park on the Rockaways, is regarded as a Jewish enclave and indeed boasts the full range of Jewish subcultures, but Table 8.7 shows that it is also home to a significant Irish-American population.

It is no coincidence that most neighborhoods (as roughly indicated by census tracts) that house high proportions of the borough's Irish and Italian Americans also include high proportions of Jewish residents, and that many of these neighborhoods line Jamaica Bay. The estuarine extension of Queens County is in every way one of the most sociologically

rich areas of the metropolitan region. Aside from the immense importance of JFK International Airport and the recreational industry centered
on the bays and beaches, here the county joins a human ecological zone
that extends from Atlantic City to Montauk Point. This urbanized, barrier island ecological zone is populated largely by New York-born people
of Irish, Italian, and Jewish ancestry, with enclaves of upper class Protestants, and black or Latino communities inserted here and there as a
result of local settlement histories.[11] Census data can identify these
ecological patterns, but many questions remain about how actual subcultures and styles of political expression develop in such places.

Class, Ethnicity, and Community Cultures

The cultures of the white communities that border Jamaica Bay (and this
is equally true of Sheepshead Bay and Gravesend Bay) are expressed
through an amalgam of ethnic and class solidarities. Despite the overwhelming middle class status and identity of communities like Howard
Beach, Breezy Point, Belle Harbor, Neponsit, South Ozone Park, and
Canarsie, there is an older pattern of blue collar community formation
that continues to exert important influences over the entire Jamaica Bay
region. These blue collar neighborhoods are the remnants of baymen's
quarters and shanty neighborhoods at the water's edge. They maintain a
unique subculture which motivates the strongest patterns of territorial
defense to be found in the region.

The outstanding example of this older, blue collar community of baymen and construction workers who are baymen in their leisure time is
the community of Broad Channel, located on Broad Channel Island in
the center of Jamaica Bay. Here about 7,000 permanent residents live in
homes typically built on tidal wetlands rented from the City of New
York. Originally settled in the late nineteenth century as a shanty neighborhood of fishermen, baymen, and poachers, this largely Irish working
class enclave is actually only the largest and most visible of a number of
similar shanty and bungalow settlements that line the shores of Jamaica
Bay. Such shanty neighborhoods predate the larger, more affluent tract
developments and housing projects built after World War II. In Howard
Beach, the Rockaways, and on the tidal creeks surrounding Kennedy
Airport are smaller versions of the Broad Channel community. These
little-known refuges of the urban working class are small but highly
symbolic communities that represent a more widely shared dream of the
workers' escape into nature. In the following passage from field notes, a
locally famous striped bass poacher from Broad Channel describes the

way local issues of development and demographic invasion are perceived in these blue collar refuges:

> Up to the fifties there were hundreds more shacks all over the bay islands.
> And not only here in Jamaica Bay. You had them all along Reynolds
> Channel [in Nassau County] and into Great South Bay all the way out to
> the Hamptons. Most of 'em were pulled down when these areas began to
> get settled after the war, but we're still hanging in here as long as we can.
> This bay used to be one of the finest fishing spots on the East Coast, and
> there's still a lot of good fish to be had all over this outer harbor if you
> know where and when to find 'em. When the Kennedy runway was built
> into the Ruffle Bar, that screwed up the whole tidal action of the Bay. This
> back half where we are got totally polluted. That doesn't ruin the fish, but
> it can sure stink up the place sometimes, especially after a heavy rainfall
> when you get all the excess sewer runoff. There's also a place we call "the
> boil" just East of the Cross Bay Bridge where all the sludge and runway
> pollution from Kennedy is pumped into the bay and you see it boiling up
> sometimes, usually at night.

What this respondent did not mention is that every time a major development project is proposed for Jamaica Bay and its shores, from expanding Kennedy Airport to new apartment housing construction or expanded recreational facilities, there is usually an opposing coalition of neighbors that brings the blue collar residents of the old shanty neighborhoods together with the residents of the more middle class communities surrounding them. These coalitions may be labeled in the press as "white ethnic," but neither ethnicity nor race has much to do with what brings Jamaica Bay people together across the social distances of status and territory. The defense of environmental quality, or efforts to force governmental agencies to improve their region or to prevent new populations from being brought into it, typically cause these coalitions to form. These are well demonstrated in the responses of people in the Jamaica Bay communities to the creation of Gateway National Recreation Area in the period from 1972 to the present.

Gateway and the Politics of a Natural Area

In 1972, Congress passed legislation creating two experimental "urban national parks." One was Golden Gate National Recreation Area in San Francisco; the other, Gateway, includes all the beaches and waters of Jamaica Bay south of the Belt Parkway as well as Floyd Bennett Field at the bottom of Flatbush Avenue. Gateway's properties also include the beaches of Breezy Point on the Rockaways, including Jacob Riis Beach, the old Robert Moses era beach park, the beaches of Staten Island from the Narrows to Great Kills, and Sandy Hook in New Jersey.

Gateway legislation was promoted by a broadly based coalition of leaders from the Jamaica Bay communities and their congressional representatives, including the late William F. Ryan and former Congresswoman Elizabeth Holtzman. Strong support for this controversial proposal also came from the Regional Plan Association and allied silk stocking groups recruited by the Parks Council, the *New York Times*, the professional planning associations, environmental organizations, and regional foundations. The proposed urban national park was controversial not because of local or regional opposition, but because the U.S. Department of Interior and the National Academy of Sciences opposed the legislation. The former feared what urban parks would do to its annual operating budget, while the latter argued that federal control over Jamaica Bay would present "formidable difficulties of transporting large numbers of inner-city residents to the most remote oceanfront regions of the metropolitan area." A better solution to the preservation of Jamaica Bay and the development of its recreational potential would be, the Academy argued, "direct federal aid to New York City for expansion of its own park facilities in Jamaica Bay."[12] But this was an extremely weak argument; anyone familiar with park issues in the metropolitan region knew that no new park lands had been added to existing acreage for almost a generation, and there was extremely little hope that a financially strapped city parks administration could get the funds necessary to preserve Jamaica Bay or the beaches of the Breezy Point peninsula on the Rockaways. The promise that Gateway would bring national park-quality recreation facilities to the people of inner-city New York won support from liberal, professional planning constituencies in Manhattan, but such appeals won few supporters around Jamaica Bay. They supported Gateway because it would preserve and restore the marshes and fishing grounds and beaches.

Some communities around the bay had a particular interest in promoting the legislation. The Cooperative Community of Breezy Point at the tip of the Rockaways would, if the legislation was passed, be forever saved from invasion by high rise beachfront development, and the beach in front of this largely Irish, middle and upper middle class community would be sold to the federal government for far more money than the community had originally paid for all the land on which their converted summer homes now rested. And the community's residents would probably get most use out of the beach, if they could maintain their influence in later phases of the actual park planning. At the other end of the Rockaway beaches proposed for inclusion in the federal park, on the east side of Riis Beach, the largely Jewish residents of affluent Neponsit would find their property interests protected by a federal presence that would vastly improve the decaying Riis Park and upgrade the quality of Jamaica Bay. Even in Broad Channel there was hope that passage of the federal legislation would finally present residents with the opportunity to purchase their land from the city. With luck they could become owners rather than squatters; this ultimately came to pass.

In consequence of these and similar community interests around Jamaica Bay, a unique coalition emerged. Composed of upper class regional and environmentalist interest groups and far more parochial and defensive Jamaica Bay community groups, this coalition acted effectively to win congressional approval of Gateway legislation. But the coalition dissolved in 1973, as soon as the legislation was passed and actual park planning began. The regional elites who saw Gateway as their victory made no secret of the fact that they hoped to see a major recreational development on the scale of Jones Beach located at the vacant navy airfield, Floyd Bennett Field. They similarly took every opportunity to remind people at planning meetings that Congress intended additional thousands of inner-city people to share the beaches of Breezy Point, the wetlands of Jamaica Bay, and the planned facilities of Floyd Bennett Field. This argument did not sit at all well either in exclusive Breezy Point and Neponsit or in Broad Channel, Canarsie, and Howard Beach. There was no federal commitment for funding new transportation routes to Gateway, nor was there support in the Jamaica Bay communities for large-scale recreational development at Floyd Bennett Field or on Breezy Point.

Only the heroic efforts of the Gateway Advisory Commission, under the leadership of Marion Haiskell, and of local Park Service managers held the warring local and regional factions apart long enough to arrive at actual park plans that represented compromises acceptable to both sides. But in the process, most of the grandiose plans for a Gateway on the scale of a Robert Moses park were scrapped entirely.

After twelve years of efforts to develop even the scaled-down plans for Gateway, regional elites could claim only one victory, the extension of two city bus lines from Brooklyn to Riis Park. For residents of the Jamaica Bay communities, on the other hand, the designation of the bay and its beaches as a National Recreation Area preserved their ways of life around the bay from further urban development. They would not have to accommodate new thousands of inner-city, minority park visitors to these areas. Local resistance to park development was motivated by the fear of added congestion on the Belt Parkway and Flatbush Avenue. But an even more frightening prospect was the idea of sharing the bay and ocean beaches with even greater numbers of blacks and Hispanics than already found their way to Riis Park and the Rockaways.

Race and Neighborhood Defense

In the summer of 1983 a group of black children from a Brooklyn day care center was playing on Miller Field, a Gateway sports area on the Staten Island coast. Suddenly, they were attacked by a gang of white adolescents and young adults from the New Dorp community. This incident was the subject of a few articles in the *Times* and a strong editorial condemning racism and racial violence. But no one mentioned then or later that this had been only one in a series of incidents of violence directed against blacks and Hispanics in the communities along New York's outer shores. In March 1982, a black subway motorman was beaten to death in Gravesend by a gang of white youths, three of whom were eventually sentenced for second degree manslaughter, a charge that carries a five-to-fifteen-year sentence. And in 1978 a gang of white youths had immolated a black subway clerk in a token booth in Broad Channel. The clerk had argued with the adolescents the day before. For revenge they poured gasoline in her booth and lighted it.

In no other region of New York City do local residents direct as much violence against racial minorities, a point underscored by the Howard Beach attack and the subsequent trials in 1987 and 1988. Racial hatred is never far from the surface in these shore communities; expressions of it can easily be brought forth in casual conversation. But is this virulent racism, then, a defining feature of "white ethnicity"? The mass media often link the term "white ethnic" with antiminority attitudes, and the evidence from the shore communities of New York would seem to link racism and neighborhood defense to expressions of white ethnicity. But there is nothing particularly ethnic about this violence. It is motivated by racial fears and the desire to defend territory; the cultural meanings of ethnicity appear to have little to do with it.

In summary, where racial violence occurs in cities in the United States it is often attributed to the fears and animosities of "white ethnics," and at first glance the evidence presented in this essay might seem to bear out that perception. Yet we could cite many examples from Northern and Southern cities in which the violent defense of territories occurs in white neighborhoods with no clear ethnic identity. What we attempted to demonstrate in this essay is the conflict due to efforts by white middle class and working class people to maintain the quality of life in their neighborhoods against the desire of inner-city populations and regional elites to make these areas accessible to minority people. This conflict appears to be especially rancorous in New York's shore communities because of their particular local histories. Many were settled as uncontrolled, squatter enclaves where blue collar people fought to maintain a foothold on the beach or marsh, and from there to enjoy life in a natural environment even as they worked in the industrial institutions of the city. Other enclaves were settled more recently by upwardly mobile people of Jewish, Italian, and Irish descent. But because all these settlements were continually subject to harsh environmental pressures, and to the demand that their natural values be shared with a larger public, their residents also tend to support highly vocal and, at times, violent defense of neighborhood territory.

The demographic and ecological analysis presented in the essay points to a clear pattern of ethnic residential segregation in these shore communities. Although this segregation pattern is by no means unique to the New York south shore, we found that there was a disproportionate concentration of middle class ethnic neighborhoods in the Jamaica Bay area. Further analysis along the same lines would show analogous areas elsewhere along the city's coast (e.g., Staten Island). But the south shores of Brooklyn and Queens have a particular history as land reclamation areas, which made them prime areas for new housing development after World War II. Because they had also been the site of fabled popular amusement areas like Coney Island and Brighton Beach, they first attracted the attention of the populations that would later transform them into residential neighborhoods. But that transformation seems to have created special barriers against the sharing of area beaches and waters with minority people. And it is this history of settlement and exclusion that makes the more universalistic efforts of agencies like the National Park Service all the more difficult and critical to the eventual development of a larger leisure culture at the city's shore.

Notes

1. See William Taylor's essay in this volume.
2. Raymond Williams, *Problems in Materialism and Culture* (London: Verso, 1984), 25.
3. Williams, *Materialism and Culture*, 25.
4. Jonathan Rieder, *Canarsie: The Jews and Italians of Brooklyn Against Liberalism* (Cambridge: Harvard University Press, 1985).

5. Rieder, *Canarsie*, 34.

6. Rieder, *Canarsie*, 263.

7. From 1973 to 1978 Kornblum was a principal planner for the National Park Service on the Gateway National Recreation project and other major federal recreation projects in the North Atlantic region.

8. The first, or immigrant, generation of Italian, Irish, and Jewish settlement in New York was typically located in Manhattan or in any of a number of industrial communities along the East River in Queens or in Brooklyn. Areas of second settlement were typically located in central Brooklyn, Queens, or the Bronx. The residents of the communities in lower Brooklyn and Queens described in this essay are most often of second, third, or now even fourth generation ethnicity.

9. Gerald Suttles, *The Social Construction of Communities* (Chicago: University of Chicago Press, 1972).

10. Gerald Suttles, *The Social Order of the Slum* (Chicago: University of Chicago Press, 1968).

11. William Kornblum, "Ethnicity at the Beach," *Ethnic Groups: An International Periodical of Ethnic Studies* 4, no. 2 (1982).

12. National Academy of Sciences, *Jamaica Bay and Kennedy Airport*, vol. 1 (1971), 13.

9

The Postindustrial Transformation of the Political Order in New York City

John Hull Mollenkopf

New York City's economy and society have undergone a profound and often painful transformation since the mid-1950s. At the end of World War II, New York was clearly a white, ethnic, blue collar, industrial city, despite the importance of its office sector. Today, high level business service activities drive the city's economy and its industrial base suffers from seemingly endless decline. The white, blue collar working class has aged and greatly diminished in size. Those of its children who remain in the city hold positions in the higher occupational ranks of the stronger economic sectors, particularly the business professions.

Within the declining goods-related sectors, minority groups, particularly Hispanics, have rapidly succeeded whites; more important, a whole new minority service working class has developed. The "new immigration" has had a major impact on the city. In short, New York City is a premier example of the postindustrial transformation that has reorganized U.S. cities since World War II.

The severe cyclical economic downturn and fiscal crisis of the mid-1970s accelerated and crystallized these secular trends. By 1986, it was obvious that the city had experienced a qualitative and not simply quantitative change since such recent and relatively calm times as the late 1950s. Economic and social restructuring had produced new, not yet fully incorporated social groups, as well as new kinds of actors in and demands on city politics. They in turn have posed a profound and unresolved challenge to the political order in New York City.

On an everyday level, the postindustrial transformation has undermined old constituencies, created new ones, and tested the operating principles of the political arena. Yet earlier political traditions and institutional patterns persist; the new forces have yet to play out their full potential impact on the political order. While it is too early to know with certainty what that impact will be, we can begin to analyze its dimensions. This essay is an initial and tentative effort to chart the contours and fault lines of New York City's emerging postindustrial political order. It concentrates on the post-1969 period, and particularly on the post-1977 recovery. Since many other studies have described such generic post–World War II trends as suburbanization, minority influx, and ghetto expansion, and the interplay between urban decay and the growth of the central business district, they will largely be assumed.[1] Other crucial issues, such as whether sectoral shifts in the economy have displaced some groups to the advantage of others, need much more research and can be described only tentatively. Finally, since political prognostication is treacherous, the following thoughts should be considered a memorandum of needed research, not a finished argument.

For the last two decades in which the postindustrial transformation has crystallized, this essay will seek to answer the following questions:

1. How has the postindustrial transformation reorganized the social and economic terrain on which New York's political order rests?
2. What tensions have thus been generated, and how has New York's political order mediated or reacted to them?
3. In particular, what are the social roots of the current dominant coalition in New York City government?
4. What are the prospects for a return of the "reform cycle" that produced a challenge to that dominant coalition?

To anticipate the conclusion, it will be argued that the postindustrial transformation has created an enormous underlying tension between a potential new majority of underrepresented postindustrial constituencies and the group interests currently represented within the political order and particularly within the prevailing dominant coalition. In essence, the political order stratifies political participation. In the past, reform coalitions have succeeded in reorganizing New York City politics to include previously underrepresented groups and interests. Today, serious obstacles retard the possibility of such a reform thrust.

The Forces of Postindustrial Transformation

The economic and social aspects of the postindustrial transformation must be distinguished when analyzing how large cities have arrived at their current condition. Large cities are economically open and strongly shaped by market forces that they cannot control, but which large cities have historically initiated. In general, they are also socially open and cannot control who enters or leaves their boundaries. Like it or not, they compete with one another for investment and markets, on the one hand, and with residents and workers on the other.

It would be a mistake to conclude, however, that outside forces totally shape cities. For one thing, the cities that invent and propagate new economic forms have a decided competitive advantage. As Lewis Mumford has observed, by concentrating and intensifying productive forces, big cities play a key role in reorganizing the system as a whole.[2] New York certainly benefits from having been the first and largest U.S. financial market and business decision-making center, which in turn affords leverage to its political institutions. Second, market forces often arouse the city's citizens, creating conflict between the community and the marketplace. Although city residents must bow to market forces in the long run, they still make vigorous and sometimes successful efforts to control the parameters within which market forces operate in the short run. Political institutions thus navigate a sea of contradictions and tensions.[3]

Economic Forces

The postindustrial revolution may be defined as the displacement of the production of goods by the production of managerial, social, and personal services as the dominant function of an urban or even a national economy. By this measure, New York City has been gradually postindustrializing since about 1919, when the absolute and relative concentration of its manufacturing activities peaked. Since that time, the garment industry and the other consumer nondurable manufacturing sectors that provided the greatest number of jobs have first deconcentrated relatively and then declined absolutely.

Table 9.1 shows that the traditional goods production and distribution activities of New York's economy have sunk to fractions of their former numbers. Apparel, with one-tenth of the city's jobs in 1950, was cut by two-thirds. Manufacturing fell almost as much. The table also shows that the 1969–1976 recessions accelerated trends that had been

Table 9.1 Nonagricultural Employment in New York City Annual
Averages, 1950–1985 (*in thousands*)

Industry	1950	Column Percent	1970	1977	1980	1986	Column Percent
TOTAL	3,469	100.0	3,745	3,188	3,302	3,549	100.0
Construction	123	3.5	110	64	77	114	3.2
Manufacturing	1,040	30.0	766	539	496	396	11.2
Nondurable	810	23.3	525	376	351	288	8.1
Apparel	341	9.8	204	153	140	108	3.0
Printing and publishing	119	3.4	121	90	94	91	2.6
Durable	230	6.6	241	163	145	108	3.0
Transportation	232	6.7	203	157	150	127	3.6
Communications	66	1.9	95	76	82	79	2.2
Utilities	34	1.0	26	26	25	24	0.7
Wholesale trade	322	9.3	302	248	246	246	6.9
Retail trade	433	12.5	434	372	368	402	11.3
Finance, Insurance, Real Estate	336	9.7	460	414	448	519	14.6
Services	507	14.6	785	783	894	1,076	30.3
Government	374	10.8	563	508	516	569	16.0

Source: New York State Department of Labor. 1950 T,C,U, and wholesale and retail employment figures estimated. 1986 Communications figure adjusted for comparability.

evident for quite some time. Only twice in more than two decades has annual employment in manufacturing risen. Goods wholesaling and movement declined steadily along with goods production. The waterfront life depicted in the 1954 film *On the Waterfront* is practically gone. One recent study shows that all goods-related employment has fallen from 35.4 percent of the total in 1969 to 21.8 percent in 1985, while personal services, information, and financial now make up almost 80 percent.[4]

Table 9.1 also shows that the market and service functions that first developed in New York's mercantile period now dominate its economy. In contrast to manufacturing, which has fallen from one-third to only one-ninth of the city's employment base over three decades, financial activities have risen from 9.7 percent to 14.6 percent of the total, other private services from 14.6 percent to 30.3 percent, and government from 10.8 percent to 16.0 percent. Together, these three service sectors accounted for almost two-thirds of the city's employment in 1986.

One major thrust behind these trends has been the importance of what Matthew Drennan and his colleagues have called the "corporate headquarters complex."[5] This grouping includes the "chief administrative office and allied," or headquarters, employment of industrial corporations, corporate services like management consulting, and ancillary services like hotels and restaurants. Within this complex, however, divergent trends may be discerned. Both the number of industrial corporations headquartered in New York and the number of people working in them have declined significantly in the last two decades; twelve Fortune 500 industrial firms left between 1976 and 1981 alone, reducing the number of those remaining to seventy-two. However, the number of headquarters of the largest banks, life insurance firms, and diversified financial firms has held steady, while banking and securities employment has burgeoned. The advanced corporate services have also grown rapidly, suggesting that their role is far more important than that of merely serving the industrial corporations headquartered in the city. Indeed, New York City is not only far and away the most important financial center in the country, it is also the premier location of the largest, most specialized, and most international corporate service firms.[6]

The main dimensions of service sector growth can be seen in Table 9.2, which recategorizes the standard presentation of sectors to make clear the relative contribution of the different kinds of services. It shows that the advanced corporate services (law, management consulting, and accounting) and banking have grown rapidly, adding well over half of the gross gains in employment. But Table 9.2 also shows that other services are important. New York has a nationally dominant concentration of book, newspaper, and magazine publishing firms, advertising agencies, television network and news division headquarters, filmmaking activities, and communications firms, from AT&T on down. Some of these activities are strongly linked with the fashion industry and such merchandising powerhouses as Macy's. (New York was, after all, the place where A. T. Stewart invented the department store.) Thus by propagating the culture of consumption, the mass media take their place alongside the capital market and advanced corporate services.

Entertainment, high and low culture, and tourism also burnish the aesthetic dimension of advanced capitalist urbanization in New York. Its rich supply of eating and drinking establishments, hotels, movie theaters, and other amusements serve resident corporate employees and visitors alike. Because many new immigrants to New York are willing or compelled to work in the restaurant industry at low wages, they in effect subsidize the corporate sector, or at any rate give it an alternative to fast food franchises.[7] Substantially more people hold officially counted jobs

Table 9.2 Nonagricultural Employment Trends for Rising Sectors in New York City, 1969, 1977, 1986 (in thousands)

Sector	1969	1977	1986	Percent 1977–1986 Annual	Percent of Services Gain
TOTAL	3,798	3,188	3,549	0.77	n.a.
Goods Production and Distribution	1,541	1,123	1,033	−0.89	n.a.
Financial Services	466	414	519	2.82	16.7
Banking	97	118	171		
Securities	99	70	137		
Corporate Services	183	228	470	11.79	38.5
Legal services	28	39	64		
Management consulting and PR	35	22	33		
Accounting	23	21	28		
Engineering and Architecture	21	16	21		
Protective services	15	20	30		
Business services	21	22	35		
Communications/Media	249	212	268	2.94	8.9
Communications	86	76	68		
Advertising	39	32	42		
Publishing	70	52	56		
Entertainment, Culture, and Tourism	185	162	201	2.67	6.2
Restaurants, bars	123	106	128		
Hotels	34	24	31		
Legitimate theater	10	14	22		
Museums	4[a]	5	7		
Education and Research	158	206	250	2.37	7.3
Elementary and Secondary	151	142	140		
Colleges	—	44	46		
Health and Social Services	198	240	343	4.77	16.4
Hospitals	104	119	129		
Other health services	47	66	101		
Social services	47[a]	55	113		
Government (Noneducational)	398	377	415	1.12	6.0
Local	254	242	285		
State	38	51	53		
Federal	106	84	77		

Source: New York State Department of Labor.

[a] Estimate.

in food service than work in the garment industry. The importance of high culture for New York goes far beyond the employment numbers indicated in Table 9.2. The legitimate theater, the museums, and the art industry are symbiotic with the communications and fashion industries and invigorate the city's powers of cultural attraction and projection. In a city whose managers and professionals and business visitors can be cosmopolitan to the point of rootlessness, these cultural amenities provide a grounding.

Table 9.2 reveals two other key pillars of the postindustrial transformation: government and private, nonprofit social services. Public sector services have experienced the roller coaster of retrenchment and recovery since 1969. From a high of 149,400 workers in 1969, for example, public elementary and secondary education fell to 124,000 in 1977, but recovered to 155,000, mostly after 1983. Government noneducational employment also fell in the mid-1970s crisis, but it too has now recovered all its lost ground, mostly in the last several years. Public services account for one of every six jobs in the city's economy. Meanwhile, the health and nonprofit social service sector grew more rapidly than any other sector except corporate services, adding one-sixth of all the gross jobs gained since the mid-1970s low point. New York's twenty-two major medical centers constitute a major export industry, training one-tenth of the nation's interns and residents. As we shall see, government and the health and social service sectors have been an important source of employment for native and immigrant black residents of New York and for other minorities.

In examining the trends enumerated in Tables 9.1 and 9.2, the importance of the mid-1970s economic and fiscal crisis cannot be overstated. The recessions of the early 1970s had a major impact on employment patterns, costing New York one-sixth of its employment, capacity to add value, and earnings. Thousands of the small firms that had characterized both nondurable and durable manufacturing were wiped out. Only subsectors with strong links to upscale markets (designer gowns, jewelry, furs) or advanced services (printing of corporate reports or stock prospectuses) could survive.

In the subsequent recovery, business services and finance clearly dominated New York's economic development. The widespread conversion of loft manufacturing space to offices and luxury residences clearly indicates their market power in the intersectoral competition for space. Their growth over the last decade has been astonishing. Even the securities industry, where employment declined because of automation as well as the bear market during the late 1960s and early 1970s, has tumbled over itself to serve the post-1977 expansion, with an average employment growth of 11 percent per year.

The economic crisis of the mid-1970s also profoundly influenced the public sector. In the volumes of the *Setting Municipal Priorities* project, Charles Brecher and Raymond Horton have given an overview of the impacts as of the early 1980s: taxes were reduced as a percentage of personal income, public spending declined in real terms, employment was pared by as much as 25 percent even in core services like police and fire, and redistributive spending was held down while public investment in economic expansion was stressed.[8] If the fiscal crisis was an implicit veto cast by capital investors against the public spending patterns of the late 1960s, then it succeeded, at least until the last few years. The crisis of the mid-1970s closed out an old era and set the stage for a new one in politics as well as economics.

At one time, it was fashionable to argue that New York City had been reduced to a social services "sandbox" or an "Indian reservation." Tables 9.1 and 9.2 show instead that New York City's economy retains powerful competitive advantages. It is the leading national money market, and one of three that dominate internationally. A large portion of its large corporate headquarters has departed for the suburbs, but New York retains twice as many as the next largest center, Chicago. The remaining companies tend to be larger and more successful than those that have left, and departing firms in the metropolitan area still consume its corporate services. Commercial banking, investment banking, corporate law, management consulting, accounting, advertising, communications, architecture, and construction all interlock with and reinforce one another. New York is the main base for the international aspects of these activities, providing a key link between the United States and the rest of the world, particularly Europe. It is extremely well equipped with the communications and transportation infrastructure that international operations require. Finally, its rich supply of cultural and consumption amenities reinforces these other advantages. New York City may have lost relative ground as other large cities develop similar strengths, but its primacy has not been threatened.

Social Forces

Social and demographic changes have paralleled and intersected this economic transformation. The decline of manufacturing, the rise of services, and changes in the organization of work within the service industries have had an enormous impact on the occupational structure of the city's labor market. Simultaneously, large demographic changes have reshaped the population inside and outside the labor force. The meeting of these two forces has reorganized the mosaic of ethnic specialization in occupations and industries.

This confluence has powerfully altered New York City's social terrain. For example, the white, ethnic, blue collar working class has been greatly reduced. An analysis of the 1980 microdata sample of the census reveals that less than one-third of all white, male, native New Yorkers of Anglo-Saxon, Irish, or Russian (Jewish) ancestry identified themselves as craftworkers or operatives, and the figure was only slightly higher for Italian Americans. The percentage for women from these backgrounds was minuscule. Thus one-sixth of all white New Yorkers could be classed as traditional workers. As the white ethnic working class has aged and decreased in size, its children have entered managerial and professional occupations. Minorities, particularly Hispanics, have replaced retreating whites within the shrinking manufacturing labor force. Even more important, a whole new white collar, largely female, working class has been created in the service sectors. White women make up about half of this labor force and tend to hold the better jobs; black and, to a lesser extent, other minority women make up a quarter of this new service sector proletariat, and their numbers are growing. (Men make up the rest). The service sectors have also produced a new managerial and professional class into which the educated children of native-born, albeit often ethnic, whites have moved. Before looking at these changes, however, let us consider shifts revealed by a comparison of the 1970 and 1980 censuses.

Numerous items stand out in this comparison, presented in Table 9.3: New York in 1980 was 26 percent less white, 11 percent more black, and 1.6 percent more Puerto Rican than ten years before. It was a much more Caribbean, Hispanic, and Asian city. For the first time since World War I, the percentage of foreign-born jumped dramatically, from 18.2 percent to 23.6 percent. If the 860,000 Puerto Ricans and the estimated 750,000 undocumented aliens are added to this figure, perhaps 45 percent of the city's population was born outside the fifty states, a figure comparable to the late nineteenth century. As Saskia Sassen-Koob has argued, New York City has led the first world's penetration of the third world, and in turn the third world has penetrated New York City.[9]

The city is also poorer, as lower income black and Hispanic households replaced better off white households. The number of persons officially in poverty rose by 19.5 percent, while the number of female-headed households rose 30.9 percent, as did the rate at which they experienced poverty. But, in a sense, the city also became richer, because the number of nonfamily, often multi-earner households increased 30.0 percent and household size fell 9.1 percent, due mostly to

Table 9.3   Census Profile of New York City, 1970 and 1980

Subject	1970	1980	Percent Change
Total Population	7,894,862	7,071,639	−10.4
Non-Hispanic White Population	4,972,509	3,668,945	−26.2
	(63.0)	(51.9)	
Non-Hispanic Black Population	1,525,745	1,694,127	11.0
Hispanic Population	1,278,630	1,406,024	10.0
Puerto Rican	846,731	860,552	1.6
Non-Puerto Rican	476,913	545,472	14.4
Asian and Pacific Islanders	115,830	300,406	159.3
Foreign-born	1,437,058	1,670,199	16.2
	(18.2)	(23.6)	
Median Household Income			
(1980 dollars)	$19,170	$16,818	−12.3
Per Capita Income	$7,397	$7,271	−1.7
Persons in Poverty	1,164,673	1,391,981	19.5
Percent Below Poverty Line			
All persons	14.9	20.0	
All families	11.5	17.2	
Female-headed with children	45.7	55.1	
Total Households	2,836,872	2,788,530	−1.7
Family households	2,043,765	1,757,564	−14.0
Married couple families	1,603,387	1,203,387	−25.0
MCF's with children < 18	774,496	535,581	−30.8
Female-headed households	353,692	462,933	30.9
FHH's with children < 18	209,006	307,709	47.2
Non-family households	793,107	1,030,966	30.0
Average Persons per Household	2.74	2.49	−9.1
Males in Labor Force	1,988,774	1,732,165	−12.9
(% males > 16)	(74.1)	(69.5)	
Females in Labor Force	1,355,654	1,435,533	5.9
(% females > 16)	(42.2)	(47.1)	

Sources: N.Y.C. Department of City Planning, first five entries, which made adjustments of census data based on microdata distributions. 1980 U.S. Census of population for the remainder.

the decline in fertility. Real per capita income thus fell only slightly. Income inequality rose, however, with the growing relatively poor minority population balanced off by the slowly declining but much better off white, multi-earner, managerial and professional households. Since 1977, per capita real incomes have been growing more rapidly than the national average, but dividends and interest have contributed more to this pace than wages or transfer payments, again suggesting a more unequal income distribution.[10] Indicative as these figures may be, more research on income distribution and income changes for different groups over time is badly needed.

What picture, then, do these figures paint? The trends resemble those for most other large central cities during the crises of the 1970s. White families departed by the hundreds of thousands, and the remaining white population aged. Minority families, particularly immigrants from the Caribbean as well as Hong Kong, Korea, and India, grew rapidly within the population. (The native black and Puerto Rican population experienced net out-migration if fertility and mortality are taken into consideration.) New York again became a city of immigrants, this time nonwhite.

Like the society as a whole, household patterns changed substantially, with nonfamily and other nontraditional households predominating over traditional patterns. Some of these new household types suffer from poverty and dependency, but not all. As women have entered the labor force and multi-earner households have formed, a new middle and upper middle class stratum of baby boom professionals has been created. Though resembling their white middle class predecessors in some respects, their lifestyles and childbearing patterns, and hence in what they want from their neighborhood and city, differ.[11] New York City reflects national patterns in the growth of this cohort: between 1970 and 1980, thirty-to-thirty-four-year-olds increased by 19.4 percent, and twenty-five-to-thirty-four-year-olds by 11.9 percent. However, Dan Chall has recently pointed out that this group grew more slowly in New York than in the nation and/or than would be extrapolated from the size of these cohorts in 1970. He also shows that the growth of high income households lagged behind the surrounding suburbs and the nation as a whole.[12] Nevertheless, the number of college-educated New Yorkers rose by roughly 50 percent over the decade, to 750,000, and the formation of young professional households has certainly accelerated since 1980.

It would be wrong to conclude that New York City's white, ethnic "Archie Bunker" population has disappeared. The city remains half non-Hispanic white; of these, approximately 33 percent are Jews of Russian and other East European extraction, 27.4 percent are of Italian ancestry, and 17.7 percent have an Irish background.[13] These groups have moved into managerial, professional, and governmental positions while retaining a hold on strongly unionized craft positions in the blue collar labor force. They certainly remain a strong, even dominant force in the city's political culture, with a conservative disposition clearly illustrated in Jonathan Rieder's study of Canarsie.[14]

These aggregate trends have taken on a specific geography within the city. Traditional centers of the black population in Harlem and Bedford-Stuyvesant have spread out, leading to racial transition in surrounding neighborhoods like Washington Heights and East Flatbush. New centers of black population also grew over the decade; middle class black families moved into Queens, for example, over the decade. The old ghetto centers were depopulated and in many instances subjected to severe housing abandonment and destruction. Hispanic settlement patterns paralleled but also diverged from black patterns. Puerto Ricans have diffused out of the traditional Hispanic cores of the South Bronx, East Harlem, and the Lower East Side. Hispanic immigrant groups, however, have settled in distinct places. Dominicans predominate in Washington Heights, overlapping with Puerto Ricans, and higher income groups like Colombians, Peruvians, and Ecuadorians have concentrated in Jackson Heights, Queens. Jamaicans and other West Indians, along with Haitians, are concentrated along Nostrand Avenue in central Brooklyn. Greeks, Indians, Chinese, and other nonblack and Hispanic immigrants have also settled in Astoria and Flushing. Soviet Jews are concentrated in Brighton Beach and to a lesser degree in Canarsie.

In the midst of the tremendous racial and ethnic succession in formerly white ethnic neighborhoods like Brownsville and Flatbush, other neighborhoods have become ethnic redoubts. Kornblum and Beshers's essay in this volume shows how the white ethnic population has settled along the city's oceanside rim, from Bay Ridge and Bensonhurst through Canarsie and South Ozone Park to the Nassau bayside. Other neighborhoods, like the Upper East Side or Riverdale, remain upper class preserves, while a few old ethnic enclaves, like Arthur Avenue in the Bronx or Greenpoint in Brooklyn, remain.

The growing young professional stratum has colonized neighborhoods initially built for the late nineteenth century upper middle class, especially those where blacks and Hispanics never fully replaced whites. This stratum also created demand for converting loft factory buildings in well located, architecturally distinctive areas, particularly those with-

Table 9.4   White Male Occupational Distribution

Occupation	WASPs	Italians	Irish	(Jewish) Russian
Manager	10.7%	8.8%	8.4%	12.5%
Professional	9.2	5.2	5.6	13.4
Technician	4.0	2.2	2.8	4.1
Salesperson	13.1	10.3	8.6	24.2
Clerical and Office	18.4	16.9	19.3	16.9
Service Worker	14.9	12.7	19.6	6.1
Craftworker	11.9	19.8	15.3	11.5
Operative	16.7	23.0	18.8	10.8
Percent Male Population	(2.15)	(16.96)	(8.18)	(4.29)

Source: 1980 U.S. Census Public Use Microdata Sample. Farming occupations are excluded; all are New York-born of indicated ancestry.

out surrounding minority population. Where the housing stock was sufficiently grand and the proximity to white neighborhoods close, however, white middle class professionals have reinvaded predominantly black neighborhoods, as in Clinton Hill, Fort Greene, and Prospect Heights in Brooklyn. Incumbent upgrading is also taking place in black middle class areas.

Where do these geographically segregated groups stand in the changing economic structure? A first distinction must be made between the declining but still dominant white ethnic groups and the various rising minority groups. Because men and women have different positions, gender must also be distinguished in each group. Tables 9.4 and 9.5 present occupational breakdowns for these groups. (Similar tables on industry are given in the Appendix.)

The declining number of white men tend, as might be expected, to occupy the higher occupational ranks, but white women more heavily populate the growing industry sectors. Minority women are similarly well positioned relative to minority men and have had a little more success in becoming managers and professionals. All white groups have better occupational and industry locations than any minority group. There are important differences among white ethnic groups, however.

Russian Jews have done best, WASPs follow, Irish are somewhat farther back, and Italian ancestry individuals trail the others. Among the minorities, blacks are currently positioned in higher occupations and more rapidly growing sectors than Hispanics; native-born groups are

Table 9.5   White Female Occupational Distribution

Occupation	WASPs	Italians	Irish	(Jewish) Russian
Manager	7.9%	5.8%	6.5%	7.3%
Professional	13.6	7.7	13.8	21.1
Technician	2.6	1.9	1.8	2.9
Salesperson	12.1	11.8	10.4	12.4
Clerical and Office	46.7	51.3	52.2	48.6
Service Worker	10.8	10.1	11.4	4.3
Craftworker	1.8	1.9	1.2	1.0
Operative	4.4	9.0	2.6	1.7
Percent Female Population	(2.35)	(16.14)	(9.56)	(5.56)

Source: 1980 U.S. Census Public Use Microdata Sample (PUMS). Farming occupations excluded; all are New York-born of indicated ancestry.

also better positioned than noncitizen immigrants. However, over the decade there is evidence that minority immigrant groups achieved more upward mobility than did natives.

Among white men, Table 9.4 shows that from one-seventh (Italian ancestry) to one-quarter (Russian Jewish) are managers and professionals. Interestingly, many men hold clerical and office administrative jobs, ranging from 16.9 percent of those with Russian ancestry to 19.3 percent of those with Irish backgrounds. From 10 to 20 percent of these men (particularly Italians) remain in craftsman positions, typically strongly unionized positions in the building trades. Except for the Russian Jews, about one in six are also in service occupations such as janitors or bartenders, which might be considered blue collar but are not industrial. Fewer than one in five are on assembly lines or operate machines.

Table 9.5 shows clearly that ethnic white women are concentrated in growing white collar occupations, particularly clerical work. All four groups of women predominantly hold "white collar working class" or "lower middle class" office jobs. More than one in five hold managerial or professional jobs, with Russian ancestry people (a proxy for Jews) doing best, WASPs doing next best, and Italians trailing the Irish. This pattern parallels and (except for the Irish) slightly trails that of the men, with fewer managers but more professionals. Even fewer white ethnic women are operatives.

Though Tables 9.6 and 9.7 indicate that minority men and women show rough similarities to their white counterparts, there are also sig-

Table 9.6   Minority Male Occupational Distribution

Occupation	NY Black	Jamaican	Puerto Rican	Dominican	Chinese
Manager	6.6%	6.0%	6.5%	4.5%	11.3%
Professional	7.4	5.5	3.1	1.8	8.0
Technician	2.0	3.3	1.0	0.6	3.0
Salesperson	5.7	5.5	5.3	7.8	6.5
Clerical and Office	22.9	15.5	11.9	8.3	7.1
Service Worker	21.6	15.5	25.0	25.8	43.4
Craftworker	9.4	20.0	15.3	13.6	6.0
Operative	22.8	23.2	30.8	36.9	14.1
Percent Total Male	(11.35)	(2.38)	(10.46)	(3.23)	(2.58)

Source: 1980 PUMS File. NY blacks are those born in New York; Puerto Ricans are island-born; Jamaicans, Dominicans, and Chinese are born abroad. Farming occupations are excluded.

nificant differences from whites and among minority groups. Among minority males, New York–born blacks and Jamaican immigrants most resemble the white males, but they are more likely to be operatives and service workers and less likely to be managers and/or professionals. Hispanics are even more concentrated in the operative and service worker categories. A surprising proportion of native black and Jamaican males have found clerical and administrative positions in offices. Blacks are generally better off than Hispanics, and Puerto Rican immigrants are better off than Dominicans.

A third of Hispanic males are concentrated in the classic but declining industrial operative category. Conversely, fewer are clerical workers and even fewer are managers or professionals. Chinese immigrant males

Table 9.7   Minority Female Occupational Distribution

Occupation	NY Black	Jamaican	Puerto Rican	Dominican	Chinese
Manager	5.0%	3.0%	3.0%	1.2%	5.3%
Professional	11.9	13.4	5.6	2.4	6.6
Technician	2.3	3.1	1.4	0.5	1.6
Salesperson	9.3	5.6	7.6	5.7	7.3
Clerical and Office	44.5	28.0	26.1	14.7	14.7
Service Worker	18.5	40.2	16.2	12.7	674.2
Craftworker	1.3	1.1	4.4	6.3	3.4
Operative	6.7	5.5	35.4	56.4	54.6
Percent Total Female	(14.08)	(3.68)	(8.67)	(3.85)	(2.52)

Source: 1980 PUMS file. NY blacks are those born in New York; Puerto Ricans are island-born; Jamaicans, Dominicans, and Chinese are born abroad. Farming occupations are excluded.

offer another contrast: almost half are service workers, mostly waiters and cooks in restaurants, but they also have the highest minority rates of managerial and professional work.

Minority women show like similarities and differences with white ethnic women. Like white women, native-born black and Jamaican women are concentrated in white collar occupations. Few are factory workers or craftspersons. Many are clerical or office workers and substantially more are professionals than is true of their male counterparts. The largest concentration of Jamaican women are service workers, many of whom provide child care. (Jamaican women are also twice as likely as Jamaican men to be professionals.) Like their male counterparts, both groups of black women differ strongly from Hispanic women. The latter are even more heavily concentrated than Hispanic males in the operatives category. Over half of all Dominican women were operatives in 1980, primarily in the apparel industry. Chinese women are also quite heavily concentrated in this trade.

Similar patterns can be observed by analyzing the distribution of the groups across industries presented in Tables A.1 to A.4 in the Appendix. These tables substantiate many of our stereotypes about ethnic specialization in the occupational order: WASP males dominate the banking and securities industries and corporate services; Italian ancestry males are important in manufacturing, construction, retailing (not all the fruit stands are run by Koreans!), and carting and goods movement; Irish ancestry males are well represented in transportation and in banking and the civil service; Russian Jews figure strongly in the apparel industry, wholesale and retail trade, and the professions, particularly doctors. As the previous discussion has made clear, white women are strongly represented in the growing business service sectors, particularly banking and the advanced corporate services, and in such areas of "women's work" as elementary education and social services. Twenty-one percent of working Russian ancestry women are in the educational system.

As with occupations, the industry specializations of black and Hispanic men and women differ. Blacks are more heavily concentrated than Hispanics in the services, particularly in government, social services, and health. All minorities are underrepresented in the financial industries, but native blacks and Jamaican immigrants, especially women, have done best. Jamaican males lean more toward manufacturing, especially nondurable manufacturing, while almost 30 percent of Jamaican females work in the health sector. (Fourteen percent are also private household workers.) Interestingly, native blacks and Puerto Ricans did better in the civil service than did black immigrants. Over 10 percent of the native black men and women work for government agencies outside the schools and hospitals, figures that are generally twice those of other groups (except for Irish males).

These figures help us to see how different groups are positioned with respect to the structural change in the economy. In general, white men occupy the best positions in the fastest growing sectors, but they also occupy senior (and, we may infer, well-protected) positions in blue collar sectors like construction, trucking and transport, and utilities. If the relationships were controlled for generation, we would undoubtedly find older workers in blue collar crafts positions and younger ones in corporate professions. Thus white men are relatively protected in declining sectors and well placed in rising sectors.

From a sectoral viewpoint, white women are even better positioned, since so few are in declining sectors. Yet women are restricted largely to clerical positions in the most prosperous sectors, like the securities industry, while their gains as professionals have often come in sectors, like education, where their ascent has been accompanied by relative and sometimes absolute declines in the salaries of these professions. Even so, women have made some gains in corporate professions like law and banking. Perhaps less well situated than white men at present, they are concentrated in sectors and occupations where demand, and thus market power, are likely to be greatest in the future.

Blacks, whether native- or foreign-born, occupy lower occupational rungs. The men tend more to be operatives and service workers and the women clerical workers, but blacks are less prevalent in manufacturing than whites and much less than Hispanics. Indeed, a larger proportion of black women hold professional positions than do white men, though they are obviously much lower status and less well paid jobs. Native- and foreign-born blacks have been much more able to penetrate the public and nonprofit services than the corporate services, which remain strongly white. Native-born black men hold fewer manufacturing and construction jobs and more public service positions.

Hispanics, especially Hispanic women, appear along with Chinese women to be worst positioned. They are heavily concentrated in the declining nondurable and durable manufacturing sectors, where they have undoubtedly replaced whites who have moved to sectors with more opportunity. Immigrant Dominican and Chinese women work in a highly competitive garment industry that probably could not survive in New York without exploiting their labor. Puerto Ricans, as citizens, have done better than Dominicans and Chinese, but not as well as any of the others, including Jamaican immigrants.

The city's changing economic structure thus creates substantial material differences of interest along gender and ethnic lines as well as along the more obvious cleavages of nativity and race in the competition for good positions in the emerging lattice of industries and occupations. Gender differences pervade all racial groups, with white and black women being better represented in the corporate service sectors but being largely excluded, at least to date, from the top occupations. Professional status has been achieved mainly in education and the social services, which have been vulnerable to retrenchment. Black women are particularly relegated to lower level service positions. But even they are better off than the Dominican and Chinese women sitting behind sewing machines. Hispanic women, whether citizen or alien, have found greatest access in declining industry sectors and are poorly represented in clerical positions in the expanding sectors.

These figures also show strong and important differences among ethnic groups. Male WASPs and Jews of Russian extraction are disproportionately represented in the professions and corporate management. Those of Italian and Irish ancestry are more heavily represented in the crafts positions and public agencies. White women are making far more progress than black women in the professions, with Russian ancestry Jews doing best and WASPs and Irish behind them; Italian ancestry women lag behind native black and even Jamaican women. Among blacks and Hispanics, blacks are doing better than Hispanics and citizens better than immigrants, although Puerto Ricans are lower than Jamaicans in the industry occupational order.

We can now summarize how the postindustrial transformation of New York City's economy has affected different groups:

1. The structural change in the economy has undermined the old lattice of occupational niches within industry sectors and created a new one; demographic trends have simultaneously diminished old groups while creating new ones. Declining groups (older white ethnics) have sought to defend their favored industry/occupational position while new groups (native and immigrant minority groups) compete to improve theirs. These new groups bring widely different assets to this competition and face different kinds of labor market barriers.

2. Race and class divisions overlap to a considerable degree. Blacks and Hispanics are both concentrated in the lower occupations and, particularly for Hispanics, in declining industries. Problematic economic incorporation is probably closely related to poverty, welfare dependency, and female-headed households. The resulting

"underclass" (a misnomer) does not seem to be diminished by overall economic growth; rather, inequality appears to be growing.

3. Manufacturing decline disproportionately harms Hispanics and Chinese, particularly immigrant workers. Their displacement will be slowed only to the extent that they accept lower wages and poorer working conditions. Their weak labor market position may put them at odds with other groups.

4. Growing minority groups are sorted across occupations and industries according to ethnicity, gender, and nativity as well as race. Black women are positioned better than black men and Hispanic women somewhat better than Hispanic men; blacks are better positioned than Hispanics. Although these groups are all weakly represented in the managerial and professional ranks of the growing advanced corporate services, they differ substantially in their position.

5. The fastest growing groups—black, Hispanic, and Asian immigrants—lack citizenship rights. Many Dominicans and Chinese are concentrated in the most vulnerable economic sectors, such as the garment industry, but the latter seem to be experiencing much more intergenerational migration to stronger sectors and occupations.

6. While the resulting new ethnic division of labor (or ethnic/occupational mosaic) may be characterized as a new form of class inequality, it is cross-cut by racial, ethnic, gender, and nativity differences. The class basis for political mobilization can thus be attenuated by intraclass divisions. While the political underrepresentation or exclusion of many groups may stem from low economic status, many are formally excluded through lack of citizenship.

The Impact on the Political Order

The differential impact of economic restructuring on various groups holds a twofold challenge for the political order in New York City. First, emerging forms of social inequality are bound to create new conflicts that will erupt, at least indirectly, in the political system. Second, the widening gap between the electorate's social base and the city's overall resident population is creating the conditions for future upheaval when excluded groups finally enter the electoral arena. This essay cannot predict how such a political development might unfold, but it can begin to assess the political impact of the postindustrial transformation by looking at how the different groups are currently located in New York's electoral arena.

Components of the Electorate

Economic and demographic trends will clearly reorganize the city's electorate over the long term. Within the resident population as a whole, whites are now less than a majority. Within that minority, the working class constituency upon which regular Democratic organizations were originally constructed has become a waning influence. Presumably, this will ultimately be reflected in the composition of the electorate. But Table 9.8 shows that this is not yet the case.

Although whites are only half of New York's population, they made up almost three-quarters of the 1980 presidential general electorate because they are older than other groups, more likely to be citizens, and registered and turned out to vote more frequently. Only registration and turnout are subject to short-term improvement in other groups, and even they are not easy to alter. As a result, over at least the next decade, a successful insurgent candidate would need to mobilize many white votes along with minority support.

Table 9.8   The New York City Presidential Electorate, 1980

	Population	Adjusted For			
		Age	Citizenship	Registration	Turnout
Whites	51.9%	56.8%	59.6%	65.6%	71.6%
		(80.5)	(91.8)	(60.8)	(54.4)
Blacks	23.9%	21.9%	22.5%	21.5%	19.6%
		(67.4)	(90.2)	(52.7)	(45.7)
Hispanics	19.9%	17.4%	14.0%	8.9%	4.8%
		(64.2)	(70.1)	(34.9)	(26.8)

Source: U.S. Bureau of the Census, CPS Series P-20, no. 370, "Voting and Registration in the Election of November, 1980," Table 3, p. 23. Adjustments in right three columns for northeastern central cities of SMSAs larger than one million. Mean values in parentheses.

THE WHITE ELECTORATE   Perhaps as much as one-third of the white population is Jewish, largely of east European ancestry. This population has become increasingly middle class and professional and has perhaps adapted best of all the groups to the postindustrial transformation of the city. Yet there are important differences within this group by generation, sex, and religious orientation. The older, more traditional groups have become more conservative, having fled or been forced from their old neighborhoods by racial succession. The 20 percent of working Jewish women who are schoolteachers are an important constituency within the American Federation of Teachers; the 1968 Ocean Hill–Brownsville dispute drove a wedge between them and blacks. This constituency has been a major and fervid supporter of the Koch administration.

Because it usually decides who will hold power in City Hall, the Democratic mayoral primary electorate is the most important. Jews made up 29 percent of the city's 1985 Democratic mayoral primary electorate.[15] As a rough guess, perhaps two-thirds of the Jewish voters might be classified as traditional and one-third are younger, nontraditional, more liberal and independent voters. Thus one-fifth of all votes come from relatively traditional and conservative Jews and one-tenth from more liberal Jews.

Other non-Hispanic white voters are typically Catholics of Italian, Irish, and other ethnic backgrounds. (White protestants account for only 6 percent of the electorate.) These Catholic households have been more defensive than Jews regarding racial transition in the neighborhoods and the labor markets, less well positioned to benefit from the expanding service sectors, and more dependent on regular Democratic political influence to guard their position. They constituted 24 percent of the mayoral primary votes in 1985. Lacking the liberal garment union tradition, they are more conservative than traditional Jews. Not since the La Guardia years have Italians been outsiders for whom only a reform administration could provide the entry point to recognition. A *New York Times* poll summarized Mayor Koch's supporters as "older voters, the less educated ones, Roman Catholics, those skeptical about unions, and also those belonging to union households."[16] These attributes accurately describe the large and dominant but nonetheless declining and threatened white ethnic residents of New York.

The remaining whites might be called the "gentry." They are the baby boom cohort, aged twenty-four to forty, highly educated, concentrated in the rapidly growing service sector professions, often in nontraditional households. Education and lifestyle distinguish this group more than income. In the ABC News exit poll, 37 percent of the electorate was twenty-five to thirty-nine in 1985, 40 percent had a college degree or more, and 19 percent identified themselves as "young professionals under 40," while 13 percent described themselves as "feminists who support the ERA."[17] Over and above the liberal Jews who fit this category, there are enough white non-Jewish baby boom professionals to make up 10 percent or more of the electorate.

White votes, two-thirds of the Democratic mayoral primary electorate, thus lean toward the conservative end of the spectrum; white conservatives by themselves constitute at least 40 percent of the electorate. Perhaps 20 percent of the electorate are liberal older Jews or baby boom professionals open to a more liberal appeal. (Such people supported reform thrusts like the Stevenson campaign, the Robert Kennedy and Lindsay campaigns, and the current reform bloc in Democratic party affairs.) Since women made up 54 percent of the primary voters and white women supported Mayor Koch less than white men did, there is a modest gender gap as well.

BLACKS IN THE ELECTORATE   Table 9.8 shows that structural reasons have put blacks at a disadvantage in the electorate: they have fewer attributes that make for frequent voting, and the electoral system has given them few candidates to be excited about. As a result, they have not achieved a political breakthrough commensurate with their numbers. The impact of reform may even have weakened their position by undermining the balanced tickets previously fielded by the regular Democrats. Black leadership appears to be highly fragmented and divided, a logical consequence of exclusion. However, the 1984 and 1988 Jesse Jackson Democratic presidential primary campaign did suggest that greater mobilization is possible.

Since 1980, voter registration campaigns have increased the number of eligible black voters by more than 100,000. The Jackson campaigns show that a strong black candidate can mobilize this increased registration. Black assembly districts showed 40 and 50 percent turnout increases in 1984 over the Democratic gubernatorial primary of 1982. If black registration and turnout were to match or exceed those of whites consistently, blacks could increase their proportion in the electorate from the 1985 figure of 23 percent. The 1985 black mayoral candidate did not, however, galvanize the same kind of participation that Jackson had a year earlier.

HISPANICS IN THE ELECTORATE   Hispanics face even more problems than blacks because they are younger, poorer, less likely to be citizens, and in a worse labor market position. Thus they are even less adequately represented. Correspondingly, as Table 9.8 shows in parentheses, they register and turn out rates less than blacks, reducing Hispanics to roughly

5 percent of the presidential general electorate. (They made up perhaps 13 percent of the mayoral Democratic primary electorate.) In Angelo Falcon's view, low participation has created a vicious circle in which Puerto Rican elected officials are vulnerable because they have a narrow constituency, and "the weakness of this elected leadership in turn serves to dampen Puerto Rican and Latino enthusiasm for participation in the electoral process."[18] While registration campaigns added many Hispanic voters to the rolls before the 1984 presidential primary, Jackson's 1984 candidacy did not elicit increased turnout. The third greatest enrollment increase occurred in the largely Hispanic 68th Assembly District in East Harlem. In the 1984 primary, Reverend Jackson won about 34 percent of a Hispanic vote that was not particularly larger than four years previously. Continuing low turnout rates, combined with the fact that the greatest Hispanic population growth is occurring among noncitizen groups, works against Hispanic influence. Yet because this group is so underrepresented, it could have an impact on the political order if it were strongly mobilized.

IMMIGRANT GROUPS   As the earlier discussion indicated, the most rapidly growing components of the minority population are neither native blacks nor Puerto Ricans but other Caribbean and Asian migrants. At present and for the foreseeable future, these groups will be excluded from the political arena. They are also nonparticipants in government in the sense that they shy away from making claims on social services, or at least on welfare. (Their impact on schools and the hospital system is more substantial.) Nor do immigrants share a unifying collective interest: Haitians differ from Trinidadians who differ from Indians or Hong Kong Chinese. Each group will make its own way in politics. Many in these groups remain strongly oriented toward home country politics, where they can sometimes still vote without having to return home. Longer term changes in the process of naturalization may encourage these groups to become a larger factor in city politics. Even so, it is not clear that they would mobilize along the same lines as native blacks and Hispanics. They might instead further fragment these racial groups.

Reshaping the Political Arena

Sayre and Kaufman argued that the conflict between revenue-providers and service-demanders was the fundamental interest cleavage in New York City politics.[19] The corporate world embodied in the Manhattan central business district pays much of the city's property and income taxes, but it lacks "resident" standing in local politics and swings at best a small number of votes in city elections. The city's corporate and managerial elite must thus find other means to influence public policy and contain the tax burden needed to finance it.

A common theme in the analysis of the fiscal crisis, whether from the left or the right, is that spending pressures outran the willingness and perhaps the ability of those with wealth and income to finance them. The events leading up to the 1975 receivership and the measures taken immediately afterward may thus be interpreted as a capital strike against the city's previous political trends. Conservative observers like Morris saw the result as a sensible retreat from unattainable goals, while radical analysts saw a capitalist attack on modest attempts to achieve social justice.[20] The implication remains that business power was able to recast the city's spending priorities through such instruments as the Financial Control Board. Others point to David Rockefeller's organization of the Partnership as an important new representative of business interests.

However successfully capital might have voted with its feet against liberal politics, it is a *non sequitur* to conclude that business is therefore well organized and politically powerful. Bankruptcy can create only a transitory opportunity for the exercise of naked economic coercion. The short run effect may be, and was, large. But over the longer run, previously competing political actors previously locked in conflict embraced long enough to take the financial and budgetary measures needed to regain autonomy. Rapid economic recovery also reduced the credibility of disinvestment as a political strategy. For business influence to survive in this environment, it must weave itself into the dominant political coalition that emerges in the postcrisis era. But as crisis subsides, so does the incentive for business unity.

Ironically, the currently reigning probusiness political climate may thus reduce the direct political influence of business. By increasing the incentive for sectors and firms to pursue their particular interests, it may lead to the disorganization of corporate interests as a coherent political force, despite the best efforts of the Partnership and the Citizens Budget Commission.

The implicit veto the corporate sector exercised over liberal politics has had one longer term effect: it has reorganized governmental spending priorities. In summing up six years of work on the priorities revealed in New York City's budgets and agency activities, Charles Brecher and Raymond Horton have argued that retrenchment enabled the city's political leaders to rise above the normal log rolling and incrementalism and shift the city's budgetary priorities. They conclude that government can react to adverse market conditions like private firms, abolishing noncore functions, redeploying resources, controlling wages, and installing new financial planning and control systems.[21] While they deplore the ensuing decline in service quantity, quality, and transfer payments to the poor, they applaud innovative management behavior.

Another view would stress city government's retreat from the social problems facing the city. Government intervention is no longer fashionable (except, perhaps, in the form of social control). As Brecher and Horton and their colleagues have pointed out, government has tilted toward the core functions of building infrastructure, protecting property, and keeping a modicum of order. The Lindsay and Johnson administrations expanded government to incorporate formerly excluded constituencies. The retrenchment period repealed this strategy without entirely rolling it back. Mayor Koch has forthrightly criticized the use of public spending to curry minority support and has presented himself as the spokesperson for the neglected middle class.

While the Koch administration dismantled the Great Society poverty agencies, it does still channel hundreds of millions of city dollars to neighborhood-based nonprofit service providers. The distribution of these funds has an evident political logic. They do not foster direct political advocacy nor are they given to challengers or critics of the administration. In general, such "third party" systems of social service seem designed to reinforce the private marketplace.[22] To use terms fashioned by James O'Connor and refined by Friedland, Alford, and Piven, city policy has shifted from social expenses and the social wage to social investments fostering private economic expansion.[23]

The most important impact of the fiscal and economic crises of the last decade, then, has been the disorganization of the political arena. In a perceptive study, Julian Baim has argued that V. O. Key's discussion of one-party Southern political systems is relevant to New York City. The decades of reform have succeeded, as Shefter argues in his essay in this volume, in undermining the dominance of regular Democratic party organizations over politics in the five boroughs. When combining the changing demographic characteristics of the city, the result is what Baim describes as "unstructured, fluid, multi-factional election contests [that] deteriorate into issueless politics where the electoral process does not serve as a referendum on critical policy issues."[24]

The absence of a party organization to represent the views and interests of those outside the dominant political coalition insulates the leaders of that coalition from having to address those issues. Instead, a politics of personalities, ethnic affiliations, and invidious intergroup distinctions arises to fill the political arena. From this point of view, a charismatic black mayoral candidacy in 1985 might only have further reinforced ethnic fragmentation, notwithstanding the positive impact she or he might have had on black participation.

Martin Shefter's important study of New York City politics and his essay in this volume make a similar argument from a more structural point of view. In his view, the Lindsay era was an ambitious attempt by the "reform vanguard" of professionals to overturn the pattern of inter-interest group accommodations characteristic of the postwar years and to insert formerly excluded black and Puerto Rican constituencies into the calculus of governance, with corporate and federal support. This attempt at overturning old interest alignments failed politically, Shefter feels, and was not consolidated, yet it undermined the status quo. In the course of the fiscal crisis, powerful actors like the banks and municipal unions could protect their interests, while those whom the reformers sought to include, and indeed the reformers themselves, could not.

In Shefter's view, the present environment is one of truncated reform: the old pluralist pattern has been eroded, recently included groups have been marginalized but not cast out, and the most powerful interests have staked out a new central position, but no permanent new patterns of accommodation have been formed. In the midst of this fluid situation, Mayor Koch ascended by pulling together those who felt most threatened by Lindsay-era reform, only to be harried by the sinful fruits of the bargains he struck with the regular party organizations of Queens, the Bronx, and Brooklyn.

It follows from this analysis that, however great Mayor Koch's political skills, his power is precarious because it is based on personal qualities as opposed to a coherent organization of constituencies sharing durable lines of common interest. It is situational rather than structural; his current allies are powerful, but perhaps he is all that ties them together. His opponents have failed to consolidate a new insurgent coalition, but perhaps the sequence of scandals will open the way. Such an effort could only succeed, however, if some of those interests now supporting the mayor were to find it sufficiently promising to risk joining a new alignment. Many others, of course, would only dig in to support him.

The Potential for a Resurgence of Reform

Theodore Lowi and Martin Shefter have described a reform cycle in New York City politics. Triggering events like scandals or fiscal crises allow interests that are unsatisfied with the prevailing accommodations, as managed by the current regular regime, to coalesce with those outside the regime. This insurgent coalition can span the spectrum from capitalists worried about the watering down of the city's paper to ethnic groups whom the regulars have failed to incorporate. In the nineteenth century, their organizational bases included the Citizen's Union, committees of good government advocates, the press, and the Republican party, joining in typically short-lived fusion administrations like those of Low and Mitchel. La Guardia followed many of these patterns, but had far broader popular support. He crafted an organizational base in the American Labor party and was able to develop a working arrangement with the New Deal.

In the latter 1950s, however, with the democratization of elections to the New York County Democratic Committee, the Stevenson campaign, and the subsequent defeat of Carmine De Sapio and the Tammany organization, the Manhattan Democratic party became the vehicle through which reformers became political insiders. As a third-term, late-blooming reformer, Mayor Wagner fostered the organization of public employees' unions. Despite his Republican partisan identity, Lindsay used contracts with community-based nonprofit service providers to incorporate black and Hispanic community groups into his political coalition, a scheme the Democrats joyfully adopted as their own. As a result, the old reform outsiders are now a new establishment, compromised by all that that entails.

The aborted challenge of the late 1960s and early 1970s has left behind a legacy of disorganization and decomposition. Around what nuclei, then, and from what sources might a new reform alignment crystallize?

It is easy to list the possible elements of such an alignment: reform clubs such as the Village Independent Democrats or the Central Brooklyn Independent Democrats; progressive labor unions such as District Council 37 of AFSCME; black reformers in Manhattan, Brooklyn, and Queens; Hispanics in the south Bronx and elsewhere, and women, particularly working women. Structural trends give these elements the advantage of growing numbers, if not wealth or status. But there are two problems with this potential alignment.

First, they do not constitute an electoral majority. Second, the interests that divide them are as great as those that unite them. Even a smoothly working alliance, however, might not produce a majority of the electorate. Mayor Koch won 51 percent of the union members, 70 percent of the Hispanics, 54 percent of the city government workers, 56 percent of the young professionals, 44 percent of the feminists, and even 37 percent of the black votes in the 1985 primary against a black and a white reform challenger.[25] Hispanic voters suggest that the conservative influence of Catholicism can outweigh the liberal influence of minority status. More profoundly, a reform coalition cannot succeed unless weighty interests defect from the present dominant coalition. Such interests provide the necessary financing, legitimacy, and media access.

Who might such defectors be? Given their legacy of liberalism, Jewish voters might be such a valence constituency. But the wedge of racial division driven into the city over the last several decades casts doubt on this possibility. Italian voters are less likely defectors, since they are generally more conservative, although Governor Cuomo has shown that a liberal Italian candidate can cut into this group. From whatever source, and for whatever reason, a sizable minority of white, ethnic, middle class voters must find it in their interest to vote for resurgent reform if it is to succeed. The growing negative rating for Mayor Koch and the operation of the wheel of time on the social makeup of the city may eventually produce enough of a new middle class to make this possible.

The second major impediment to reform lies in the differences among the potential allies and the fact that the political arena presently reinforces such differences. Table 9.9 presents a sobering set of relationships for those awaiting the rainbow coalition. It comes from work by the Legislative Task Force on Reapportionment relating demographic and voting patterns when (as in the 1977 Democratic mayoral primary) each group can vote for a candidate of its own background.

Table 9.9   Correlation between Race of Candidates and Voters in the 1977 Mayoral Primary

Candidate	Population Percentage		
	White	Black	Hispanic
White	0.903	−.773	−.517
Black	−.741	0.940	−.012
Hispanic	−.573	0.114	0.862

Source: Roman Hedges and Jeffrey Getis, "A Standard for Constructing Minority Legislative Districts: The Issue of Effective Voting Equality" (Nelson Rockefeller Institute of Government, SUNY Albany, Working Paper No. 6, 1981), Table 1. Data collected for candidates of three races across 4,105 groups of election districts with boundaries coterminous with census blocks.

Table 9.9 clearly shows that each group strongly favors candidates of its own background: whites vote against blacks and Hispanics; blacks and Hispanics vote against whites; and blacks and Hispanics do not particularly vote for one another. Indeed, in examining districts with concentrations of both blacks and Hispanics, Hedges and Getis found that "the proportion of Hispanic residents has a negative effect on the vote going to a black candidate."[26] It may be argued that these relationships hold only for elections in which each group has its own candidate. Close inspection of heavily Hispanic assembly districts in the 1984 primary reveals, however, that Jackson got under 40 percent of the Hispanic vote and that his candidacy produced no mobilization effect. Results from the 1985 mayoralty and borough presidency races are perhaps even more disheartening.[27] These data suggest that groups can be mobilized only by charismatic candidates from their own background, but that such candidates might induce countermobilization in other groups. An insurgent white candidate might offer a way out of this catch-22, but this prospect is not particularly palatable to minority groups who feel they have been politically marginalized for too long already. A racially balanced slate might overcome such objections, but reformers have shown little capacity to generate such cross-racial support relationships. A woman candidate might be able to use gender issues to bridge racial and ethnic differences.

Other divisions are also important. In particular, it will be difficult to overcome the class differences between the young urban professionals and the minority groups. Shefter and others have argued that the public employee unions' pension investment in the city's bailout has made them hostage to the status quo, or at least has led to a working accommodation with the city's leading bankers that they do not want to jeopardize. Finally, within all the constituent groups there are serious problems of fragmentation by ethnic subgroup and leadership factions. Tensions are evident, for example, between native blacks and West Indians, and there are certainly many differences among the Hispanic nationality groups.

Despite these problems, the potential sources of mobilization for a new reform insurgency are persistent. The Koch administration has shown a capacity to alienate even its supporters, although perhaps not systematically enough to do itself in. It certainly has alienated its opponents, and may do so vigorously enough to convince opposition leaders to overcome the differences among their constituencies. Time and socioeconomic change will steadily diminish constituencies' support of the mayor's alignment and will expand the potential opposition, a process that immigration reform and the spread of citizenship might hasten. The various out groups may find ways, as blacks did with the Jackson candidacies, to overcome the demobilization induced by the current structural arrangements of local politics. Any revitalization of the national Democratic party in 1988 or 1992 would surely help. The interest that public service providers and recipients share in the adequacy of public services and the potential organizational capacity of nonprofit service providers will also be constant factors. Finally, a liberal ideology will continue to be a natural response to the growing social problems of the postindustrial transformation.

Conclusion

As with the complex new forms of inequality in New York's ethnic division of labor, we are left, then, with a complicated picture of political stratification. In gross terms, the electorate, not to mention elected officials as a group, does not fully represent New York City's residents. It remains two-thirds white, while the city's resident population is less than half white. But, like the economic position, the political position of underrepresented groups varies a great deal, and these differences impede them from forming a collective challenge. Political stratification also operates at higher and more subtle levels than in the electorate that underlies them. But even in the electorate, present political patterns seem to inhibit rather than encourage the expression of the interests of those who are underrepresented or excluded. The political order thus mirrors and reinforces economic differences.

Ironically, some minority groups may be making better progress at penetrating higher occupations and growing industries than at the higher reaches of the political order. As the electorate becomes progressively distant from the populace, this is likely to create increasing tensions. Just as immigrant Jews and Italians overcame Irish political dominance, in considerable part through the reform cycle, new groups will, to the extent the political order is genuinely democratic, make their impact. In contrast to the experience of the Jews and Italians, however, contemporary excluded groups seem to lack the organizational vehicles, whether in the decaying regular party organizations or the moribund reform establishments, to achieve their political breakthrough.

Notes

1. See, for example, the 1927 Regional Plan studies of the metropolitan area or the volumes of the New York Metropolitan Region Study of the late 1950s. The latter are summarized in Raymond Vernon, *Metropolis 1985* (Cambridge: Harvard University Press, 1960).

2. Lewis Mumford, *The City in History* (New York: Harcourt, Brace, Jovanovich, 1961), 34.

3. John Mollenkopf, "Community and Accumulation," in *Urbanization and Urban Planning in Capitalist Society*, ed. Michael Dear and Allen Scott (New York: Methuen, 1981), 319–38; Martin Shefter, *Political Crisis/Fiscal Crisis* (New York: Basic Books, 1985), 4–12; and Frances Fox Piven and Roger Friedland, "Public Choice and Private Power: A Theory of the Fiscal Crisis" (unpublished paper, June 1981).

4. Rosalyn Silverman, "Trends in New York City Employment—A Different Perspective," *The Regional Economist* 4, no. 2 (Spring 1986): 1–4.

5. Matthew Drennan et al., *The Corporate Headquarters Complex in New York City* (New York: Conservation of Human Resources Project, 1977); Drennan, "The Economy," in *Setting Municipal Priorities 1982*, ed. Charles Brecher and Raymond Horton (New York: Russell Sage, 1981), 55–88; and Drennan, "Local Economy and Local Revenues," in *Setting Municipal Priorities 1984*, ed. Brecher and Horton (New York: New York University Press, 1983), 15–45.

6. John Mollenkopf, Thierry Noyelle, and Robert Cohen, "The Growth of Corporate Legal Services, Management Consulting, and Investment Banking in New York City" (New York: Policy Analysis Division, New York City Office of Economic Development, April 1984).

7. Tom Bailey, "A Case Study of Immigrants and Other Workers in the Restaurant Industry" (New York: Conservation of Human Resources Project, Columbia University, July 1982). Eating and drinking establishments are one of the largest and most rapidly growing of the service sectors, yet the location quotient for covered employment relative to the rest of the country is only 0.7. Since we know that New York in fact has more restaurants than the national average, perhaps as much as 50 percent more, this suggests that there may be as many off-the-books jobs in this industry as there are on-the-books jobs.

8. See "Expenditures," in Brecher and Horton, eds., *Setting Municipal Priorities 1984*, 68–96, for an overview of their findings, as well as their "Introduction" to *Setting Municipal Priorities: American Cities and the New York Experience* (New York: New York University Press, 1984), 1–11.

9. Saskia Sassen-Koob, "Exporting Capital and Importing Labor: The Role of Caribbean Migration to New York City" (New York University Center for Caribbean and Latin American Studies, Occasional Paper 28, December 1981).

10. See John Mollenkopf, "Economic Development," in *Setting Municipal Priorities 1984*, ed. Brecher and Horton, 136, for further discussion of this point.

11. Kathleen Gerson, *Hard Choices* (Berkeley: University of California Press, 1985), offers a definitive analysis of this development.

12. Dan Chall, "Neighborhood Changes in New York During the 1970s—Are the 'Gentry' Returning?" *Federal Reserve Bank of New York Quarterly* (Winter 1983–1984): 38–48.

13. Steven Schwartz, "The Demographic Evolution of the Jewish Community in New York City as a Policy Issue" (M.A. thesis, City University of New York Graduate Center, 1984); 1980 census breakdown on ancestry.

14. Jonathan Rieder, *Canarsie: Jews and Italians of Brooklyn Against Liberalism* (Cambridge: Harvard University Press, 1985).

15. "City Democrats Shout 'Encore' to Koch," *Daily News*/Channel 7 Eyewitness Poll, September 1985.

16. *New York Times*, April 15, 1984, B10.

17. *Daily News*/Channel 7 Poll, September 1985.

18. Angelo Falcon et al., *Latino Voter Registration in N.Y.C.* (New York: Institute for Puerto Rican Policy, August 1982), 8.

19. Wallace Sayre and Herbert Kaufman, *Governing New York City* (New York: Norton, 1961), 45–53.

20. Charles Morris, *The Cost of Good Intentions* (New York: Norton, 1980); and William Tabb, *The Long Default* (New York: Monthly Review Press, 1984).

21. Brecher and Horton, "Introduction."

22. For a further discussion, see John Mollenkopf, "The Politics of Racial Advancement and the Failure of Urban Reform: The Case of New York City" (paper presented at the Center for the Study of Industrial Societies, University of Chicago, April 1985), and Lester Salamon, "Partners in Public Service: Toward a Theory of Government–Nonprofit Relations," forthcoming in *Between Public and Private*, ed. Walter Powell (New Haven: Yale University Press).

23. James O'Connor, *The Fiscal Crisis of the State* (New York: St. Martins, 1973); and Roger Friedland, Robert Alford, and Frances Fox Piven, "Political Conflict, Urban Structure, and the Fiscal Crisis," in *Comparing Public Policies*, ed. Douglas Ashford (Beverly Hills: Sage, 1977).

24. Julian Baim, "Southern Politics, New York City Style" (paper presented to the 1983 Annual Meeting of the New York State Political Science Association), 1.

25. *Daily News*/Channel 7 Poll, September 1985.

26. Roman Hedges and Jeffrey Getis, "A Standard for Constructing Minority Legislative Districts: The Issue of Effective Voting Equality" (Nelson Rockefeller Institute of Government, SUNY Albany, Working Paper No. 6, 1981), 11.

27. John Mollenkopf, "New York: The Great Anomaly," in *PS* (Summer 1986).

APPENDIX

Distribution of Industry Sector of Employment by Ethnicity and Gender

Table A.1   White Males

Industry Sector	WASPs	Italians	Irish	(Jewish) Russian
Manufacturing	10.2%	10.8%	7.7%	12.8%
Nondurable	4.3	4.2	3.3	6.3
Apparel	1.2	2.1	0.6	4.1
Printing	1.4	0.9	1.7	0.9
Durable	5.9	6.6	4.4	6.5
Construction	4.8	8.1	6.4	2.8
Transportation	10.5	14.9	13.0	8.0
Communications and Utilities	4.9	6.3	7.9	1.9
Wholesale Trade	5.1	6.0	4.9	10.2
Retail Trade	9.5	13.9	9.2	13.1
Finance, Insurance, Real Estate	15.4	12.2	15.7	10.1
Banking	4.3	3.9	4.8	1.5
Securities	4.8	3.4	3.7	3.1
Advanced Corporate Services	7.6	3.6	4.8	11.2
Bars, Restaurants, and Hotels	4.9	3.3	5.0	2.5
Health Services	4.3	2.9	3.1	4.8
Hospitals	3.4	2.4	2.5	3.9
Education	7.0	3.7	4.5	9.7
Social Services (nonprofit)	1.6	0.7	0.9	1.4
Public Agencies	6.0	7.3	11.2	5.4

Table A.2 White Women

Industry Sector	WASPs	Italians	Irish	(Jewish) Russian
Manufacturing	9.1%	14.0%	7.5%	9.7%
Nondurable	5.0	9.6	3.5	6.6
Apparel	2.6	7.5	1.5	4.7
Printing	0.6	0.3	0.4	0.7
Durable	4.1	4.4	4.0	3.1
Construction	1.0	1.0	0.7	0.9
Transportation	3.1	4.0	3.4	2.2
Communications and Utilities	2.7	3.1	5.1	1.2
Wholesale Trade	5.1	5.0	3.7	7.3
Retail Trade	13.2	15.4	11.5	11.4
Finance, Insurance, Real Estate	19.3	21.7	20.8	11.0
Banking	7.8	9.7	8.0	3.0
Securities	4.2	3.8	4.0	1.8
Advanced Corporate Services	6.8	5.6	6.7	10.6
Bars, Restaurants, and Hotels	4.0	4.0	6.0	1.5
Health Services	8.3	7.5	13.3	8.1
Hospitals	6.3	5.9	10.5	5.9
Education	13.6	9.5	11.6	21.0
Social Services (nonprofit)	4.0	1.8	2.0	4.6
Public Agencies	3.7	3.6	4.3	6.0

Table A.3 Minority Men

Industry Sector	NY Black	Jamaican	Puerto Rican	Dominican	Chinese
Manufacturing	9.7%	15.2%	24.5%	32.5%	16.7%
Nondurable	3.8	4.2	8.1	16.3	12.2
Apparel	1.7	2.1	4.7	10.3	11.4
Printing	0.6	0.1	0.1	0.6	0.4
Durable	5.9	11.0	16.4	16.2	4.5
Construction	4.4	10.6	4.0	3.3	1.6
Transportation	13.7	9.1	8.3	3.8	2.4
Communications and Utilities	3.8	2.5	2.0	0.7	0.7
Wholesale Trade	4.1	4.1	5.7	4.9	3.2
Retail Trade	10.7	11.1	10.8	13.8	6.9
Finance, Insurance, Real Estate	10.0	11.1	10.8	13.8	6.9
Banking	3.6	4.0	1.8	0.8	1.3
Securities	1.2	2.0	0.6	0.4	1.0
Corporate Services	2.5	1.9	0.9	0.3	1.7
Bars, Restaurants, and Hotels	5.1	5.0	8.3	17.2	51.0
Health Services	6.9	11.4	7.9	3.3	1.0
Hospitals	5.7	8.9	6.7	2.2	0.6
Education	5.1	2.9	1.4	1.0	2.6
Social Services (nonprofit)	3.8	2.1	1.4	0.9	0.6
Public Agencies	10.3	2.3	4.5	1.0	0.7

Table A.4 Minority Women

Industry Sector	NY Black	Jamaican	Puerto Rican	Dominican	Chinese
Manufacturing	6.9%	6.6%	38.5%	65.2%	67.3%
Nondurable	3.5	3.5	25.0	46.6	64.7
Apparel	2.4	3.1	19.8	40.0	64.2
Printing	0.1	0.1	0.1	0.1	0.0
Durable	3.4	3.1	13.5	18.6	2.6
Construction	0.5	0.4	0.4	0.4	0.0
Transportation	3.9	1.1	1.8	0.8	1.2
Communications and Utilities	4.5	1.2	1.2	0.5	0.5
Wholesale Trade	2.2	1.9	3.5	2.8	2.3
Retail Trade	10.4	8.9	8.8	7.2	5.9
Finance, Insurance, Real Estate	13.3	15.1	7.7	4.0	5.1
Banking	6.3	9.1	3.0	1.7	2.6
Securities	1.5	1.6	0.9	0.5	0.8
Corporate Services	3.0	2.0	1.6	0.5	1.1
Bars, Restaurants, and Hotels	4.4	4.3	4.0	3.5	6.1
Private Household	2.2	14.1	1.2	2.3	0.8
Health Services	15.5	29.9	10.8	3.3	2.1
Hospitals	12.7	22.1	8.9	2.5	1.5
Education	9.2	3.0	7.1	1.4	2.4
Social Services (nonprofit)	9.5	7.2	4.9	1.9	0.3
Public Agencies	11.0	2.8	4.4	0.8	0.8

Source: 1980 Census Public Use Microdata Sample (PUMS). Definitions are the same as Tables 9.4–9.7. Retail trade figures exclude eating and drinking establishments.

PART **IV**

Conclusions

10

Metropolitan Life and the Making of Public Culture

Thomas Bender

What has long been needed in studies of New York and other great cities is some integrating concept to help scholars—whatever their discipline and specialization—pull together what is known and enable them to orient their future work better to the larger community of scholars studying the same city. The series of conferences out of which these essays emerged sought to address this problem. Each of the essays seeks to reach beyond the discipline and problems that initiated it. But it is as a group that one best appreciates the accomplishments of these essays. Their collective implication is the suggestion of a way to guide scholarship toward an eventual synthetic analysis of New York or other great metropolises.

In my own discipline of history, the emphasis in New York City studies has been on the pieces—on various groups or processes, too often in isolation from one another. Such work is at once necessary and limiting. At this point, I think we need a stronger focus on what is in some sense common (though surely variable) to New Yorkers: the notion of the public realm—as a spatial, cultural, and political phenomenon.

Recent historical writing on New York and other cities has tended to assume, sometimes without much reflection, that the experience of work in the context of industrialization provides the core experience that unifies the disparate elements of urban life.[1] Although the social history of industrialization is a topic of fundamental importance in its own right as well as a key element in the making of city culture, it is not the same

261

as the social history of urbanization.[2] To the extent that the concept of industrialization frames the revival of interest in New York City's history, it has been limiting and, to a degree, distorting. Industrialization does not distinguish great cities from other places: Manchester, Pittsburgh, even Amoskeag, New Hampshire, variously exemplify the social history of industrialization. We must recognize that urbanism and industrialism imply very different questions.

Great cities like New York—or London or Paris or Rome—invite analysis of the making of city life and culture. The social relations of production are not irrelevant to this task, but they are not central.[3] Cities generate a public culture, made up of life in the streets and other public places, embracing a wide range of institutions of culture that, whether privately owned or not, provide an arena for the making, inscribing, and interpreting of public experiences.

It could be argued that a focus on the structure and experience of play and leisure might teach us more about the dynamic of great cities than would a focus on work.[4] When William R. Taylor, in his essay in this volume, points to the centrality of play and the near absence of discussions of work in the texts of urban culture he examines, he rightly reads the urban quality of New York, a distinctive quality it does not share with mere industrial centers. It is in this peculiar element of urban life, a highly developed and enormously complex public life—in which the political and economic cannot be dissociated from the cultural—that the dimensions of contest and order in metropolitan life are to be located. This makes the political dynamics of the metropolis infinitely more complicated than in any industrial town.

The modern city is marked by its capacity to generate public life, not as a periodic and formalized public ritual, as in the medieval and early modern city, but as an ongoing aspect of ordinary daily life.[5] Great cities of the nineteenth and twentieth centuries still share with earlier cities and with smaller human settlements rich configurations of personal networks in which the lives of individuals are rooted. These patterns of association have not dissolved in modern times, much conventional wisdom notwithstanding, but rather have come into relation with a novel and more complex pattern of impersonal association.[6] What characterizes the modern metropolis is the creation of a significant culture of impersonality, a social world of strangers in continuous but limited association.

This quality of impersonal association gives the modern city its peculiar definition. The emergence of this impersonal world transforms the meaning of society, culture, and politics. If the origins of this transformation can be traced well back into the colonial era, the essays in Part I by Peter G. Buckley and Amy Bridges chart, in different fashions, its flowering in the antebellum years.

The image of the market provides us with a rich metaphor for acquiring a qualitative understanding of the modern city and its culture. Max Weber, who identified the modern city with the market, observed that the market "is the most impersonal form of practical life into which humans can enter with one another." As Weber always understood, it is an arena of a characteristically modern form of power.[7] These qualities of the modern market are paradigmatic of broader qualities that I associate with the notion of city culture. I refer particularly to the pattern of exchange among strangers and to the subtle patterns of exclusion, distortion, and blockage that define these exchanges.

In the market, as in the modern city, there is an "incomplete integration" of participants. People enter and withdraw from the market, including the marketplace of public culture, without relinquishing other structural attachments. The values and local commitments brought to the central place of public culture affect the meanings and results associated with that experience. At the heart of the metropolitan experience, then, is a mechanism that connects, without destroying, mixed and homogeneous urban collectivities.[8]

Smaller *gemeinschaftlich* groups defined by various categories—sometimes empowering, sometimes constraining, based upon class relations, gender relations, ethnic identity, family and kinship networks, spatial distributions, and the like—come into contact in the public life of the city. Their coming together in fact constitutes the public culture of the city.

This culture is contested terrain. Much of the city's social dynamic derives from attempts to possess and appropriate that terrain. The topographical quality of this image is appealing, since cities are distinguished from society generally by their peculiar conjuncture of spatial and social relationships. But the notion need not be restricted only to territory. Whether the arena is the city's public space or its social institutions (for example, schools or newspapers), the prize for the actors is relative influence, legitimacy, and security for the meanings they give to civic life. The result for the collectivity is what I call public culture, a local configuration of power and symbolism, always in some flux, yet understood and either accepted or challenged by all local groups of social actors.[9] A focus on the making, inscribing, and meaning of the public realm is a way of pulling together the many strands of experience that must be incorporated into any synthetic understanding of the city.

The concern of these essays with economic, political, and cultural history suggests yet more. Here we see that phenomena we conventionally call *culture* are in fact political once they are framed within the notion of the making of public culture. The political becomes difficult to distinguish from the cultural.[10] And when one speaks, as William R. Taylor does, of the hegemonic possibilities of commercial culture, all conventional categories are confounded in the historical analysis as well as in the historical process itself.

The connotation of the *public* changes from sector to sector. In economic analysis, the "public" is interventionist, generally representing a nonmarket principle of resource allocation. In politics, the "public" refers to political expressions of diverse interests through governmental institutions, interests mobilized by various strategies. In the cultural realm, the notion is at once more expansive and less well bounded conceptually. It may mean publicly subsidized cultural activity, but it may also mean cultural activities (e.g., vaudeville or public sculpture) open to a diverse audience on either a commercial or a not-for-profit basis. The "public" in all these permutations represents an arena where different interests, commitments, and values collide and resolve themselves into a reciprocal, multivoiced, perhaps even carnivalesque civic sense that is shared as a *relation*, not as sameness or consensus.

A focus on public culture can enable urban history to establish the various degrees to which identifiable groups participate in the public world, always attentive to the terms of this participation. Unlike the older pluralism that also stressed interaction in a somewhat narrower conception of public life, such a history would not assume that all relevant groups are represented in public.[11] It would rather ask why some groups and some values are so much—or so little—represented in the historical construction of the public realm.

If the modern city and its distinctive experience are defined by the simultaneity of multiple meanings and actions in public, then public life is a constitutive arena where these meanings and interests are brought into contact, sometimes as conversation, sometimes as confrontation. Smaller units of life are not in this devalued; rather, the transaction between the whole and its parts is stressed. This relationship between the parts and the whole, the periphery and the center, even the private and the public, is reciprocal. The point is to explore this relationship. But if one seeks to grasp the city, rather than one of its parts, this process is best scrutinized from the point of view of public culture, not of these segmented cultures.

The focus, then, would be on the interplay of the interior cultures (the world of private life, the cultures of homogeneous groups) and the exterior, contested culture of the city's public life. How does the interior realm of various cultures affect the larger world of public life? How do the character and quality of public relationships in turn affect private life? Such an angle of vision can capture a distinctive and important quality of modern urban culture: the constant movement between local cultures and public culture, between the homogeneous sectors of the periphery and the heterogeneous, contested center.

Always, however, there is a "problem" to be addressed in the analysis of public culture. It represents a contest—and one that is not fairly waged. The stakes, moreover, are high: "the public interpretation of reality." Particular social groups, seeking power and recognition, want, in Karl Mannheim's phrase, "to make their interpretation of the world universal." This thrust by all groups, but most obviously and effectively by the powerful, seeks to define for themselves and *for others* a public culture that looks very much like their group values writ large.[12] In achieving an interpretive, analytical, and moral orientation to this contest, one realizes the promise of the study of public culture.

The essays in this volume reveal that the formation of culture and society in New York and the structuring of order is far too complex to be captured in a simple bipolar analytical model—rich and poor, capital and labor, native and immigrant, elite and mass, establishment and the people, or any other conceivable pair. Such bipolarities generally define the rhetoric of social history, with its concern for understanding the changing social relations of industrialization; urban history, however, requires a multiplex approach.

One finds in these essays repeated reference to rather striking economic inequality. Yet the clarity of these statistical facts is considerably reduced in the formation of individual identities and public culture. To understand the relative social and political stability in a city so desperately unequal in its social structure, we must understand the making of metropolitan culture much better than we do at present.

New York after the 1820s has been a prototypical modern metropolis in its combination of democratic ideology and its multiple axes of social identification and division. Most urban scholarship on New York and other large cities has concentrated on the various elements—women, immigrants, workers, blacks, architects or planners, bankers, and so on. Too much of this literature seems self-referential. When it does assume any relational perspective, these relations tend to be bipolar (men and women, for example, not men, women, Democrats, garment workers, and movies).

Yet, we must be careful; we must not go from bipolarity to bricolage.[13] Historiography, like the city itself, may become simply unmanageable if one too enthusiastically multiplies such distinctions. But the focus on public culture seems to offer a means of acknowledging complexity in a relational sense without being overwhelmed by it. The focus on the construction of the public realm allows the scholar to approach what is "common" without sacrificing the fact and the fundamental significance of difference.

The demographic and economic foundations of the modern city of New York as it began to take form in the first half of the nineteenth century is elaborated in this volume by Diane Lindstrom. It is important to recognize not only the great disparities of wealth and the labor market segmentation that she outlines, but also the cultural vitality suggested by her enumeration of data relating to immigration, the proliferation of newspaper readers, travelers, and letter writers. Here the city is actively creating its own culture out of the most diverse materials. We do not get, however, a clear sense of how these elements are given public form. There is little sense of geography and no indication of the spatial elaboration of economic and cultural development. Nor do we get a sense of the real or proposed relations of public authority and private power in the shaping of the city's economy and society. But surely that is a key question to be explored: What was the contemporary theoretical and practical claim of the public on the social and economic processes Lindstrom describes? What was the relative importance of private and public decisions in shaping the physical and social development of the city?[14] Without answers to such questions, we lack the knowledge needed to understand the making of public culture.

The extreme inequality documented by Lindstrom provides the essential context for the work of Amy Bridges and Peter G. Buckley. One cannot but be struck by the language of bipolarity in their reconstruction of political and cultural life. But equally striking: simultaneous with these perceptions, social practice in public, whether in the political or cultural realm, dissolved that language into a much more diverse, messy, even confused process of social formation. The diffuseness of social practice seems to have undermined the language of bipolarity in the interest of stability. By what mechanisms did this occur? Here we want to know much more about the transactions between public and private. In that inquiry we want to know how the political and cultural were related, or not related, to each other. How did political practices and cultural expressions articulate with economic processes to dissolve the destabilizing potential of gross inequality?

Before about 1820, as Bridges and Buckley both suggest, the line between public and private was indistinct, as was that between the Patriciate and the Town. The emergence of democratic claims coincided with the advent of a contentious public sphere. Paradoxically, however, the emergence of a democratic ethos and a vital public sphere seems to have somehow depoliticized economics and culture. In Jacksonian America the confrontation of competing political interests typically resulted in the dispersion of power, removing the issue from the realm of politics to that of private decision and conscience. Economics and culture, as a consequence and in a way recognizable in our time, tended to become self-referential and self-legitimating. The firmer the boundaries of the public sphere, the more difficult its connection to other social processes, something that might at once intensify and broaden the contest over meaning while reducing its material consequences. If such a paradox is inherent in this process, we need much more historical understanding of it, for its implications would be of considerable theoretical and practical import.[15]

Both Bridges and Buckley show the public gradually becoming at once an arena for and the substance of an ever-broadening contest. Political machines and public spaces both offered a place for men and, to a lesser extent, women to bring their private *gemeinschaftlich* interests and values to the contest over the definition of public power and meaning. Public space and the machine were the key sites for inscribing public culture in a modern democratic city.

So fearful are we of seeming to be provincial boosters that we seldom realize that public life, whether in the streets or in the formal political sense, was created in its specifically modern image in New York. Here we find—before any other city—diversity, egalitarianism, and mass suffrage producing a city contentious but not insurrectionary. These qualities make the study of New York peculiarly interesting and significant. The weakness of its traditional social forms made the American metropolis, even while still on the periphery of the Atlantic world, precociously modern.

If public culture was first formed in New York before the Civil War, it seems to have been significantly restructured between, roughly, the 1880s and the 1930s. In politics, Martin Shefter shows in this volume that the notion of the public, at least in reform ideology and practice, became directly opposed to that of the machine.[16] If defenders of the machine might have located the contest among diverse interests and values *within* the machine, Shefter argues that by the time of Fiorello LaGuardia the machine had come to represent a "special interest" in opposition to the "public interest." Pluralism replaced the machine when a variety of channels to power were developed through which organized interests (of which the machine was reduced to only one) interacted with one another, rather than with the machine. With this development, the center, the arena, of the public shifted and probably became more sectoral and functional (e.g., education, sanitation, real estate, and so on) rather than localistic and spatial in its component parts. Such developments subtly undermine the place-specific basis of city culture and city politics.

Much the same shift is evident in the city building process as recounted by Emanuel Tobier: larger and more organized actors were increasingly brought into the more pluralistic city-planning process. In the cultural realm, William R. Taylor effectively describes an analogous process in his inferences about the transition from popular, or, as I would call it, city culture, to mass culture. In this process the location and reciprocal association with streets and neighborhoods is attenuated by 1930.[17] The dissolution of public culture in the nineteenth century sense is suggested in yet another way: if Taylor is correct in using the word *pastiche* to describe what he finds, and if, as he suggests, every reader is practically free to "read" whatever versions of the city's culture he or she desires in the compendious hodgepodge of the newspaper, then it may be that nothing beyond the most trivial cultural matters provides the basis for a common culture, even understood as relational difference rather than sameness.[18]

The essays in Part III, by Norman and Susan Fainstein, William Kornblum and James Beshers, and John Mollenkopf, address the issue of public culture less directly. Yet insofar as they touch upon matters surrounding the making of such culture, they raise questions not so much as to its restructuring as to whether it continues to exist at all. We read of an economy structured by translocal institutions, of failed popular political movements, of the apparent inability of various subordinate groups to find a place in public, and of an aggressive defense of neighborhood space in the boroughs. At the same time, unmentioned in the text but directly related to the transformations the essays consider, is Times Square. This great example of a heterogeneous center, a place famous for the making of city culture out of diverse elements, has become a symbol of fear and urban failure. It is about to be transformed under municipal and state auspices from a public square to a post-modern corporate campus. The erosion of public values along the periphery of the city in Jamaica Bay thus finds its parallel in the center. At the periphery, however defined, the forces toward sameness have always been strong, but the greatness of the city lay in the means whereby the center could transform homogeneous elements into a heterogeneous public culture. The current efforts of the political, civic, and economic elites of the city to transfer a public space from all groups to one group strikes at the moral ideal of city culture. It may even mark the exhaustion of the ideal.

Is metropolitan culture a phenomenon of the past? Is the city still a place of multiple voices in public? Of *gemeinschaftlich* groups engaging one another in a public place and thus inscribing for themselves and others a multidimensional public culture? Or have politics and culture ceased to be a part of a complex and reciprocal urban process? Have politics and culture become, as Debra Silverman has argued in a recent book, a version of Bloomingdale's fashion and consumer fantasy, with no relation to the actual peoples, circumstances, and experience of metropolitan life?[19] Such a phenomenon, whatever its sources and dimensions, is a denial of the historical understanding of metropolitan culture offered at the beginning of this essay.

It may well be that the era of the great city, the metropolitan city, as Jane Jacobs has warned us repeatedly, is over, after a career of, at best, two centuries.[20] In studying New York City historically, we define metropolitan culture by its great examples. In the process, however, we may also discover how different this rapidly receding metropolitan experience is from our own. But that fact, too, may enable us better to grasp emergent cultural and political forms, thus clarifying our contemporary circumstance.

Notes

1. Here I refer even to such a fine book as Sean Wilentz, *Chants Democratic: New York City and the Rise of the American Working Class* (New York: Oxford University Press, 1984).

2. Although she begins with the assumptions of the social history of industrialization, Christine Stansell moves toward the social history of urban culture in her *City of Women: Sex and Class in New York, 1789–1860* (New York: Knopf, 1986). See also Peter G. Buckley, "To the Opera House: Culture and Society in New York City, 1820–1860" (Ph.D. diss., State University of New York, Stony Brook, 1984).

3. This point is well made by Gareth Stedman-Jones, *Outcast London* (New York: Pantheon Books, 1984).

4. See the stimulating recent work of Kathy Peiss, *Cheap Amusements: Working Women and Leisure in Turn-of-the-Century New York* (Philadelphia: Temple University Press, 1986). Also, it is this focus that makes Theodore Dreiser's *Sister Carrie* one of the great urban novels.

5. See, for example, Edward Muir, *Civic Ritual in Renaissance Venice* (Princeton: Princeton University Press, 1981); and Natalie Z. Davis, "The Sacred and the Body Social in Lyons," *Past and Present* 90 (1981): 40–70.

6. This argument is fully developed in Thomas Bender, *Community and Social Change in America* (Baltimore: Johns Hopkins University Press, 1982).

7. Max Weber, *Economy and Society* (New York: Bedminster Press, 1968), 636. See also Max Weber, *The City* (New York: Free Press, 1958); and Max Weber, *Max Weber on Law in Economy and Society* (Cambridge: Harvard University Press, 1954), 196.

8. Hans Paul Bahrdt, "Public Activity and Private Activity as Basic Forms of City Association," in *New Perspectives on the American Community*, 3rd ed., ed. Roland Warren (Chicago: Rand McNally, 1977), 28–32.

9. In a series of recent essays, I have been gradually elaborating my thinking on this notion as a general historiographical issue. See Thomas Bender, "The New History—Then and Now," *Reviews in American History* 12 (1984): 612–22; "Making History Whole Again," *New York Times Book Review* (October 6, 1985): 1, 42–43; "Wholes and Parts: The Need for Synthesis in American History," *The Journal of American History* 73 (June 1986): 120–35; and "Wholes and Parts: Continuing the Conversation," *The Journal of American History* 74 (June 1987): 123–30.

10. See Jean H. Baker, *Affairs of Party: The Political Culture of Northern Democrats in the Mid-Nineteenth Century* (Ithaca: Cornell University Press, 1983).

11. For the conventional pluralism to which I refer, see David C. Hammack, "Problems in the Historical Study of Power in the Cities and Towns of the United States, 1800–1860," *American Historical Review* 83 (April 1978): 323–49.

12. Karl Mannheim, "Competition as a Cultural Phenomenon," in his *Essays on the Sociology of Culture* (London: Routledge & Kegan Paul, 1956), 196–98.

13. For an example of where we might end up if we indulge a penchant for multiplying axes, see the brilliant yet problematic work of Theodore Zeldin, *France, 1848–1945*, 2 vols. (Oxford: Oxford University Press, 1973–1977).

14. See, for a good beginning, Hendrick Hartog, *Public Property and Private Power: The Corporation of the City of New York in American Law, 1730–1870* (Chapel Hill: University of North Carolina Press, 1983).

15. Here the "free speech situation" that Jurgen Habermas idealizes as the definition of the public sphere may in fact undermine his political intent. For his earliest formulation, originally published in 1946, see his "The Public Sphere: An Encyclopedia Article," *New German Critique* 3 (Fall 1974): 49–55.

16. It is important to remember, strange as it may seem in the context of the present Koch administration scandals, that New York, for most of the twentieth century, including the Koch administration, has been a "reformed" city. See Theodore Lowi, "Machine Politics—Old and New," *The Public Interest* 9 (1967): 83–92.

17. On this point, see the illuminating work of Robert L. Snyder, "Voice of the City: Vaudeville and the Birth of Mass Culture in the Neighborhoods of New York City, 1880–1930" (Ph.D. diss., New York University, 1985).

18. Here, whether or not the possibilities for readings are as utterly open as the term *pastiche* suggests, the role of "desire" in interpretation as developed by

some literary critics deserves the attention of students of urban culture. See the rich critical writings of Peter Brooks, *Reading for the Plot* (New York: Knopf, 1984).

19. Debra Silverman, *Selling Culture: Bloomingdale's, The Metropolitan, the White House, and the Merchandising of the New Aristocracy* (New York: Pantheon Books, 1986).

20. See Jane Jacobs, *The Death and Life of Great American Cities* (New York: Vintage, 1961), and, especially, her more recent *Cities and the Wealth of Nations* (New York: Random House, 1984).

11

The Place of Politics
and the Politics of Place

John Hull Mollenkopf

Two themes in this volume intertwine to produce an interesting paradox. One concerns the declining ability of party organizations to moderate or stabilize the explosive potential of class inequalities produced by New York City's development. In the mercantile and industrial eras, the regular county party organizations provided the central means for mediating such conflicts. They forged inter-class and inter-ethnic political accommodations, selectively articulated some forms of political expression while dampening others, and provided the only route to ongoing political power. The regular party organizations still exist and exercise influence today, but they contrast greatly with the situation a century, or even fifty years, earlier. At best they are one of many means of striking inter-class and inter-ethnic accommodations, if indeed they do so at all. Their organizational roots in the city's new minority working class are weaker and more tenuous, and they certainly cannot claim to be the only, or even the most important, route to political power.

The other theme concerns the state's capacity to shape physical and economic development. In contrast to the oblique influence the state exerted through the 1811 street plan, the Erie Canal, or the subway system, today state intervention is direct and extensive. Two paradoxes thus arise: as the state has become stronger, the historical mechanism for mediating class conflict over its actions has progressively weakened; and, despite increasing tensions produced by the weakening of the regular county party organizations and the fact that class inequality is as

273

great as ever, the potential for those outside the political establishment to challenge it has, if anything, declined. These apparently contradictory trends are worth pondering.

The Place of Politics

The first theme is a variant on a classic Madisonian concern: How can political participation and party competition be structured in a way that both selectively represents the city's evolving interests and blunts the formation of factional cleavages around the issue of property? Madison argued that limited government, the separation of powers, and federalism would limit the tyranny of a propertyless majority. Taking a different approach, Amy Bridges and Martin Shefter (in this volume) have shown that party competition and machine politics cut across and constrained class divisions from the start in New York and other large cities. And while Madison feared political excess, Bridges and Shefter have the opposite concern, that the party system represented the underlying range of interests in a selective, partial, and perhaps debased manner.

Bridges and Shefter suggest that this tendency was variable and complex, however. While the party system dampened some political expressions of working class interests, it facilitated others. The "machine" encouraged expressions of mass sentiment and working class culture that promoted party strength, while suppressing forms of interest expression that challenged the dominant regular party organizations. Bridges convincingly argues that the American party system, as exemplified by New York City's Democratic party, patterned working class political participation in a distinct way compared to the form it took in Britain or might have taken in New York and the United States if white male suffrage and party competition had not preceded the formation of the urban working class. Shefter's essay and his other work have convincingly elaborated this theme of simultaneous representation and exclusion. Katznelson has made a similar point with regard to black political representation.[1]

Marx thought that the concentration of workers in increasingly class-divided cities would lead to a direct challenge to capitalism. Bridges suggests that the New York Democrats absorbed this challenge with relative ease. Tammany made the establishment of New York City as a dominant one-party island in the antebellum political system a profitable enterprise. Lindstrom makes clear that this was not for want of sharp and growing class inequality, and Buckley shows that workers did develop distinct and vital cultural zones of their own.

Tammany (and after 1898 the regular Democratic organizations in Brooklyn and the other boroughs) was thus able, through selective representation and the striking of cross-class accommodations, to contain the potential consequences of class inequality until at least the 1930s. But with the New Deal and the La Guardia years, and even more in the 1960s, this began to change. Shefter recounts how reform episodes progressively weakened the role of party chieftains in striking accommodations among the important interests and political forces of the city. During the New Deal, local administration fell into the hands of fusion Republican Fiorello La Guardia for more than a decade, while reformers became a major force in the local and national Democratic party. Most agencies were "reformed" by giving special access to nonparty interest groups and constituencies.

This trend continued after World War II. Shefter and the Fainsteins describe how regular Democrats paid the "price" of support for Robert Moses' autonomous public works empire in order to secure business acquiescence in their return to power in City Hall. Mayor Wagner campaigned successfully for reelection in 1961 against the county leaders who had previously promoted his career. Mayor Lindsay was the archetype of the reform outsider, while Mayor Koch began his career as the Village Independent Democrats' candidate in 1963 to block Carmine De Sapio's return to a district leadership.

By the late 1960s, Tammany Hall, the oldest continually existing political organization in the world, was effectively bankrupt, had sold its Union Square headquarters to the ILGWU, and was headed by De Sapio's former chauffeur.[2] The local political clubs on which the county party organizations had been built were far fewer, and even the survivors were in decline.[3] Richard Croker and Charles Murphy, Tammany's greatest chieftains, would surely have been astounded and dismayed by such a turn of events. Reform had made regular party leaders peripheral players in the postwar "pluralist" regime, especially in New York's political core, Manhattan.

The decline of regular Democratic organizational influence has not been complete, however. Regulars may have been banished from the core, but they remain a force on the periphery. Most New Yorkers, including most blacks and Hispanics, reside in the outer boroughs where a few strong assembly district political clubs keep regular county party organizations in power. Despite recent scandals, they still control the borough presidencies and the lower reaches of the representative system, especially in the city council and the judiciary.

By controlling these rungs of the political system, the regulars can block or delay initiatives from the reformed center and extract patronage in return for their cooperation. These resources can be used to compete against borough-level minority challengers, to win minority votes, and to foster "plantation politics" in which minority leaders become beholden to the regulars.[4] The regulars have so far managed to bring a good many successful black and Hispanic insurgents into their fold. Of the seven black and three Hispanic Council members, no more than two can be considered independents. Bronx, Brooklyn, and Queens regulars have defeated minority challengers for the borough presidencies, and their ally, Mayor Koch, secured an impressive number of minority votes against a black challenger in 1985.[5]

This lingering influence must be distinguished, nevertheless, from the more pervasive power that regular organizations exercised before the 1950s. Today, these organizations do not appear deeply enough rooted in minority working class neighborhoods to dictate their future political development. Instead, their political capacity derives from the white ethnic enclaves on the city's rim where organizations such as the Thomas Jefferson Democratic Club may be found.

As a result, their ability to pattern minority political mobilization is limited. Bronx regulars could prevent Assemblyman Jose Serrano from unseating the incumbent borough president only by resorting to numerous "election irregularities." The Queens regulars could not dictate the successor in the late Congressman Joe Addabo's majority black south Jamaica district. A black insurgent coalition has made considerable inroads in Brooklyn, unseating corrupt black politicians associated with the regular organization. Future demographic trends do not bode well for the social base of the regular organizations.

Despite continuing regular Democratic party influence in the outer boroughs, regulars must therefore be clearly distinguished from their "machine" predecessors. Because they do not control access to citywide offices or set overall policies, they are no longer central to the securing of the cross-class accommodations that undergirded political stability in the past. If anything, today they contribute to and reinforce New York's class and racial inequalities. Nor are they champions of the increased social spending that might promote cross-class accommodations. Reform critics may well decry how earlier machine politicians managed their constituencies, but they cannot deny that such Tammany leaders as Al Smith pioneered social welfare measures which, in turn, promoted the regulars' strength in working class constituencies. The regular organizations use their current influence over government operations to protect their white, middle class, homeowning constituencies.

If the regular party organizations do not promote cross-class and inter-ethnic accommodations, then what prevents these considerable underlying class and racial tensions from being loudly and directly expressed? Does some other political mechanism achieve what the political machines used to accomplish?

The forces of reform certainly do not promote such cross-class and cross-race accommodations. In the past, white liberal reformers pursued their own political interests by goading the regulars to bring new groups into city employment and appointive and elective office. The La Guardia administration did this for Jews and Italians in the 1930s, and the Lindsay administration did it for blacks (and, to a lesser extent, Hispanics) in the 1960s. Middle class white liberals needed the support of outgroups to gain their own ascendancy. Today, however, reformers are little better than regulars at providing entry points to excluded groups. The middle class Jews who fueled reform in previous decades, for example, *are* the establishment today. Middle class professionals now enjoy direct access to the agencies and policy arenas that interest them. They consequently show little interest in mobilizing working class minority groups.

V. O. Key once pointed out that factional competition simply does not represent minorities and other outgroups as well as party competition does.[6] Neither the regular nor the reform faction of the Democratic party is now interested in mobilizing potentially challenging groups, but no other potential vehicle for political mobilization is either. The Republican party shows no interest in fusion, and the Liberal party is little more than a convenient ballot line. Nor do nonparty organizations offer more prospects for crystallizing an insurgent coalition of outsiders.

The public employee unions, caught up in their own processes of racial transition, have been thrown on the defensive by the fiscal crisis, and are too dependent on established politicians to challenge them frontally. Trade unions in other sectors dominated by the emerging majority of minority groups are either economically extremely vulnerable, like the ILGWU, or nonexistent. The many community-based service delivery organizations and community groups cannot act as an independent political force either. In short, the political leadership of a potential insurgent coalition is weak, fragmented, and divided, and lacks a way to heal these conditions.[7]

The net result seems to be that the political organizations that Bridges and Buckley describe as once having promoted accommodations across classes have been replaced by spatial and political separations that Kornblum and Beshers describe well. The civic culture that Bender perceptively evokes as a main focus for historical analysis has become deeply fragmented. The political system is less representative of the city's actual social base and the reform cycle less capable of producing the political development needed to cope with new forms of inequality.

The resulting political stability is frustrating to the discontented in the short run, but perhaps ultimately brittle.

The Politics of Place

The state's growing capacity to shape urban development contrasts clearly with regular party decline. In the antebellum period, the state merely provided a framework in which market forces were given free play; any sense of artisanal rights and guild privileges went quickly by the boards. While the Erie Canal, the Croton water supply system, Central Park, the Brooklyn Bridge, and the construction of the subway system after 1900 were publicly financed, the commissions that built them were essentially under elite private control; the subways were privately owned, though regulated.

The golden years of city growth described by Tobier continued the earlier pattern. The pathbreaking 1916 Zoning Act was designed to prevent the sky-blocking overbuilding of Lower Manhattan through setbacks and the intrusion of loft factories and their workers on upper class commercial and residential districts through land use controls. It was thus a form of self-protection for property owners.[8] Extension of the subway influenced development even more strongly, but it too was in private hands until well into the Great Depression.

As with the decline of the regular party organizations, the New Deal represented a "fault line" in government influence over the city's physical development. Beginning in 1933, and especially in the 1950s, New York City built a prodigious amount of publicly owned and publicly subsidized nonprofit housing, culminating in over 110,000 public housing units, another 80,000 Section 8 units, and 138,000 Mitchell-Lama units, sheltering one household out of eight.[9] Extensive rent regulation became a permanent feature of the New York City housing market in the mid-1940s as well.

Parallel to this direct intervention in the housing market, independent public authorities, under the aegis of Robert Moses and Austin Tobin, "recaptured" central business district land for "higher and better" uses and constructed the metropolitan bridge and highway network.[10] Unlike the earlier commissions sponsoring public improvements, these new authorities represented genuine expansions of state capacity. Their actions spatially reorganized the city to accommodate postindustrial economic activities, the automobile era, and a new middle class suburban lifestyle. Market forces would have produced these results, but massive state intervention undoubtedly hastened this transformation. And while business influenced these agencies, they developed much greater autonomy and capacity than did the organizations that had built the canals and bridges a century before.

The political and economic logic that framed this intervention is a matter of debate. The Fainsteins argue that national economic forces and federal policy produced essentially similar outcomes in all cities, that capital was "directive" in the initial phase, and that New York differed only by anticipating national patterns in a more liberal way that resulted in more social housing. Each of these points is open to serious challenge. Joel Schwartz has recently shown, for example, that liberals and radicals contributed substantially to Moses' power, undermining the Fainsteins' argument about the "directive" nature of this era.[11] The notion that cities are mere creatures of larger forces can also be challenged.[12] Indeed, New York City's economically pivotal location has enabled its political system to extract more local taxes and to grow larger than is true of most other cities.

Whatever the causal mechanics, however, the result is clear: in New York City, government intervenes pervasively in the urban development process. Indeed, it can be argued that intervention is now broader, and market forces more conditioned upon it, than ever before. The president of the Real Estate Board recently argued that no major project could go forward in Manhattan without substantial public subsidies because it could not compete with the many other projects that do have such support. Multibillion dollar examples include Battery Park City and the 42nd Street Development Project.[13] Almost as if the lessons of protest against urban renewal in the 1960s had been forgotten, massive redevelopment is also under way in downtown Brooklyn, with an aggregate construction value also approaching a billion dollars.

Meanwhile, the production of social housing is nearly at a standstill. This state of affairs is symbolized by the current economic development mission of the Urban Development Corporation, initially established to build subsidized housing. Mayor Koch's proposed $4.2 billion housing program may invigorate the future production of moderate income housing, but the prospects for better housing are quite dim for the quarter of New York's population that falls below the official poverty line.

Interrelationships and Consequences

It is tempting to argue, following Friedland, Piven, and Alford, that political party decline was a precondition for the growth of state intervention in the urban development process. They argue that state economic development activities must be "structurally segregated" from social programs and insulated from popular political accountability.[14] But this view is problematically functionalist: a contradiction "must" be resolved in a certain way. To be truly convincing, this argument must show how and why structural segregation is actually socially constructed. A causal relationship cannot simply be deduced, as the Fainsteins do when they assume that New York City's political patterns are simply imprinted by systemic economic and political imperatives.

On the face of it, it seems unlikely that large corporations and other pro-growth interests would attack the party system in order to promote state intervention to foster economic transformation. In general, as long as they could benefit from contracts, contributions, and payoffs, regular party organizations have happily promoted development even when public opinion opposed it. The Fainsteins and Caro's study of Moses' tactics make it quite clear that his "structurally segregated" activities cohabited nicely with machine politics. For their part, developers have shown no lack of interest in making contributions to the regulars as well as to the erstwhile reformer mayor.

The link between regular party decline and growing state influence over development must therefore be more complicated. Shefter and others have suggested that business dismay over graft, inefficiency, and lack of action on development projects contributed the reform agenda of establishing independent development agencies. This provides a starting point for explaining the relationship between growing state intervention and party decline, but much more work remains to be done.

If the causal link between these trends remains unclear, their practical consequences for the city do not. Declining party control over political access, the growing disjuncture between the dominant political coalition and the city's actual social makeup, and the absence of a mechanism to promote reform have reinvigorated the politics of capital investment. At least for the time being, a new pro-growth coalition dominates New York City politics.

The results may be read in the unprecedented rate of change in the city's neighborhoods and central business district. More office buildings are being constructed than in any other city, the real income of the upper half is rising strongly, and gentrification has picked up its pace. Once-scorned areas like the Lower East Side and Harlem have experienced dizzying real estate speculation.

Owing to the political trends discussed, this new form of pro-growth politics retreats not only from the late 1960s and early 1970s but from the New Deal. Few mechanisms remain from the Great Society era to restrain or provide community influence over development projects. Community boards cannot block projects, and "project area committees" and "maximum feasible participation" are no longer mandated. The remaining community development corporations are mostly scrambling for a decreasing supply of public funds by supplicating themselves to established political powers. Rapid central business district construction has been accompanied by a worsening of housing prospects for the bottom quarter. In contrast to the 1950s or even the early 1970s, the city is building almost no public housing.

The city's capital stock is also being renewed in a more private and less social way than was true in the New Deal. Indeed, New York's public spaces are still living off New Deal capital investments, be they neighborhood pools, Riis Park beach, or the Brooklyn Public Library. Some New Deal facilities have recently been renovated, but many others are in disrepair. Clearly, no new program of communally oriented public works on a New Deal scale is in the offing. Whatever their faults, the strength of regular Democratic party organizations in the New Deal era probably had something to do with the public-regarding nature of its public works program.

The truncated nature of contemporary political organization in New York undoubtedly contributes to the private orientation of state intervention in the development process. Many observers have expressed qualified hopes that community organizations would emerge as a liberal force in urban politics, but this result has not been realized in New York. The political engines that drove increases in social spending, community-based provision of new kinds of services, and a policy reorientation toward the neighborhoods in the late 1960s are now in low gear, if not disengaged.

This conclusion poses a most interesting research question. Scholarly opinion has generally classified (and national public opinion has often vilified) New York City as an archetypically liberal city. The Al Smith and the Franklin Roosevelt wings of the New York Democratic party both helped define modern political liberalism in America. New York's Jewish socialist trade union tradition was at one time pervasive. The Fainsteins' favorable analysis of the Lindsay administration is testimony to the city's contribution to Great Society politics during the late 1960s. The city has been a hotbed of radicalism, whether of the old left or of the new. It has also been a major source of national leadership for black and Hispanic civil rights movements. Today, these traditions appear to be largely moribund. How and why this came to pass must surely be a significant question for social scientists as well as a matter for deep political introspection.

Notes

1. Martin Shefter, "Political Incorporation and the Extrusion of the Left: Party Politics and Social Forces in New York City," *Studies in American Political Development* 1 (1986): 50–90; and Ira Katznelson, *Black Men, White Cities* (New York: Oxford University Press, 1973).

2. Warren Moscow, *The Last of the Big-Time Bosses: The Life and Times of Carmine De Sapio and the Decline and Fall of Tammany Hall* (New York: Stein and Day, 1971), 159–86.

3. Norman Adler and Blanche Blank, *Political Clubs in New York* (New York: Praeger, 1975).

4. Angelo Falcon, "Black and Latino Politics in New York City: Race and Ethnicity in a Changing Urban Context" (Institute for Puerto Rican Policy, 1985); and Basil Wilson and Charles Green, "The State of Black Politics in New York City" (John Jay College, CUNY, 1985).

5. John Mollenkopf, "New York, The Great Anomaly," *PS* (Summer 1986).

6. V. O. Key, *Southern Politics in State and Nation* (New York: Vintage Books, 1949), chap. 14.

7. John Mollenkopf, "The Politics of Racial Advancement and the Failure of Urban Reform: The Case of New York City" (paper presented at the Center for the Study of Industrial Societies, University of Chicago, April 1985) explores this point further.

8. S. J. Makielski, Jr., *The Politics of Zoning* (New York: Columbia University Press, 1966), 11–40.

9. Elizabeth Roistacher and Emanuel Tobier, "Housing Policy," in *Setting Municipal Priorities: 1981*, ed. Charles Brecher and Raymond Horton (Montclair, N.J.: Allanheld, Osmun, 1980), 145–80; and *New York Times*, April 21, 1983, B4.

10. Aside from the Fainsteins' essay, in this volume, see Robert Caro, *The Power Broker* (New York: Knopf, 1974); and Jameson Doig, "To Claim the Seas and the Skies: Austin Tobin and the Port of New York Authority," in *Leadership and Innovation*, eds. Jameson Doig and Irwin C. Hargrove (Baltimore: Johns Hopkins University Press, 1987), 124–73.

11. Joel Schwartz, "Tenant Radicals, Urban Liberals, and Redevelopment in New York City, 1937–1953" (paper presented to the annual meeting of the Organization of American Historians, New York City, April 1986).

12. For example, Rufus Browning, Dale Marshall, and David Tabb's *Protest Is Not Enough* (Berkeley: University of California Press, 1984) shows great vari-

ation in local political and policy outcomes despite larger economic and federal policy uniformities.

13. For an excellent discussion of the Forty-second Street Development Project, see the special issue on the redevelopment of Forty-second Street, *City Almanac* 18, no. 4 (Summer 1985), Susan Fainstein, guest editor.

14. Roger Friedland, Frances Fox Piven, and Robert Alford, "Political Conflict, Urban Structure, and the Fiscal Crisis," in *Comparing Public Policies,* ed. Douglas Ashford (Beverly Hills: Sage, 1977).

12

Reflections on Space and the City

Ira Katznelson

Max Weber had little to say as a social theorist about New York, Chicago, St. Louis, and the other large cities he saw during his visit to the United States in 1904. But he made clear in his diary entries that these cities served as a metaphor for capitalist modernity: magnificently though frightfully fragmented, "a mad pell-mell," extraordinarily unequal, characterized by "a tremendous intensity of work," loosely integrated, composed of a mosaic of nationalities each in its own territory, yet marked by an uncaring individuality. "Undoubtedly one could take ill and die without anyone caring!" He was struck too by the way in which an unequal social structure was inscribed in space, and by the extent of the geographic divisions between work and home: "When they finish work at five o'clock, people must often travel for hours to get home. . . . With the exception of the better residential districts, the whole tremendous city—more extensive than London!—is like a man whose skin has been peeled off and whose intestines are seen at work."[1]

Weber's astonishment was quite characteristic; it was no more than the common sense of the time. More than a half-century earlier, Peter G. Buckley shows, the "awful separations," the stark contrasts between squalor and luxury, had defined a new kind of representational mapping of New York that contrasted the new canvas of space and class with an "olde New York" of a functionally integrated city with a vibrant, cross-class public life. No longer, mid-century observers insisted, did the city possess a consistent set of social, cultural, and political standards. Like these earlier figurative interpretations of the city by New

Yorkers, Weber's shocked representation reflected, and his mapping and reading of urban space confirmed, a view of reality common to most of the leading social theorists of the late nineteenth and early twentieth centuries. The modern city was new and terrifying.

The city as such was neither central to, in a descriptive sense, nor manifestly the main subject of, such great theorists as Marx, Durkheim, Weber, Toennies, and Simmel. Each dealt with the city, of course, but only as a small part of the larger project of coming to terms with an industrial, capitalist, state-centered modernity. Just the same, the large modern city was an inescapable and constitutive element of all their considerations of these hallmarks of the modern world.

Each understood in his own way a point made more recently by Raymond Williams, when he wrote that "city life, until our own century, even in a highly industrialized society, was still a minority experience, but it was widely and accurately seen as a decisive experience, with much more than proportionate effects on the character of the society as a whole."[2] The large city—as a central arena and symbol of modernity; as the product and locale of such fundamental social processes as state making and capitalist development; and as the generative locale for the formation of collective identities and collective action—thus provided an inescapable setting and subject for nineteenth and twentieth century social theory, albeit a setting and subject usually only tacit or implicit.

We shall see that the principal way students of the city constructed these analytical and cognitive maps suffered in part from an insufficient and distorted appreciation of space as an integral element of economic, social, and political life. The main source of this distortion has been a key strand of nineteenth and twentieth century social theory focusing on the connections between social differentiation and social order. The result has been a portrayal of the history of the modern city in terms of a rupture between preindustrial cities characterized by a simple, integrated, homogeneous organization of space and industrial, capitalist cities characterized by an unintegrated, heterogeneous, disorganized patterning of space.

An important example of this kind of treatment can be found in Stephen Kern's *The Culture of Time and Space, 1880–1918.* Using these two coordinates, he reconstructs the decomposition of certainty in the late nineteenth century. Kern understands space as consisting of three elements: form (an amalgam of shape and area), distance, and direction. In the four decades straddling the turn of the century, distances contracted, the city spread and concentrated its direction, and its form altered in numerous ways. Kern shows how both the humanities and the social sciences tried to come to terms with the resulting plurality of spaces. This attempt was exemplified by the cubist movement in art, which put the heterogeneity of space onto a single painting, and negated "the traditional notion that the subject of a painting . . . is more important than the background."[3] Within the city, the new organization of form, distance, and direction signified the demise of the traditional hierarchies of class and politics. This vision of a radical break in city space and social relations was rooted in basic changes in the city as an economic, political, social, and symbolic construction.

Modern big cities are a post–sixteenth century phenomenon. From the eleventh to the sixteenth centuries towns grew at a rather slow, even pace. They were nodes of trade and craft production within feudalism's system of parcelized sovereignty. Each town, like each of the basic units of feudalism, fused political, economic, and symbolic power; in Max Weber's terms, a "fusion of fortress and the market." Each was an administrative center and a place where economic activities were based on principles of market exchange.

In *The City* Weber studied the urban centers of feudalism because he wished to join the debate about whether medieval towns were in fact goads to capitalist development and precursors of larger sovereign nation-states. He identified the town's specificity by contrasting it with the Oriental city, where, for reasons of the strength of such ascriptive ties as religion or caste, autonomous urban communities did not develop; and with earlier Western cities of antiquity, whose economies were based on war and plunder, not on the rational market capitalism characteristic of the medieval town. Weber thus concluded that neither the Oriental nor the ancient Western cities could have led to modern states and capitalism. The medieval Western city, by contrast, was conducive to the development of both.[4]

We will see how Weber's analysis of the feudal town hints at an alternative to what came to be the dominant approach. Here, the relevance of Weber's portrait is not so much whether he provides us with a persuasive way to study the city, or whether he was right in suggesting that the medieval city proved the undoing of feudalism (this debate continues to have a very lively existence). Rather, it is the fused, ordered character of the towns with which he dealt; for it is just this unity that could not survive the transition from feudalism to capitalism through mercantilism.

The first postfeudal modern cities were political capitals, the homes of royal courts: London, Paris, Amsterdam, Antwerp, Seville. Their fate was tied to absolutist states and to a mercantile international economic order. The societies in which they were embedded were characterized by a new division of property and sovereignty and by a concentration of both in explosively growing urban centers. Indeed, it is this very characteristic that allows us to define the modern city in terms of spatial implosion of (merchant and industrial) capital and of political power. We shall see that these most basic social processes of the post–sixteenth century Western world have been most fundamental to the creation of modern cities, and that these cities have been key elements in the reproduction of both capitalism and modern states.

In these cities the internal unity of the towns described by Weber was threatened not only by changes in size and density which breached the old walls and reorganized ancient quarters, or by more complicated relationships within the dominant classes now that political authority and private wealth-seeking were established as related by distinctly autonomous activities. What also challenged the old unities was the beginning of new patterns, in space, between places of work and places of residence. Fused in the workshops of the medieval city, work and home began to separate for the political and economic elites of the capital cities. Merchants who traded on a world scale began to construct homes away from the center; in turn, state officials increasingly began to work in the new office blocks of the crown at the city center.

The second group of modern cities, the industrial centers built in the nineteenth century at the sites of old villages, like Manchester, or on empty prairies, like Chicago, even more dramatically altered the traditional organization of urban space. The industrial cities were built as places of work according to the logic of capitalist accumulation. And even in the older mercantile centers and political capitals—London, Paris, New York, Berlin—the pace and character of change were astonishing.

What were the new cities of the nineteenth century like? The various portraits of New York City below show a city of high indeterminacy and of bewildering alterations to established ways of life and patterns of social relations.

New York City's commercial, financial, and manufacturing urban base supported an explosive population growth, from just 60,000 inhabitants in 1800 to over 1,100,000 by the eve of the Civil War. New York began the period as a leading commercial and trading center, and it maintained that position; just after the turn of the century it became the country's largest city. Diane Lindstrom indicates how the combination of improvements in communications and trade enhanced the city's commercial supremacy which, in turn, helped New York become the financial capital of the country. New York, she also shows, became a major, and rapidly growing, manufacturing center in the antebellum period. With textiles, ready-made clothing, and printing and publishing in the lead, New York developed a robust manufacturing sector that took advantage of the city's large market close at hand.

Both Lindstrom and Amy Bridges indicate how, in this variegated economic setting, the nature of work altered radically. The labor process was characterized by the decline of artisanship, a reorganization of skills, and the development of a modern, wage-labor working class; in short, by the development of a highly segmented, differentiated labor market. The demand for unskilled labor was fueled by very high rates of in-migration, mostly of people in their teens or twenties; by 1860, New York was mainly a city of people who had been born outside the United States. The new occupational structure, Bridges stresses, overlapped and reinforced the division between natives and immigrants. Most Germans were wage workers in trades that had been proletarianized; and the most common jobs for Irish newcomers were as laborers or domestics. By contrast, most craft work was performed by the native-born, who also filled elite and upper class positions. These divisions were reinforced, Lindstrom shows, by growing and dramatic inequalities in wealth and income.

The antebellum period likewise witnessed enormous changes in political institutions, the character of political leadership, and the meaning of citizenship. Bridges demonstrates that machine politics was characterized by a sharp increase in partisanship, leadership by career politicians, and the importance of contracts and patronage as the currency of politics. The antinomy of machine and reform came to be the characteristic solutions at the local level to the integration of a population divided by class and ethnicity into a mass franchise democracy. These political forms, Bridges argues, were the product not of a set of distinctively American social conflicts, but of a distinctively American context, the unusual conjuncture of the simultaneity of industrialization and the introduction of a widespread suffrage.

Changes in population, work, and the units of political activity were embedded in and expressed by the dramatic reorganization of the urban form, whose most characteristic shifts were the accelerating and fundamental separation of work from home and the emergence of ethnic- and class-specific neighborhoods and zones of the city. The rapidly growing city, Peter G. Buckley demonstrates, became increasingly divided, as "population and riches were spread unevenly over the procrustean grid of new streets laid out in the Commissioners plan of 1811." We can see these changes in the graphic portraits Buckley presents in his essay of the destitution of the Five Points and the grandeur of the Fifteenth Ward surrounding Washington Square.

This stark contrast was the most visible and dramatic result of three interrelated and overlapping historical processes entailed in the separation of work and home. First, the household ceased to be the main unit or location of production. Even if just next door, people went somewhere outside their homes to earn a living. Second, whole areas of large towns and cities came to be devoted *either* to residential use *or* to factory production or commercial and financial functions. Although primitive compared to the late nineteenth and early twentieth century patterns discussed by Emanuel Tobier, these concentrations of new kinds of workplaces transformed the physical form of the city and the social geography of work and production. Third, the residential areas of the city became increasingly homogeneous in both the Marxist and Weberian senses of class. With the division of city space into separate districts defined by their functions, and with the growing homogeneity of the residential areas, the city came to be defined, and to define its residents, in terms of the residents' connections to the now increasingly autonomous markets for labor and for housing. The job and the residence became distinctive commodities to be bought and sold by the discipline and logic of money and the marketplace. Older bonds were no longer determinative.

Within the physical city, patterns of daily life were shaped by a new transportation technology and new paths to and from work; by a centralization and demarcated definition of cross-class public space; indeed by the very emergence of class, in both the Marxist and Weberian senses, at the workplace and in the residence community, as the building blocks of the urban, industrial, capitalist social structure.

In the embrace of these changes, the physical city began to define patterns and zones of activity, and within them, not just new spheres of inequality but also new spheres of freedom. For working people, the various separations of work and home made possible the development of a spatially bounded, institutionally rich, independent working class culture in their neighborhoods of the city, and, at the same time, it impelled cultural producers, as William R. Taylor demonstrates, to create new commercial cultural forms capable of appealing to the various new social groups and classes of the industrial city. This was a culture of pastiche, that dramatized "the discontinuity, the kaleidoscopic variety, and the quick tempo of city life," and which had the capacity to appeal in different ways to each class and stratum in the city's diverse population.

The consumption of this new mass culture went hand in hand with the development of segmented, regionalized group and class cultures. For if working people were free from property, they were now also free, once they had left the workplace, to create something of an autonomous culture. As the city was reorganized in space, the places where people lived became increasingly homogeneous. The capacity of people to buy or rent real estate determined where they might live. As a result, the parts of the city became settlements of people sharing class attributes in Weber's sense of the capacity to consume goods and services offered in the marketplace. From the more macroscopic perspective of the city as a whole, however, urban areas were now much more heterogeneous than they once had been.[5]

It should not be surprising that the massive shifts in urban form and social geography, taken together, proved a puzzle for various social groups and classes and for social theorists. Neither should it surprise that the breakup of the more integrated city prodded many theorists to develop new principles of order, group cohesion, and social control. The main result of this quest was the paradigm of differentiation, which became the centerpiece of many major works of social theory in the late nineteenth and early twentieth centuries. This world view was more than just one new cosmology; it provided the most important grammar and vocabulary for representing the new city and its new patterns of social space.

The results of massive shifts in the nineteenth century city that so shocked such observers stimulated the interpretation that social differentiation is the hallmark and "the inevitable product of social change." In this view, summarized by Charles Tilly, "the state of social order depends on the balance between processes of differentiation and processes of integration and control, with rapid or excessive differentiation producing disorder."[6] From this vantage point, rapid social change and its disorienting possibilities are the central general processes of modernity. This perspective is condensed in such dichotomous pairs as Maine's status and contract; Durkheim's mechanical and organic solidarity; and Toennies's *Gemeinschaft* and *Gesellschaft*.

To be sure, these antinomies are not identical. Toennies, for one, stressed the new importance of the market for urban differentiation. For him, the contrast between precapitalist and capitalist cities lay in the new pervasive Gesellschaft, which he conceived to be an

artificial construction of an aggregate of human beings which superficially resembles the *Gemeinschaft* in so far as the individuals live and dwell together peacefully. However, in the *Gemeinschaft* they remain essentially united in spite of all separating factors, whereas in the *Gesellschaft* they are essentially separated in spite of all the uniting factors. . . . Everybody is by himself and isolated and there exists a condition of tension against all others. . . . Nobody wants to grant and produce anything for another individual, nor will he be inclined to give ungrudgingly to another individual if it not be in exchange for a gift or labour equivalent that he considers at least equal to what he has given.[7]

Durkheim by contrast referred to the new order in terms of the movement from relations of constraint ("mechanical solidarity") to relations of shared values ("organic solidarity") that produce authentic forms of cooperation in the small-scale settings of the new differentiated city.

These, of course, need not be contradictory positions. The new urban neighborhoods of nineteenth century cities were profoundly shaped by market forces in real estate, for example, which often tore social bonds asunder. At the same time, many of the homogeneous neighborhoods created as a result of the operation of local real estate markets became homes to people who shared so many attributes that the development of quite dense and solidaristic networks of social organization was facilitated.

From an analytical perspective, what is most striking is that both the view of differentiation as *"Gemeinschaft"* and the view of differentiation as "organic solidarity" share a world view and an interpretation of what was meant by the massive changes in capitalism, the state, and the city. Charles Tilly has enumerated the key principles of this perspective:

1. "Society" is a thing apart; the world as a whole divides into distinct "societies," each having its more or less autonomous culture, government, economy, and solidarity.

2. Social behavior results from individual mental events, which are conditioned by life in society. Explanations of social behavior therefore concern the impact of society on individual minds.

3. "Social change" is a coherent general phenomenon, explicable *en bloc*.

4. The main processes of large-scale social change take distinct societies through a succession of standard stages, each more advanced than the previous stage.

5. Differentiation forms the dominant, inevitable logic of large-scale social change; differentiation leads to advancement.

6. The state of social order depends on the balance between processes of differentiation and processes of integration or control; rapid or excessive differentiation produces disorder.

7. A wide variety of disapproved behavior—including madness, murder, drunkenness, crime, suicide, and rebellion—results from the strain produced by excessively rapid social change.[8]

This orientation was given its greatest plausibility by the changes experienced in the city, which appeared to conform to this metadescription of reality. The richest, and most influential, development of this perspective, at least for subsequent treatments of urbanism, was made by Georg Simmel, and it is important to examine his contribution.

Simmel's corpus is in part an attempt to come to terms with the metropolitan culture of Berlin. One of the best known of his essays, "The Metropolis and Mental Life," published in 1903, dealt with the impact of the city as such; and by his own testimony his major works, including his first book, *Social Differentiation* (1890), and *The Philosophy of Money* (1900), were animated by shifts in the character of city life. "Berlin's development from a city to a metropolis in the years around and after the turn of the century," Simmel observed, "coincides with my own strongest and broadest development."[9] Much more so than his main contemporaries, Weber, Sombart, and Toennies, Simmel concentrated on contemporary experience, including that of the customer and the resident of the big city. His central questions concerned the elaboration of market relations in the differentiated city and their effects on social relations.

In his first book, Simmel stressed how with increased differentiation the total individual dissolves into elements; the result is the construction of human ties of a more varied sort with people who share partial traits and relationships. As a consequence, new group relations become possible, and there is an acceleration of forms of social interaction. A decade later, in *The Philosophy of Money*, Simmel maintained this perspective and, in an important addition, linked it explicitly to exchange relationships in urban society, a perspective developed even more fully as an urban analysis in "Space and the Spatial Structures of Society," which composes the penultimate chapter of Simmel's *Sociology* (1908). The themes in this chapter are also taken up in "The Metropolis and Mental Life." In these works the key elements of a sociology of differentiation in space are elaborated: impersonality, detachment, isolation, segmented friendships, commodification of relationships, and, above all, the significance of boundaries. Perhaps the most brilliant contribution lies in Simmel's use of these elements to discuss alternative ways that social relationships may get anchored in space. He contrasts the medieval city from which it was difficult to exit with the residential mobility of the twentieth century city. Although this freedom exists, Simmel observes, particular social groups become anchored to distinctive territories. These spaces tend to get named, thus individualized as separate; and each of these territories tends to have one or more special buildings (church, marketplace, school, transport center) that give it a focus, a hub of activity, an identity, and a boundary.

This way of seeing urban space had profound implications for thinking about social and political order in society. For if society was now internally differentiated, then it had to face basic new problems of social control. An integrated society could be self-regulating, but a differentiated one might dissolve into disconnected fragments.

These themes were developed most clearly with regard to their implications for a modern urban-based civilization in the political sociology of Louis Wirth, who, together with his Chicago School of Sociology colleagues, was deeply influenced by Simmel. When Wirth wrote a preface to a revised edition of Robert Park's famous 1915 essay, "The City: Suggestions for the Investigation of Human Behavior in the Urban Environment," he singled out Simmel's urban essay as "the most important single article on the city from a sociological viewpoint." Wirth's own 1938 essay, "Urbanism as a Way of Life," resonates with Simmelian themes, albeit on a selective basis.[10]

Wirth's critique of the city left out Simmel's insight that metropolitan differentiation makes possible unparalleled individual and group self-development through the creation of new, relatively homogeneous, "free" social areas. Instead, Wirth underscored the problems differentiation poses to social cohesion. In his argument, the city is more than just a fragmented social and spatial order; it is also a divided and disorganized moral order. In this sociological analysis, Wirth highlighted an older, conservative lament. Thus, for example, Carlyle in 1831 had described industrial city dwellers as "strangers. . . . It is a huge aggregate of little systems, each of which is again a small anarchy, the members of which do not *work* together, but *scramble* against each other."[11]

Wirth sided rather more with Toennies than with Durkheim. Primordial integrative ties had been replaced by more artificial, secondary ones. Shared values had been shattered. The fragmentary and partial normative features of city life could not maintain social control (in the sense of the capacity of the society as a whole to regulate itself in accordance with shared aims). The consequences could be seen in political disorganization and in an increase in such pathological behavior as personality disorders, crime, and weakened family life. In this analysis Wirth presented in refracted form elite fears of contact with the new immigrant working class masses, which were most often expressed in metaphors of health and disease.

Urban differentiation and its negative consequences were likely to get worse over time, Wirth thought, because spatial fragmentation and the

cesses, it becomes clear that the differentiation problematic itself is fundamentally flawed. Thus, for example, if we were to become interested in Weber's problem of state building and in the relationships of citizens to state authorities, we would immediately face the reality that the construction of modern nation-states is as much a story of the concentration of sovereignty in the center as it is a story of differentiation. Or, if we were to concentrate on Marx's problem of the development of modern capitalism and on the relationships of employers and their work forces, we would have to deal with the profound concentration of production and the implosion of capital that are hallmark characteristics of capitalist industrial development.[14] Indeed, one way to think about the modern city is as the concentrated locus of power and capital.

By contrast to this kind of orientation, the differentiation versus order model is a very blunt analytical instrument. It simplifies the modern experience and reduces it to the familiar dichotomies of traditional and modern, individual and society.

With regard to cities, the differentiation perspective presents a plausible social and spatial representation, but at the very great cost of closing off questions about the fundamental social processes that affect and shape city life, about the networks of relationships that, in their great variety, define urbanity and its contradictions, and about the enormous range of alternative patterns of spatial relations, class formation, and collective action that characterize the modern city. We have only to read Tobier's chronicle of the massive changes in the nature of land use and economic functions in central Manhattan, the Fainsteins' description of radical shifts from period to period in the role of government in the development of the built-form, Shefter's tale of how the reform-machine antinomy was replaced by interest group politics, and Mollenkopf's and Kornblum and Beshers' assessments of interactions among processes of migration, shifts in local production, and markets understood in the context of the world economy, neighborhood spatial patterns, and electoral politics to see the cumbersome character of the differentiation-order problematic and its inability to account for the variety and sources of the dynamics of urban change.

The new and changing mix of uniformity and variation in nineteenth and twentieth century New York was neither a process unto itself nor simply the result of autonomous urban factors. Rather, most fundamentally, differentiated urban patterns were the product of very large scale processes that surmounted the agency of the city dwellers they affected. These included such essential features of capitalism as uneven development in space as a result of highly concentrated industrialization, a radical shift in the new scale of work and production, and a tendency to convert land into real estate. Also in the sphere of the economy, there was a massive expansion and extension of the market into all spheres of civil society, free time, and personal expression.

The city was also a dependent result of a new role for the state, which created the organizational framework necessary for capitalist market-places and which, through its use of fiscal incentives to builders and through direct development, planning, and regulation by building codes and zoning, gave direction to the production of the physical city. At the same time, the modern nation-state centralized power in the city and helped stimulate its growth and shape. Municipal government fur-ther reinforced the new segregation of city space by invoking its powers to tax, police, and administer in ways that were differentiated by social geography.

Let us return to Weber's *The City*. Although he did not write a compa-rable analysis for nineteenth and twentieth century cities, the way he approached the subject of the medieval town presents a very fertile example of the social process-network alternative to the differentiation perspective.

A central theme of the study contrasts the Occidental and Oriental city in terms of key differences in the nature of interactive groups: guilds and territorial associations in the West; clans and castes in the East; and between the ancient and medieval cities of the West in terms of the relative importance of military clans in the ancient city and occupational associations in the medieval city. Further, Weber locates these groups and the networks in which they were embedded in terms of such basic social processes as the development of rational economic activity and of the emergence of autonomous bases of political authority. What finally distinguished the medieval from the ancient city was the political triumph of those groups that were the carriers of rational, market-centered, capitalistic economic activity. Thus, for Weber, the sociological and historical dimensions of urban analysis fuse in a much more richly textured way than the simple dichotomies of the differentiation-order perspective could possibly allow.

Or, consider Marx. Each of his three main analytical projects—an understanding of epochal transformation; a model of the logic of the capitalist economy; and the development of social theory concerned with the relationships between capitalist development and such other social processes as politics, kinship, and culture—suggests issues for urban analysis significantly deeper and more varied than the differentia-tion orientation. How is city space a constitutive element of capitalist relations of production and consumption? How is the differentiation of urban space shaped by the logic of capitalist accumulation? What is the relationship between a fragmented city space and class formation?

I do not mean to suggest that the issues that produced and gave force to evolutionary differentiation theory are no longer with us, for they are still our issues: anonymity and alienation; the ways the city insinuates itself into intimate relations and into civil society; the circulation of material goods and images; the milling of crowds; the dissolution and construction of human bonds. We still want to ask whether the city is a unified experience or a mere division and assemblage of disordered elements, and if these, separately and together, constitute a barbarism or an appealing spectacle or, more likely, an amalgam of both.

If we accept Thomas Bender's challenge to make central the analysis of contests over public culture (the systems of meaning and symbol that interpret power and place in the city), and if we concede, within this frame, that the questions produced at the turn of the century by social theorists concerned with grappling with the new divisions within cities remain good questions, they cannot be confronted, I have tried to suggest, by the direct and seductive route of the differentiation problematic. When we examine urban space, let us remember to inquire about the social processes that produced the landscape we see, and about the various social relationships that bind the people in the factory, the office, the neighborhood, the park, and in the other arenas of city life. In so exploring, we will do better to recall the methods and perspective of Max Weber as the remarkable analyst of medieval towns than his stock imagery, horror-stricken jottings as a tourist in the New World.

Notes

1. Citations from Marianne Weber, *Max Weber: A Biography* (New York: Wiley, 1975), 285–87.

2. Raymond Williams, *The Country and the City* (New York: Oxford University Press, 1973), 217.

3. Stephen Kern, *The Culture of Time and Space, 1880–1918* (Cambridge: Harvard University Press, 1983), 8.

4. Max Weber, *The City* (New York: Free Press, 1958).

5. For a stimulating consideration, see David Ward, "Social Structure and Social Geography in Large Cities of the U.S. Urban-Industrial Heartland," *Historical Geography Research Series* 12 (December 1983).

6. Charles Tilly, *Big Structures, Large Processes, Huge Comparisons* (New York: Russell Sage, 1984), 50.

7. Ferdinand Toennies, *Community and Association* (London: Routledge & Kegan Paul, 1955), 33–34, 64–65; and Emile Durkheim, *The Division of Labor in Society* (New York: Free Press, 1964).

8. Tilly, *Big Structures*, 11.

9. Cited in David Frisby, *Georg Simmel* (London: Tavistock, 1984), 34.

10. Louis Wirth, "Urbanism as a Way of Life," *American Journal of Sociology* 44 (July 1938).

11. Cited in Williams, *The Country and the City*, 215.

12. Cited in Williams, *The Country and the City*, 215–16.

13. Tilly, *Big Structures*, 23.

14. There is a useful discussion of dedifferentiation in Charles Tilly, "Reflections on the History of European State-Making," in his edited collection, *The Formation of National States in Western Europe* (Princeton: Princeton University Press, 1975).

Name Index

Subject Index